PALM TREES IN THE SNOW

Gloria Maria Strassburger

Published by Antilles Pearl Press

No part of this publication may be reproduced, stored in retrieval system, or transmitted in any form or by any means, electronic, mechanical, photocopying, recording, or otherwise, without written permission of the author.

First Edition: 2011

All rights reserved.
Copyright © 2011 Gloria Maria Strassburger

Printed in the United States of America
ISBN: 978-0-692-23883-7

To Amy and Ana,
mis niñas lindas
and to Devin and William,
my sweetest joy—
May you always treasure your heritage
but most importantly, your freedom.

Excerpt from my grandfather Bibi's letter
to my mother, Ninina, written two weeks
before he left the island.
La Habana, Cuba, May 21, 1961

Dentro de todas las preocupaciones que tenemos, la carta de Gloria ha sido como una sonrisa dentro de la tempestad. Tiene vena de escritora y ojalá yo pueda ver sus triunfos literarios como escritora de costumbres y de sentido humorístico. Con la lectura de su carta muchas de las nubes negras de mi pensamiento se han disipado como cuando sale el sol después de una tempestad.

Within all the worries that we have, the letter from Gloria has been like a smile within the tempest. She has a writer's vein and God grant that I may see her literary triumphs as an author of customs and with humorous sense. With the reading of her letter many of the black clouds of my thoughts have dissipated, like when the sun comes out after a storm.

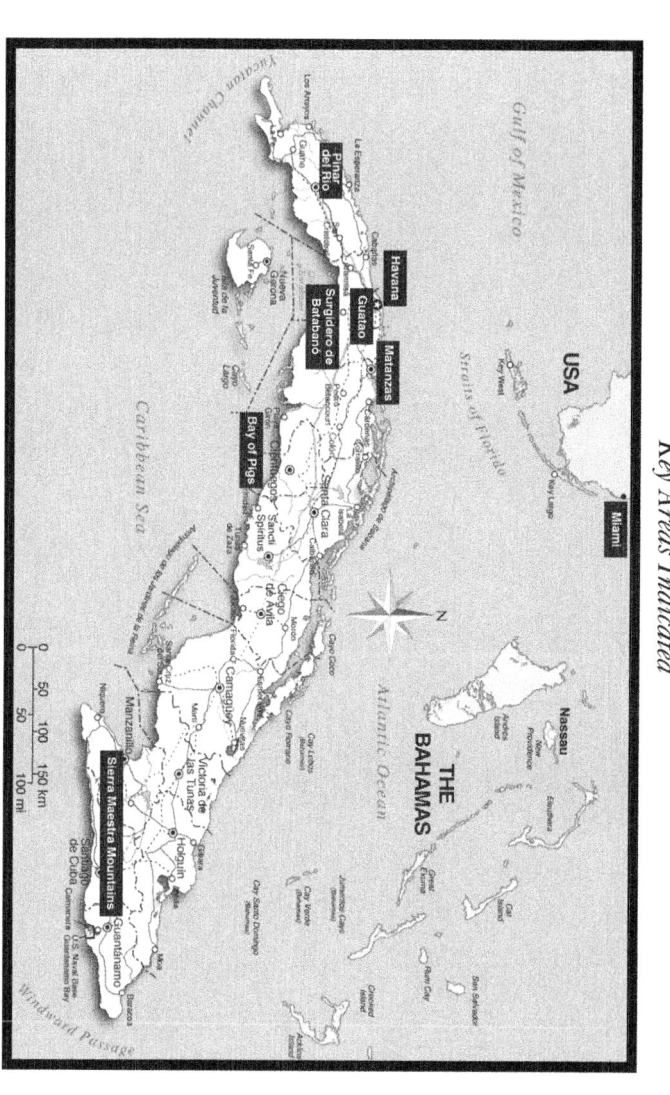

Prologue

Kawama. I pronounce the aboriginal word slowly, my lips forming each syllable with a familiar pleasure. The word evokes my first, vivid memories of Cuba and my father. I feel the lambent sun on my face, the warm, white sand, fine like sugar, enveloping my feet as I walk on Varadero's pristine Kawama Beach with my father. I am five years old, and my hand is snuggled inside his. I look up at his bronzed face. He is tall and handsome, looking out at the transparent, turquoise Caribbean. The morning sun shimmers over the water. I see his smile under his mustache. I smile, too.

A wind rises, swaying the palm fronds. We stroll past a few thatched umbrellas; it's quiet, except for the occasional squawk of a *gaviota* gliding by and the lapping of mischievous waves that turn to foam as they reach our feet. I stomp on the water-soaked sand and splash both our legs. Papi scoops me up in his strong, tanned arms.

"Let's go in the ocean," he says, his voice tight with excitement. My arms are hooked around his neck. I hang on as we approach the roaring waves; a big one is getting closer and closer. My father puts me down. I am waist-high in the ocean, but he stands right behind me and doesn't let go of my arms. "Here it comes," he yells.

"Papi-i-i," I holler, jumping nervously in the water, laughing. Just as the wave is ready to engulf me, my father lifts me up. I feel the exhilarating push of water crashing against my body as I grab on to his neck again. From my safe perch, I look down at foam and water splashing all around us. We laugh together.

Suddenly, a school of small fish barrel into us, frantically swimming through Papi's legs. My father knows what this means. Holding me tight, he bolts out of the ocean onto the beach. A lifeguard runs past us blowing his whistle, yelling the dreaded alert: "*Tiburón*, everyone out of the water, now!" Within minutes, a dark shadow swims swiftly through the shallow waters where my father and I had been playing.

"*Salao*," I hear Papi say, as he watches the shark swim back out to sea. *Unlucky.* I can't comprehend what this means or what has led my father to say it. But my mind quickly dismisses it as a little crab scuttles sideways in front of us.

"¡*Mira*, Papi, *un cangrejito*!" I point at the disappearing hole in the sand. But my father is silent. He holds my hand limply now and looks straight ahead, at nothing, as we head back to our cabana.

It is 1953. While my thoughts are busy with the beach and my approaching first day of kindergarten—making new friends, liking my teacher—a young rebel is feverishly poring through books on politics, history, and economics in his prison cell. While I unknowingly come closer to the emotional hurricane that will destroy my childhood, Fidel Castro is building the revolutionary hurricane that will destroy Cuba.

Palm Trees in the Snow

Chapter One

My Mother and Father

My Mother

Habana, 1939

Ninina awoke to the noisy exchange of the tropical birds' morning calls. She instinctively slid further under the sheets. A breeze billowed the canopied mosquito net, scenting the room with the fragrance of jasmine, rosebushes, and gardenias blooming in her mother's garden. Gardenia was Ninina's favorite flower. She closed her eyes, tempted to stay in bed a little longer. Across the hall, the radio blared a lively *danzón*.

"Milly, turn the radio down, will you? I'm not awake yet!" Ninina hollered. The door flung open.

"It's about time you woke up!" Milly landed next to her, face flushed. At fourteen, she was almost over the lanky stage. Her disheveled dark curls tumbled around her shoulders, framing her *cascabelera* expression of youthful exuberance.

"What were you doing in there, anyway?" Ninina muttered.

"Oh, practicing my new steps. I plan to dance with the handsomest boy at the party tonight," Milly said decisively while piling her hair in an upsweep. "What do you think?"

"Too grown-up for you," Ninina called after her sister, who flounced from the room to answer the phone. Ninina was getting over a head cold and was having second thoughts about going to the Elsners' housewarming party. The Elsners were close friends of her parents. What had originated as an intimate group of family and friends to help christen their palatial new home had escalated into a social affair. Ninina glanced at the new dress hanging outside her closet door. Letting out a sigh, she reached for her robe.

"*Buen día*, Nini," Carmen, the housekeeper, greeted her as she stopped by the kitchen doorway and popped her head in. "Are you hungry this morning, or will you just be having your *café con leche* and toast?" Carmen, a proud mulatta, supervised the household servants. An attractive woman in her late thirties, she wore her long black hair braided in a low, netted bun. Her white linen uniform was ironed to perfection.

The aroma of her father's *torrejas*, French toast, was enticing, but Ninina had to fit into her new dress that night. "*Sí*, Carmen, *café con leche* and one piece of toast only, *por favor*."

Carmen had been Ninina's doting *tata*, or nanny. Growing up, Ninina loved to sit on a kitchen stool while her *tata* prepared her *merienda*, a late-afternoon snack. She would listen to Carmen's stories about her slave ancestors, who, during the late 1500s to mid-1800s, had been imported from Africa by the Spaniards ruling Cuba to replace the lost Siboney and Taino Indians who had inhabited the island.

My Mother and Father

These Native Americans were peaceful and industrious people, but the Spaniards worked most of them to death in fields and mines. Others died from diseases brought by Europeans, and many were tortured and killed for sport. By 1570, the entire race of these gentle people, who gave the island its name, was eradicated. African slaves became the Spaniards' new workforce for the powerfully emerging sugarcane industry. Over the centuries, a strong class distinction based on race was established in Cuba. The descendants of African slaves, the Afro-Cubans, were now primarily fieldworkers and servants in white upper-class people's homes, with little opportunity for social or economic advancement. It was a fundamental part of life on the island: the poor were shockingly destitute, and the rich were ostentatiously wealthy.

Ninina strolled into the sunny dining room, where atrium doors gave onto a peaceful inner courtyard and her mother's flower garden in full, glorious bloom. Her parents were having their breakfast. She kissed them good morning and sat next to her father. He greeted her, putting down the morning paper.

"*Ay*, Papi, I feel awful with this cold. Do I really have to go to the party tonight?" Gustavo saw the alarmed look on his wife's face and let her answer.

"¡*Pero, niña, claro que sí!*" Mercedes' coffee cup clattered as she placed it on its saucer. "It will be a wonderful party. You get to wear your new dress and meet new friends. You'll feel better by tonight, *ya verás*," her mother concluded. Ninina looked pleadingly at her father.

"Mami is right, *m'ija*." He poured more syrup over

his *torrejas*. "You're seventeen now, and it's good for you to meet more young people besides your girlfriends at school." It was always Ninina's father who made her see what she had to do. It was the way he looked at her, the wisdom in his eyes, the sincerity of his words.

Gustavo E. Perea was a proud Cuban *caballero*, a gentleman. Tall, with brown hair and a fine mustache, he had hazel eyes framed by wire-rimmed glasses. Well educated, highly articulate, and knowledgeable in the arts, business, and politics, Gustavo was the vice-treasurer of the I.C.E.A., the Cuban Institute of the Stabilization of Sugar in Havana. This influential job brought him much respect and admiration, but his family was his life.

Gustavo's wife, Mercedes, was a slip of a woman, barely five feet tall. Cheerful and chatty, she wore her dark hair, swept with gray, in a wavy bob. Her world revolved around her Gustavo and their four children. She ran the house with a spry energy and the loyal help of Carmen. A devout Catholic, Mercedes volunteered with several charitable organizations to help the poor.

Her mother was still chattering about the party when Ninina finished her breakfast and walked out to the courtyard. The blooming gardenias were luminous in the late morning light. Plucking the prettiest one, she brought it to her nose, breathing in its heady scent. Then, hooking the flower over her right ear, Ninina found herself daydreaming about meeting a handsome young man at the party. If anything, it would be fun to watch her sister at her first party, dancing her heart away with a handsome boy of her own.

"Milly, hurry up and get out of the bathroom!" Pucha

yelled at her sister from her bedroom across the hall. The Perea girls scrambled into each other's rooms, borrowing makeup, bows, shoes, and jewelry.

Pucha, the oldest, was eighteen. She dashed into Ninina's room in a near panic, her chestnut hair still bobby-pinned into *moñitos*: "Nini, have you seen my pearl necklace? I can't find it anywhere!" She swayed in front of the mirror, fluffing up the skirt of her new rose-colored organza dress while sucking in her stomach.

"Have you checked with Milly? That's where I found my silver barrette," answered Ninina. As if on cue, Milly ran into the room wearing Pucha's pearl necklace.

"*Oye*, Pucha, can I borrow your pearls *por favor*? Mine are so childish. Don't yours look great with my orchid dress?" Milly stopped her prattling and glanced at her other sister, while Pucha snatched her pearls off Millly's neck. "Nini, your dress—¡*qué belleza*!" Ninina was quietly evaluating herself in front of a large oval mirror. The blue long-sleeved jersey dress clung subtly to her curves. An ivory appliqué laced its front, from neckline to waist and across the shoulders. Ninina's wavy brown hair was highlighted auburn from the sun, and her *moñitos* had turned out just right tonight.

"*Niñas*, your father is waiting for us, *vámonos*." Mercedes hurried into the room. As the sisters filed past her, a grumbling Milly asked her mother to help her with her own pearl necklace.

The Perea family lived in Vedado, one of the oldest residential districts in Havana. Their leafy, tree-lined avenue was flanked by massive homes made of European marble and stone. Elaborate wrought-iron gates guarded the properties. The mansions were adorned with wide windows, designed with colorful Andalusian tiles and intricately carved wooden front doors.

The chauffeur turned onto Calle del Castillo, ending the short ride to the Elsner home. Hearing the live music, Milly's eyes lit up with excitement. A marble staircase and sparkling crystal chandelier welcomed the guests as they entered the mansion. The alluring fragrance of expensive perfume and tropical flowers filled the air.

In the courtyard, young couples revolved under the starry night to the lively *boleros* and *danzones* being played by the band. Servants passed silver trays with *saladitos*, appetizers that the young people were eagerly sampling. Ninina spotted two girlfriends at the end of an arcaded corridor. Making her way toward them, she walked past an illuminated garden. The scent of gardenias brought to mind her daydream.

***

My Father

Rancho Boyeros airport was a zoo by noontime that Saturday. Rolando Fernández was returning home to Havana from North Carolina, where he had been the best man in a friend's wedding. He bought a paper and headed for the airport's front entrance, where the family chauffeur awaited him, standing next to the white Mercedes.

Rolando was the first-born child of José and Clara Fernández. Despite the affection she felt for her son, Clara was uncomfortable around Rolando, unsure of herself as a mother. But when she gave birth to Emma soon after, Clara's motherly nurturing suddenly emerged. She felt a natural preference for her daughter.

Rolando's father was born in Cangas de Onís, a village in Asturias, Spain. The son of a fisherman, José Fernández came to the island of Cuba as a young man to learn the trade of sponge fishing. By the time he married Clara, an aristocratic beauty from Havana, he owned a fleet of sponge-fishing boats in the village of Batabanó, where Rolando was born. As the business prospered, José expanded in other ventures and started an international lumber and construction company headquartered in Havana, where he settled with his young family.

Rolando began his education at the Maristas Catholic School in Havana. It was common practice for wealthy Cuban families to enroll their children in boarding schools. Daughters were matriculated in exclusive Catholic convent schools, the sons in monastery schools. Oftentimes, sons were sent to the United States to receive the best higher education. Rolando's experience was unusual. When he was in third grade, his mother convinced his father to send him to the United States to be educated. At age nine, Rolando attended St. Joseph's Boarding School in St. Augustine, Florida. He remained there until he graduated high school.

Rolando continued his education in America, graduating with honors as a lieutenant from Georgia Military Academy. Although José had given in to his wife's insistence on educating their oldest son abroad, he missed Rolando terribly and demanded that his son finish his career education in Cuba.

Rolando was accepted to the University of Havana in the fall of 1938, where he majored in law and business administration. He excelled in sports, particularly football, and was the team's quarterback. He loved music, dancing, and foreign languages. Reading was a passion, and he was a gifted writer.

The Fernández family lived in La Víbora, an exclusive suburb of Havana built in the mid-1800s. The neighborhood's architecture—columns with decorated friezes, ornate balconies, stained-glass windows, and wide-marbled stepped verandas—gave it an elegant, traditional appearance.

The Mercedes entered the Fernández home's circular driveway and stopped by the front portico. Rolando's mother was sitting on a caned rocker, fanning herself with her delicate *abanico*.

"*Hola, mi hijo.*" Clara stopped rocking and dabbed the perspiration on her face with a lace handkerchief.

"*¿Qué tal*, Mamá?" Rolando bent down to kiss her cheek as she held his arm. José Fernández had seen his son arrive from his study window and came out to welcome him.

"So, how was the wedding?" He gave Rolando a hearty pat on the back. "Good to have you back, son." After a brief exchange with his parents, Rolando got up to go inside when his mother enthused, "I'm glad you got back in time for the Elsner party tonight, Rolando."

"What party, Mamá?" He shot her an aggravated look. "I was planning to relax and stay home tonight, maybe catch a late movie with Manuel."

"Rolando, this is a huge social event." Clara stopped fanning herself and closed the *abanico* on her lap. "Señor Elsner is a good friend of your father's."

"Besides," José interrupted, "it sounds like a great party. A live band, dancing, and lots of young people your age."

My Mother and Father

He raised his brows and looked at his son mischievously.

"Papá, I'm not going anywhere until I take a nap," Rolando said. "I'll go, but I won't stay long." He grabbed his bag and walked in the house. Clara tapped her *abanico* against her palm, and with a flick of the wrist, the fan opened up. She glanced at her husband, smiled, and began to fan herself.

As soon as he entered the Elsners' glittering foyer, Rolando wished he had gone to the movies instead. A sea of strangers surrounded him. He drifted toward the sounds of music coming from the courtyard, where the band was playing "As Time Goes By."

Instantly feeling more comfortable amidst the younger crowd dancing, Rolando scanned the area for a familiar face. He recognized the boisterous laughter of a university pal. Rolando approached Arturo and joined the group, but his eyes were riveted to the girl smiling next to his friend.

Rolando flashed Ninina a disarming smile as they were introduced. She noticed that her girlfriends were gaping at the striking young man. Rolando had just turned nineteen. Six feet tall, with an athletic build, he had thick, black hair and a trimmed mustache that accentuated his warm smile. The band began to play Le Cuona's "Siboney."

"I love this song," Rolando said, reaching out to Ninina. "How about a dance?" They had danced to two songs by the time they had traded their personal histories. Listening to Rolando describe his lengthy education abroad made Ninina wonder how a mother could be without her young son for so long.

Dinner was served *al fresco*, and the delicious aroma of

paella valenciana permeated the air of the balmy starlit night. Cozy tables with fresh flowers and candles surrounded a luminous fountain in the center of the courtyard. While they ate, the band played a popular Spanish song called "*Muñequita Linda*"—"Pretty Little Doll." Rolando was humming the words as he leaned close to Ninina.

"This song will always remind me of you," he whispered. She smiled. To think she had almost given in to her cold and stayed home that night! Ninina found Rolando different from the few Cuban boys she knew. Maybe it was his American education that made him seem so suave and mature.

Doing what was customary in America, Rolando asked Ninina for her phone number. But she declined, adhering to Cuban etiquette, which required that a young man meet a young woman's parents for approval prior to calling her by phone and courting her. By the end of the evening, Rolando had an invitation to meet Ninina's family.

The following Saturday, when Rolando arrived at the Perea home, Ninina's parents, her sisters, and her brother and two of his buddies were sitting on the front porch. Even Carmen was standing by the door. Ninina came bounding down the porch steps to meet Rolando.

After introductions, the conversation unavoidably turned to Rolando's education in America. To Cubans, the U.S. represented advancement, all things modern, and an opportunity for economic development. (To Americans, Cuba was an exotic tropical island, a place to vacation and make a fortune with their businesses.) The island's developing sugar trade made it possible for Cubans to travel often to America for business, vacation, and especially education. But the many wealthy families who sent their children to be educated abroad often had problems when they returned home. Having been under American influence for a prolonged period of time, their children often changed their habits, ideals, morals, and even their religion. Gustavo and Mercedes were concerned that Rolando, who dressed in American clothes and had obvious American preferences, had given up the Cuban customs. Trying to approach the subject delicately, Gustavo jovially asked him, "So, Rolando, do you feel out of place on our little island now, after being in America for so long?"

Rolando's face turned serious as he looked squarely at Gustavo. "I am grateful for the education and cultural experience I received in America." He paused, noticing everyone was listening to him. "*Pero yo soy Cubano*—I am Cuban, and will be until the day I die. My heart belongs to my homeland forever." His eloquent passion took them aback. At that moment, Ninina knew that Rolando Fernández had clinched their courtship.

José Fernández loved boating, deep-sea fishing, and being by the ocean. He owned a large yacht called Arenas del Mar, which he docked at the Havana Biltmore Yacht Club. The famed Biltmore encompassed miles of sandy white beaches lined with pine and palm trees. Often on weekends, he and his sons, along with family and friends, would take the Arenas out marlin fishing for the day. On a warm Sunday afternoon in early March 1939, Rolando picked the opportunity to introduce Ninina to his family.

The high masts in the marina bobbed in the breeze as they approached the dock. José Fernández welcomed Ninina warmly and complimented his son on his good taste.

She instantly liked José. He was short and stocky with crinkly, graying hair and glasses. He had gentle eyes. The yacht's engine rumbled to life, and the ship began heading slowly out to sea. On the top deck, José steered his vessel inside a glass-enclosed cabin. Nearby, two crewmen were busy tending the ropes and rigging. Laughter and music floated from the yacht's living quarters on the second level. The radio was playing "Serenade in Blue" by Glenn Miller. Two servants waited on the family and their guests, offering trays of drinks and appetizers. Ninina and Rolando climbed up the narrow steps to the promenade deck, where Ninina came face to face with Clara Fernández.

"Rolando, have you seen Manuela? We need more Champagne." She ignored Ninina and turned her cheek to Rolando for a kiss.

"Mamá, this is Ninina Perea." He gave his mother a quick peck.

"Ninina? That can't be your real name." Clara raised her hand, shielding her eyes from the glare off the water while her gaze focused on Ninina.

"My name is Celia," Ninina replied. "But my family nicknamed me Ninina, and that's the name I go by." She raised her chin a bit.

"Ah, *ya veo*. Well, you two have fun," Clara said coolly with a tight little wave of her hand. "I must find Manuela now." She turned and walked back to her waiting guests.

While the yacht was anchored at Varadero Beach, Ninina and Rolando stood on the main deck, perched against the railing. Through the dazzle of sun on the water, they watched a couple of sea gulls dive-bombing at a passing school of fish.

"Big fish coming," Rolando said, seeing the fish race by. From the top deck a crewman yelled *"¡Tiburón!"* just as the shadow appeared in the clear waters. With its dorsal fin above surface, the shark swam close to the yacht, so close Ninina could see its steely eyes.

Rolando watched intently. *"Estoy salao,"* he said, as if to himself. "Old fishermen claim it's a jinx to see a shark up close in the water—to look him right in the eye. Something bad is going to happen to me." He leaned his upper body over the railing. "I wonder what would happen if I jumped in the water right now," he said in a wooden tone. Ninina pulled away and looked into his face.

"Rolando, don't even think such a thing!" Startled, she grabbed his arm. He kept watching the shark as it swam farther out to sea. "Rolando!" Ninina was almost yelling now, trying to get his attention. He turned and looked at her blankly for a moment. Then his eyes softened and he gently hooked her hair behind her ear.

"Muñequita linda," he said, draping his arm around her shoulders and drawing her closer to him. As Rolando gazed out at the horizon, Ninina looked around her self-consciously. A peripheral movement on the top deck caught her eye. Clara was watching them. For a brief moment the two women looked at each other. Then Clara shifted her focus to her son. Slowly, her head shook from side to side as she turned to join her laughing friends.

Chapter Two

Muñequita Linda

Ninina and Rolando's courtship was a whirlwind of dinners, movies, parties, country club dances, sports events, and day trips to the beach and countryside. Ninina was always chaperoned by her parents or close relatives, in accordance with the strict etiquette observed during that time.

A favorite outing was spending a day at Valle Viñales, a scenic spot in Pinar del Río, the capital of Cuba's westernmost province, with a group of friends. The impressive *mogotes* of Valle Viñales were massive, soaring green mountains that rose out of fertile valleys laden with palm trees. In the early morning mist, these huge mounds resembled sleeping giants, giving the place a mystic feeling. Fields of yellow-green sugarcane, pineapple, and tobacco mantled the surrounding hills.

After their picnic lunch, the couples would go for a hike in the hills, exploring caves and secluded coves while the chaperones stayed behind and visited.

In May 1939, Ninina's maternal grandmother, Abuelita Sofía, celebrated her eighty-first birthday. The Perea family invited Rolando to come with them to her home, El Jardín, for a family gathering. The morning of the party, Ninina accompanied her mother to La Gran Vía. Mercedes had ordered a birthday cake from the popular bakery in Habana Vieja. Old Havana was the city's colonial section, with turn-of-the-century mansions whose ornate balconies blazed with cascading, crimson bouganvillea. The chauffeur drove onto Calle de las Palomas, a narrow cobblestoned street. A high stone wall stood at the end of the road. At the entrance, above immense wrought-iron gates, a sign read "Mazorra."

"Pedro, what is this place, do you know?" Ninina asked the chauffeur, gazing out the car window.

"Señorita, it's a place for *locos*," he replied, looking at her from the rearview mirror. "You don't want nothing to do with that place!" he said, shaking his head.

"Mamá, do you know anyone in Mazorra?" She turned to her mother, who was checking the shopping list.

"No, but you must always say a prayer for the people in there whenever you drive by." Mercedes crossed herself as she spoke. Ninina looked out the window one last time as the car turned the corner. Through the gates she could see the sanatorium's barred windows.

It was always a happy occasion going to El Jardín, where the Perea family spent many of their weekends. El Jardín was Abuelita Sofía's *finca*, a country plantation in the village of Artemisa in the province of Pinar del Río, eighty miles from Havana.

Sofía and Lucilo Palacio owned three plantations in this province. La Merced grew sugar cane, La Paulina tobacco, and El Jardín, where they made their home, manufactured bricks for local construction companies. After Lucilo's death,

Muñequita Linda

Sofía was unable to run all three plantations on her own. She decided to sell the properties, except for El Jardín, home to the Palacio family for generations. There she remained with her staff of maids, cooks, gardeners, and a caretaker.

The scenic two-hour drive covered vast beaches, miles of white sand embracing the turquoise Caribbean Sea. The tropical greenery was sprinkled with royal palm trees, la Palma Real de Cuba, their heavy fronds cascading from atop gleaming white trunks. Ninina's father always pointed them out.

The rich farmlands of Pinar del Río produced much of the island's tobacco. During harvest season, *los guajiros*, the peasant farm workers, could be seen carrying the tobacco leaves, which hung from long wooden poles perched on their shoulders. They walked slowly, two by two, their tanned skin covered in loose cotton shirts and their sun-wrinkled faces shadowed under straw hats.

The car drove past many *bohíos*, thatched-roof huts of bamboo and palms, where the *guajiros* lived with their families. By their front doors, flowers bloomed in large olive-oil cans. The penniless *guajiros* lived in Cuba's isolated countryside and worked the land owned by the rich upper-class. The deep rural silence of the morning was broken by voices of children at play. Ninina watched them running barefoot and shirtless, their young bodies darkened from the sun, playing carefree in the heat of a tropical summer day. She waved at them, but they did not wave back. Their eyes were fixed on the fancy chauffeured car passing by.

Five blocks long, the *finca's* entrance was lined on both sides with fields of pineapple. Beyond was a thick green field of tobacco. There were many framboyáns, or Royal Poinsettia—willowy trees bursting with vibrant red blooms on feathery leaves. At the end of the driveway stood a white mansion wrapped by a columned veranda. Nearby, a carriage house and barn housed the horses that Lucilo, Ninina's grandfather, had enjoyed riding up until his death.

Entering the foyer of the plantation, Rolando felt a sense of family tradition. In contrast to his family's scrupulous home environment, El Jardín, though equally elegant, had a welcoming warmth and vitality that was unfamiliar to him. Instead of the latest European line of furniture, there were *taburete* chairs, made of the island's tropical hardwood, with leather seats and backrests, mingled with native mahogany and cane rockers, some specifically handcrafted for children, and a *tete-a-tete*, a conversational settee. Family portraits from past generations to present filled the walls.

Abuelita Sofía appeared at the top of the stairs. Standing proudly, she held on to the banister. The skirt of her black dress swayed as she took each slow step. For the past six years, since the death of her husband, Sofía honored the mourning custom of *de luto*, wearing black. On special occasions, she wore something white with the black. Around her shoulders rested an ivory *mantilla* made of Spanish lace, and her abundant white hair was coiled on top of her head in a chignon, ornamented by a silver *peinetta*. Through her wire-rimmed glasses, her fiery dark eyes were glowing with joy.

Rolando sprinted up the steps to reach her. He gave her his arm. "*Feliz cumpleaños*, Doña Sofía. I have been looking forward to meeting you."

Sofía smiled as happily as a child and placed her hand on his right cheek. "You must be Rolando, and I can see why my Ninina is so happy. Welcome to El Jardín." Rolando was entranced by the softness of her hand and the sweet scent of her perfume. He helped her down the rest of the stairs while Sofía patted his arm gently.

"*¿Qué tal, mi amor?*" she greeted Ninina, reaching out to embrace her granddaughter.

"Abuelita, how pretty you look! *Felicidades!*" Ninina kissed her grandmother on the cheek and hugged her tight.

The family filled the house with a contagious gaity. Milly's piano playing and off-key singing livened up the living room. Presents were piled around Abuelita Sofía's favorite cane-backed rocker. After a lunch of *arroz con pollo*, Sofía blew out three candles symbolic of past, present, and future on her enormous birthday cake.

Walking around the *finca*, Rolando and Ninina wandered into Sofía's flower garden, shaded by an arbor of Indian laurel. The brilliant red flowers on the framboyán trees glistened in the late afternoon sun.

"I love this tree," Ninina said as they came upon a colonial ceiba. "My grandfather and I always sat under it to rest after horseback riding." The ancient tree's immense trunk had cave-like openings the children loved to crawl into while playing hide and seek. Mossy vines hung from the python limbs, which spread out like a huge umbrella.

They sat on the velvet lawn shaded by the majestic tree. Rolando leaned back against the trunk. Ninina kicked off her espadrilles and felt the cool grass between her toes. She snuggled against Rolando's shoulder. Her mood grew quiet.

19

"I miss Abuelo." Ninina's voice broke off. "You would have liked him. He had the heartiest laugh."

"*Mira*, you know what? I have something I hope will cheer you up." Rolando took out a small box from his pants pocket. Opening it up, he showed it to her and said, "Will you marry me, *muñequita linda?*" Ninina blinked back tears, looking at a sparkling diamond set on a platinum diamond band. Rolando took the ring and gently put it on her finger. "Perfect fit! So, it has to be a yes," he told her with a devilish smile.

"¡*Sí*, Rolando, *sí, sí, sí*!" She threw her arms around his neck, and under the venerable ceiba tree, they kissed and pledged their love to each other. As Ninina clung to Rolando, she looked up at the branches and closed her eyes. A soft breeze was rustling the leaves. For a moment, she thought she heard Abuelo Lucilo's laughter.

The wedding was set for December 1942. Both families agreed that the couple should wait for Rolando to complete his education before marrying. While Rolando studied and learned his father's business, the political scene in Cuba was shifting quickly.

The island had endured numerous political upheavals since the Spanish American War in 1898, when it won independence from Spain, ending four hundred years of domination. The turmoil continued under the leadership of the men who subsequently ruled Cuba, starting with its first president, Estrada-Palma, followed by the ruthless dictator General Machado, then Céspedes, Grau San Martín, and Mendieta. Each leader promised changes that would heal the island's political wounds, but each man seemed more corrupt than the previous one until Fulgencio Batista came to power in 1940.

All hopes were placed on this young mulatto, who was known for his fiery speeches. During his first term in office, he made great democratic and social progress, vowing to help the Cuban labor movement become one of the most powerful and effective in the world. The Cuban people clung to his promises for peace and stability on their island while World War II was raging in Europe. The U.S. fully supported Batista's government. The island's white upper class benefited from this courtship and from their president's partiality toward Cuba's wealthy.

Cuban law required couples to be married in a civil ceremony prior to a church wedding. Rolando and Ninina's civil union took place on December 2, 1942. Three days later, they were married in Belén Chapel in a private Jesuit school in Marianao, Havana. Ninina wore an ivory satin gown trimmed with French lace. Her grandmother Sofía's gold crucifix hung around her neck, and she carried a bouquet of gardenias. Rolando looked a debonair groom in his black tuxedo.

The couple spent a two-week honeymoon touring the island of Cuba by train. They began their married life in the small town of Bayamo in Oriente province. Rolando worked full-time at his father's lumber business, and his position required him to oversee the wood exportation from the company's site there. They lived in Hotel Bayamo in the quaint country town, so different from the hustle and bustle of Havana. While Rolando was at work, Ninina spent her time embroidering, reading, writing letters, and listening to the radio. Sometimes she sat on the front porch swing visiting with the hotel owners and other guests.

Bored and homesick, Ninina counted the minutes until her husband got home. She looked forward to their dining out, often followed by a movie and romantic moonlit walks home. Rolando was attentive and loving, and their adjustment to married life was easy. When the newlyweds returned to Havana after two months, they were expecting their first child.

The couple settled with Ninina's parents in Marianao until their daughter María Elena was born in November 1943. After an excruciatingly long labor, the baby was delivered with the umbilical cord wrapped around her neck, her face blue, barely breathing. Miraculously, she survived.

"I will never let anything happen to our baby again, Ninina," a distraught Rolando vowed to his wife at her hospital bedside. He checked on the baby constantly and incessantly asked the doctor questions about her health.

In January 1944, Rolando and Ninina bought their first home, in La Víbora. They had several servants and, as was the custom in upper-class families, Ninina hired a *tata*, a live-in nanny for the baby. Ninina had known Consuelo all her life. She was the younger sister of Carmen, Ninina's former nanny and now her parents' housekeeper. As a little girl, Consuelo had often accompanied her sister to work, taking the bus from Habana Vieja to the Perea home in Vedado. On such days, Consuelo helped Carmen with menial household chores, but mostly she played with Ninina. Sweet-natured and quiet, with limpid green eyes, Consuelo was only two years older than Ninina, and the girls became inseparable.

Consuelo loved her friend's dolls. Ninina let her pick

one of her favorites and they played *cocinaditos* in the courtyard, pretending to cook for their babies with cut-up leaves and flower petals. Carmen would often give them a little flour, to which they added water and made wonderful gooey pretend pies and cakes. While playing one day, Consuelo was combing her doll's hair and asked Ninina, "When you have a real baby someday, can I be her *tata* and live with you?"

"You have to be very good with children, like my *tata* Carmen is," Ninina told her, sounding serious. Consuelo nodded, softly patting the doll's hair. "*Vale*, so you can be my baby's first *tata*, and when *you* have a baby," Ninina smiled brightly, "they can be friends like we are."

Consuelo became an orphan at a young age. She was born in a village on Cienfuegos Bay, where her father worked as a fisherman. When she was six years old, his boat capsized during a storm. Two days later, his bloated, limbless body, tangled up in the rigging of a broken mast, washed up on shore.

Her mother was overcome with grief and deep depression and was unable to care for her daughters physically or emotionally. Near poverty, fifteen-year-old Carmen took over as the family caregiver, doing laundry and housecleaning for pay. Their mother spent her days sitting on a rocker on the front porch of their seaside bungalow. Staring out to sea, she would say to her daughters tonelessly that she was waiting for their Papi to come home.

One day, following a heavy rainstorm a few weeks after her father's death, Consuelo's mother kissed both girls tenderly and hugged them for a long time before going for a walk on the beach at sunset. As Carmen helped her little sister to bed, Consuelo pointed out their bedroom window:

"*Mira*, Carmen. Mami is going for a swim." The girls watched as their mother slowly walked into the restless ocean. Consuelo stood on the porch as her sister ran toward the shore, screaming to her mother, whose head had already disappeared under the mounting waves.

After their mother's death, Consuelo and Carmen went to live with their grandmother in Habana Vieja. For weeks Consuelo would speak to no one until one day her *abuela* made her a rag doll. The little girl poured her life into her *bebé*, slowly emerging from her emotional trauma. Consuelo cared for the dolly with an uncanny tenderness that astonished her *abuela*. She grew up loving children and prepared to be a *tata*. Unlike her older sister, who had an outgoing personality, Consuelo was demure, mature for her age, and fiercely loyal to those she cared for.

Ninina kept her word and hired Consuelo as nursemaid to María Elena. But when Consuelo came to live with them, Rolando continued to hover over the baby, hawking the nanny's every move with the child. Ninina reassured him of Consuelo's skills. She assumed her husband's behavior was characteristic of a new father and that his exaggerated concern was caused by how close they had come to losing María Elena.

One day, Rolando came home and presented his wife with a small velvet box.

"How sweet, Rolando!" Ninina smiled at the unexpected gift. "What's the occasion?"

"It's something to help keep the baby safe," he said, and watched as Ninina opened the little box. She frowned.

"Rolando, what does this mean?" Ninina's voice was

unsteady. She stared at the gold pin with the words "Please do not kiss me" engraved on it.

"I don't want people slobbering all over María Elena every time they see her. She'll catch some awful disease," he cried out breathlessly. "I want her to wear this pin all the time, I mean it!"

"Rolando, be reasonable," Ninina urged. "People are more thoughtful than that. They wouldn't…"

"I don't care," he exploded. "She's wearing it all the time." There were tiny beads of perspiration on his flushed face. "Only you and I can kiss María Elena, no one else, no one!" he yelled. "I want Consuelo to wash her hands before holding the baby and to boil the water for her baths."

"Rolando, stop this!" Ninina pleaded. "There's no need for all these precautions. The baby is healthy, and Consuelo is an excellent nanny." There was a knock on the French doors to the living room where they were. It was Consuelo, bringing baby María Elena to her parents after her dinner.

"Consuelo!" Rolando thundered, glaring at the young woman. "Did you wash your hands before touching María Elena?"

The nanny looked startled. "*S-s-s-í, caballero*, my hands were clean." Her voice was just above a whisper as she glanced nervously at Ninina.

"If I ever see my daughter not wearing this pin, you will leave our home immediately. Ninina, tell her what she has to do," Rolando threatened and stormed out of the room. The baby started to whimper. Ninina took her from Consuelo's arms, and the *tata* began to sob.

"Señora Nini, what have I done wrong?" she asked. "I

am a clean person. I bathe every day. I try my best to do a good job with María Elena." Ninina hugged her with her free arm while trying to quiet the baby.

"Consuelo, please, it's not your fault. *El caballero* is overly concerned with María Elena's health, that's all." She tried to comfort her, but her friend was inconsolable.

"Señora, I don't know if I can work like this. No, Señora, I don't," she said, choking up, and left the room. The baby stopped crying and cooed in the comfort of her mother's arms. Ninina sat in a wicker rocker by the window overlooking her garden and gently rocked her daughter.

She turned to look at a honeymoon picture on the table beside her. In it, she and Rolando smiled radiantly. Ninina put the picture face down on the table and gave her sleeping baby a kiss.

Ninina convinced Consuelo to stay on, promising her that she would talk to her husband and stop him from hounding her about María Elena's care. Rolando backed off at Ninina's insistence, but Consuelo felt intimidated by him.

After the pin incident, other oddities began to surface. Rolando refused to eat meat and certain foods for fear of poisoning.

"*Pero mi amor,* who would want to harm you?" an astounded Ninina asked.

"Don't you see?" He pushed the *bistec* to the side of the plate. "That Consuelo has the cook against me now, too."

"No, Rolando, that's not true. You're imagining things." But he would not listen to her and became even more agitated. Ninina soon realized it was no use reasoning with her husband.

She began to find scattered pieces of paper throughout the house on which Rolando had written incomprehensible notes. The first one was in the bathroom hamper. *Papá is checking up on my work,* he had scribbled. *Everyone in the office is watching me.* Consuelo found one on the living room floor. *I will die of food poisoning in this house.*

One evening, Ninina found another scrap of paper under Rolando's pillow. *Maids coughing, much bacteria in the house… check weather…* She sat at the edge of the bed and dropped her arm on her lap, holding the rumpled bit of paper in her hand. Something inside gripped her hard. *What is happening to Rolando? This is not normal.*

At Ninina's parents' home for dinner one night, Rolando brushed off the maid serving him *palomilla*.

"None for me, thanks," he told her. Mercedes overheard him and looked perplexed.

"Rolando, you love *palomilla*. Don't you feel well?"

"It's too risky, Mercedes," he answered in a low voice so the others could not hear. "I can't take a chance." Then he resumed eating his black beans and white rice. Mercedes shot a quick glance at her daughter, who had heard their conversation. Ninina quickly put her index finger to her lips and shook her head. Her mother nodded and passed her the rolls.

After dinner, while Rolando was outside smoking a cigar, Ninina asked her parents to come into the study with her. Gustavo closed the door behind them.

"I need to talk to you about Rolando," Ninina blurted as soon as they were in the room.

"What's the matter with him?" Mercedes asked pointedly. Gustavo was also concerned. He had noticed Rolando's moody behavior.

"There's something wrong with him," Ninina said. "He thinks someone wants to poison him, and he's driving Consuelo crazy with his demands about caring for María Elena. I don't know what to do." She began to twirl the wedding band on her finger. "He's irritable most of the time and hasn't been able to do his job well at work, either."

"*Mi vida*, you need to talk to his parents. There are doctors who can help him," Gustavo reassured her. "You must get to the bottom of this, the sooner the better." He reached out for his daughter's hand, stopping her ring twirling. "Your mother and I are here for you, and we will do whatever is necessary to help you." His voice was steady yet urgent. Mercedes pushed back some wisps of hair from Ninina's face.

"Ay, *hija*, I will pray for both of you," she said, giving Ninina a hug.

Ninina's eyes were brimming with tears. "It's so strange. I don't know why he's acting that way." Her voice quivered as she looked at her father. "I'm really scared, Papi."

Gustavo held both her hands firmly. "Tomorrow, Nini. You call José tomorrow."

With the help of her in-laws, in the fall of 1947 Ninina arranged for her young husband to see the first of many psychiatrists. A drug treatment for several weeks to calm his disturbed state of mind did not help. The psychiatrist next recommended that Rolando undergo an electric convulsive treatment. He explained how a carefully regulated electric current would pass through the head, producing convulsions and unconsciousness. It would shorten the periods of his depression so that he might seem free of the disorder, but it would be a temporary remission, a quick fix. It was not a cure and would not prevent further attacks.

Ninina was horrified by the thought of bolts of electricity attacking Rolando's body while he lay strapped to a bed. She refused. It was her father-in-law who convinced her otherwise, pointing out that this was the best psychiatrist in Havana and that many of his patients had responded well to the treatment.

Rolando's first electroshock treatment was successful. Immediately after, he seemed his normal self once again, but the side effects were harsh; his body was left exhausted and he suffered transitory memory impairment. The psychiatrist recommended a restful vacation to help Rolando recuperate.

In December 1947, Rolando took Ninina, Consuelo, and the baby to Miami for a two-week vacation. They rented a small villa by the ocean, and it was like a second honeymoon. Rolando enjoyed being with his family and praised Consuelo for her good work with the baby.

Back home, he was calmer and more rational, able to work productively again. He took Ninina to baseball games, boxing (a favorite for them both), and tennis matches. They had an active social life with their families and friends. Ninina was filled with hope and optimism.

María Elena was four years old by now—a lively little girl, thriving and happy in Consuelo's care. One day during this tranquil time, in January 1948, Ninina was watching her daughter play in the garden and suddenly felt nauseated.

"Consuelo, I think Ramona uses too much garlic, don't

you?" she asked, putting one hand on her stomach as she grimaced.

"No, Señora Nini, I love Ramona's cooking." Consuelo looked at Ninina and frowned. "I have noticed lately you complain about a lot of things you eat," she said, watching Ninina's face grow pale. "Why, the other night you did not finish your *carne asada*, your favorite," she went on while tying María Elena's shoelace. Ninina abruptly got up.

"Consuelo, I think I'm going to throw up," she announced, putting her hand on her mouth and rushing toward the house.

"¡*Ay, que bueno, niñita*!" an ebullient Consuelo said to the little girl, reaching out for her hand. "*Ven*, it's time for your *merienda*. Let's go see how your Mami is doing." Watching the child skipping ahead of her, she said to herself, "Soon there will be another little someone for you to play with."

* * *

La Virgencita de Abuelita

Rolando was ecstatic with the news of Ninina's pregnancy. He pampered her and was sympathetic about her morning sickness. With Consuelo's vigilant help, he made sure she ate right. He was getting along with Consuelo and now fully trusted her with the care of his wife and daughter.

In February 1948, Rolando and Ninina moved to Vedado so he could be closer to his doctor and the medical center. Their new home was an elegant mansion, its property enclosed by a wrought-iron fence and elaborate front gates. Ninina was happy living in Vedado, with her parents and Abuelita Sofía, who now lived with Mercedes and Gustavo, nearby. Sofía had suffered a severe bout of bronchitis the previous year while living at El Jardín. She developed an alarming high fever from a secondary infection, which left her partially deaf. At eighty-six years old, her fragile health and physical condition forced her to sell her beloved *finca* and move in with her daughter.

It was difficult to let go of El Jardín, with its myriad family memories. Mercedes was devastated. She was born at El Jardín; it was home. She had celebrated her civil marriage to Gustavo there in a beautiful ceremony in her mother's flower garden. And there, the extended families had gathered most Sundays since she was a child. But the sacrifice was necessary in order to give her mother the best possible care during the last years of her life.

The day the *finca* was sold, Gustavo went out to join his wife in the garden. Mercedes was gathering the last bouquet from her mother's flowerbeds before leaving El Jardín forever. Through her quiet tears, she said to her husband, "*Ay*, Gustavo, who will tend Mamá's garden now?" They sat in the gazebo where they had first kissed as husband and wife.

"Bebita," he said, using his nickname for her, "I promise someday you will have another *finca* with a garden. We will carry on El Jardín's tradition and gather with our family every weekend." Mercedes leaned her head on his shoulder.

"*Dios quiera que sí*, Gustavo," she sighed, and the thought comforted her.

Sofía had settled in with her family and spent most of her days in her large, airy bedroom, which had atrium doors opening out to a patio. Her weakening eyesight still allowed her to read, but the arthritis was problematic, especially in her legs and hands. Sofía used an earpiece resembling a small trumpet and learned to read lips and sign language. In the corner of her room was her cane-backed *sillón*, cushioned with pillows. Next to it, a small altar held a statue of the Blessed Mother, Our Lady of Mercy, to whom she prayed a rosary daily.

Ninina visited her grandmother often, many times bringing little María Elena with her. One sunny day in February 1948, they stopped by for a visit after shopping in Habana Vieja. Sofía's face lit up when she saw them.

"*Ven, niña linda, ven acá.*" She gestured to her great-granddaughter to come sit on her rocker with her. "*Y dame un besito bien rico.*" With open arms, the little girl complied and gave her a kiss.

"Belita, these are for you," chattered María Elena, handing Sofía a fragrant bouquet of jasmine. "I picked them myself," she yelled proudly into the trumpet Sofía held to her ear.

"*Pero* María Elenita, how did you know these are my favorite flowers?" She hugged the child, who squirmed next to her.

"I just knew it, Belita," María Elena replied, wiggling her feet and hugging her dolly with delight. Ninina embraced and kissed her grandmother and took the flowers to put them in water. She placed the vase by La Virgencita, as Sofía called the Blessed Mother. At the foot of the statue, a lit votive candle shone brightly. Ninina then sat by Sofía and stroked her grandmother's arm.

María Elena held her baby doll in midair. "Belita, do you like my new dolly? Mami bought it for me at the store." Sofía took the doll in her gnarled hands.

"She is precious, *mi querer*," she said. Holding the doll

brought memories of how her Virgencita came to be a part of her family. She recalled when she and Lucilo were newlyweds living in El Jardín. Every Sunday they attended Mass in a little church in the nearby village of Artemisa. On a side altar was a beautiful statue of Our Lady of Mercy, to whom Sofía was devoted. Every week she lit a votive candle to the Blessed Mother and said a prayer for special intentions: a loved one's health, job, marriage, or personal concerns.

One night, a terrible fire burned the church to the ground. Lucilo and a group of men from the village helped to clean up the ruins. Sorting through the rubble, Lucilo came upon what was the altar of the Blessed Mother. All that remained was the small statue laying on a pile of ashes, her beautiful face blackened with soot. The clothing had been burned off, but she was intact. Lucilo carefully gathered the statue in his arms and, wrapping it in his jacket, took it home to his wife.

Sofía called it a miracle that the statue had survived the fire. She painstakingly cleaned her, retouched her eyes and lips, and, using her own dark brown hair, created locks to frame the delicate virgin's face. She then sewed her a long dress of ivory silk and Spanish lace. On the Blessed Mother's head, Sofía draped part of the ivory *mantilla* she had worn on her wedding day. A silver crown with a small crucifix held it in place.

Lucilo and Sofía returned the statue to the parish priest and told him what had happened. Aware of her deep devotion to Our Lady of Mercy, the priest told Sofía that the Blessed Mother now belonged with her. As he handed back the statue, Sofía was overcome with emotion. At that moment, she vowed that her Virgencita would always remain in her family.

Lucilo turned a small alcove in their bedroom into an oratory for his wife's precious Virgencita. The petite statue was always surrounded with fragrant flowers and a lit votive candle or two. To honor her devotion to La Virgen de las Mercedes, Sofía named her only daughter Mercedes.

María Elena tugged at Sofía's shawl, interrupting her reminiscing.

"*Mira*, Belita, *batidos*," she yelled excitedly into her great-grandmother's earpiece, seeing her grandmother walk in the room with their *merienda*.

"¡*Y empanaditas de guayaba*!" Mercedes added cheerfully, carrying a tray of *batidos de mamey*, her and her mother's favorite fruit shake, and a plate of warm guava pastries. She gave Sofía her medication, then handed her mother the frosty drink.

"Let's celebrate four generations of Palacio women." Sofía toasted her *batido* to her daughter, granddaughter, and great-granddaughter.

Three days later, Ninina's beloved grandmother died peacefully in her sleep.

Chapter Three

Yvonne

Ninina stopped pruning her roses. She stood on the narrow path in her flower garden and felt the warm fluid streaming down her legs.

"Rolando, my water broke," she announced calmly. "I think it's time."

Rolando tossed down the sports section of the newspaper and bounded down the porch steps. "Are you okay? Do you feel faint?" he asked, helping her walk inside the house. His face was ashen.

"I'm fine," Ninina assured him. "Let's go to the hospital and see what God will send us this time." She winced as a jab of pain shot through her abdomen.

Five years after María Elena's difficult birth, Ninina *dió a luz*, gave to the light, another girl in September 1948. After only three hours of labor, followed by a problem-free delivery, I weighed in at a robust and healthy 10.5 pounds.

"She looks like she's three months old," an exuberant Rolando told Ninina as she was wheeled into her room from delivery. There were tears in his eyes as he held her hand and kissed her. "She's perfect, Nini." He kissed her hand. "Thank you."

"María Elena will be so happy," Ninina said, groggy

35

with exhaustion. "She wants a little sister."

"What do you say we call her Yvonne?" Rolando smoothed the hair off Ninina's forehead. She perked up.

"Yvonne? Is that an American name?"

"No, it's French." Rolando kissed her hand again. "Don't you love it? I think it suits her fine."

"I don't know, Rolando," she replied wearily. "It sounds so foreign. I thought maybe we could name her Sofía after Abuelita." But Rolando wanted something different, not family-related. Ninina gave in for the time being, and for the first two months of my life I was called Yvonne.

A woman named Veronica was hired to be my live-in nursemaid. She was efficient and vivacious, doted on me, and got along well with Consuelo. Veronica had a lilting voice and loved singing to me. Her hands always smelled of *agua de violeta*, which she generously applied to my hair as she formed *un kiki*, a curl, on the top of my head. "¡*Mi niña linda!*" my *tata* always called me, especially when admiring her work of art on my hair.

A week before the baptism, my mother brought up the subject of my name.

"Rolando, we need to talk about the baby's name."

"What's wrong with Yvonne María?" He sounded surprised.

"Well, I just don't like the two names together." My father was deeply devoted to the Blessed Mother and wanted to give his daughters the name María. My mother liked the idea, but not with the name Yvonne.

"How about María Cristina, or better yet, Gloria María?" she suggested. Rolando took off his glasses, closed his eyes, and pressed the bridge of his nose.

"Okay, *muñequita linda*." He looked up at her and smiled. "Gloria María it is."

One afternoon, in the fall of 1950, when the *tatas* were preparing to take María Elena and me to the park, my father heard Veronica cough.

"Veronica, are you sick?" He startled her. "Why are you coughing?" My mother looked up from her letter writing.

"No, *caballero*, I am not." Veronica was holding me in her arms. "My sinuses act up this time of year, that's all." She was not timid like Consuelo, and she looked my father right in the eye.

"I don't want you to touch my children with that cough," he instructed as he briskly took me from her arms. Veronica looked at Consuelo, then at my mother, and shook her head.

"Rolando, *por Dios*," my mother said emphatically. "She's not sick." But my father would not listen to reason. From that day forward, he scrutinized every move the *tata* made. He watched her feed and bathe me and sat on the porch while she took me out to play. He hounded Veronica constantly, as he had done with Consuelo, and insisted she wash her hands often.

"*El caballero es un bicho raro*," Veronica commented to Consuelo as they sat down to dinner one night. "I can't deal with this *mierda* any longer."

"Yes, he has problems," Consuelo said as she ate her *picadillo*, "but *el caballero* has a good heart. Señora Nini needs our help, Veronica."

The following morning Veronica went to her room to gather her laundry. As she approached the doorway, she heard a noise. Peering through the open door, she saw my father inspecting her uniforms in the closet. Incensed, she stormed to the kitchen where my mother was.

"Señora, I can't go on working here," Veronica burst out, flapping her hands around. "*El caballero* is driving me crazy. He's in my room now, going through my clothes." By the time my mother reached the *tata*'s room, my father had left. She returned to the kitchen and saw Veronica taking off her white apron.

"If you could give me my wages, Señora," she said, throwing the apron on the kitchen table. "I am leaving right now."

"No, Veronica, please." My mother tried to assuage her. "Sit down and we will talk about this."

"Please kiss *mi niña linda* goodbye for me." Veronica's eyes glistened. "*Lo siento*, Señora," she said as she left the room.

After Veronica quit, my father's eccentricities intensified. He would not eat his meals unless my mother tasted them first. He had fears of persecution and became extremely protective of his children. He continued receiving electroshock treatments, a dreaded experience for both my parents. Each session left him exhausted and confused.

In addition to the electroshock, the doctor tried hypnosis, but nothing worked. My father hardly slept, could not go to work, and refused to leave the house. He became withdrawn, confused in his speech and thinking, and he feverishly wrote notes to himself. His progressive breakdown climaxed when he locked himself in the bathroom and threatened suicide. He would not listen to my mother's pleas to open the door. In a panic, she called my grandfather

José to come help her. Hearing his father's voice, my father unlocked the door.

"Papá, help me." He slumped in his father's arms and cried. My mother then called the psychiatrist, who recommended immediate hospitalization.

"Nini, don't let them hurt me," my father pleaded. "I'm going to die if they take me there. They want me dead." His eyes were wild with fear. "You are the only one I can trust."

"Rolando, I will go with you." Ninina held her husband like a child as they sat at the edge of their bed. Her voice faded out as she fought back tears. "You need help."

My father was diagnosed with paranoid schizophrenia, and the doctors gave my mother no hope for a cure. The treatment options were a lobotomy or permanent hospitalization in a sanatorium. She vehemently refused both. The only alternative now was continued treatment with sedatives, which would cure nothing but keep him calmer when his behavior became dangerously disturbed or aggressive.

My mother became *una viuda en vida*, a widow in life. She realized that her gentle and loving Rolando would never fully return. His behavioral deterioration was advancing at an alarming pace. What was happening to him? How much worse could it become? The only assurance the doctors could give her was that the mental disorder was permanent. My father would be an emotionally sick man for the rest of his life.

My mother accepted her future as God's will and prayed for the strength to face the oncoming difficulties. She was resigned to take care of her husband any way she could.

After my birth, my mother had become concerned about

getting pregnant again. When given my father's diagnosis, she worried that the illness might be hereditary. She was fearful of bringing more children into their lives and of how Rolando's illness would affect them. The Catholic Church dictates that married couples should not prevent the conception of children; to do so is a sin. Both staunch Catholics, my parents discussed this issue. My father resisted my mother's proposal of practicing the rhythm method, a form of natural family planning the Church condones only if there is a "grave reason" to postpone pregnancy. My mother believed, without any qualms, that schizophrenia would certainly qualify, but my father could not deal with the guilt and did not cooperate.

My brother was born in June 1951. Shortly after the birth, as my mother held her sleeping infant, she thought of her husband in the psychiatric clinic. She recalled the first time she had seen the Mazorra institution on her way to pick up Abuelita Sofía's birthday cake and the dreadful impression it had made on her. Her Rolando, in a place like that. *He should be here with me now, holding our first-born son,* she thought. The baby stirred. His face was blurry through her tears.

"José Rolando," she said to him. "I think your Papi will like that name for you."

Following the birth, my mother was determined to practice the rhythm method. Discussing her decision with a priest during confession, she was told she was committing a sin, from which he could not absolve her. She walked out of the confessional in shock. How could the Church not accept her situation as a "grave reason?" How could she continue having babies with a schizophrenic husband?

Kneeling in front of the altar, she asked God to forgive her the sin she had to keep committing. My mother continued attending Sunday Mass, but she did not receive Communion. She knew she could not, being in a state of sin. It destroyed her spiritually, but she did not give up her faith. Her love of God was separate and went deeper than the Church's dictates. In her heart she knew God understood her problem and forgave her.

By August, my father's condition had improved enough for him to go home. The doctor informed my mother that with the medication he could have symptom-free periods during which he could handle the stresses of everyday life, but he required constant monitoring. Gradually, my father returned to work and seemed happy to be home with his family. My mother welcomed the peace that came with this, even if it was temporary.

In early 1952, Fulgencio Batista overthrew the Cuban government with a bloody *coup d'etat* and became the island's dictator. During his first term in power, Batista had been revered as a man of the people. When his presidential term ended in 1944, he left behind a country prime for democratic rule. But the two corrupt leaders who succeeded him, Grau San Martín and Prío Sacarrás, ruined the good work Batista had done for the island. The Cuban people gave up on the idea of democracy; it was their broken spirit that prompted Batista to come out of retirement in Key Biscayne and return to power.

With Batista at the helm again, my family was filled with optimism, remembering how good things were when he was president. Cuba prospered during Batista's second term in office. He encouraged foreign investment in the island and established badly needed public works. He allowed American organized crime to take over Havana, controlling most of the major hotels, casinos, and popular nightclubs in the island's capital. American tourism was high, and U.S. businesses flourished, especially in Havana.

As a wedding gift, my mother's parents had given the couple three acres on Avenida de los Mangos, in a quiet country suburb of Havana. Unlike the ornate, iron-gated mansions of Vedado, these homes were modern and unpretentious, with extensive acreage. During this wave of prosperity, my father built my mother her dream house. Despite his illness, he was enthusiastic and totally involved with the project, though at times he was heavily sedated.

Soon after Batista's *coup*, my mother discovered she was pregnant again, this time with twins. My brother was barely nine months old. She was overwhelmed with the news and concerned how my father would react.

"Oh yeah? When is that going to happen?" my father asked her impassively when she told him. He kept looking over the architect's blueprints in front of him.

"End of September," my mother answered anxiously, watching his reaction.

"I can't deal with this, Ninina," he said irritably. "I have too much going on with the building of this house." He slammed the papers on the dining room table. A dark expression unknown to my mother veiled his face. "You've been spending a lot of time with that gardener," he scoffed. "Are you sure they're mine?"

"*Por Dios*, Rolando, how can you say that to me? Rolando, look at me," she yelled, but he ignored her and kept reading the blueprints. My mother ran out of the room to their bedroom and slammed the door. She dropped on the bed and sobbed.

There was a soft rapping on the door. "Señora Nini, may I come in?" Before getting an answer, Consuelo walked in, sat on the bed next to my mother, and put her hand on her shoulder.

"Señora...Nini, don't upset yourself. *Mire*, think of those babies you're carrying," she said imploringly, giving my mother a handkerchief from the night table.

"¡*Ay*, Consuelo! What's going to happen now?" My mother sat up and blew her nose. "Five children and a sick husband." Her voice was small. "I don't know who he is anymore," she sighed, shaking her head in despair.

"Señora, you will get through this," Consuelo said, squeezing her forearm. "I will be here to help you, *siempre*."

"Consuelo." My mother looked at her childhood friend. Consuelo's green eyes were doleful. "I am so grateful that you're here."

My father remained indifferent to my mother's pregnancy.

During the construction of the house, my mother waged a battle with a difficult term. The babies were large and her weight ballooned. Her legs swelled from water retention. The skin on her abdomen was stretched so thin it hurt to the touch. She slept sitting up in a recliner. At her doctor's insistence, she was hospitalized for the last month of her pregnancy.

My grandmother Mercedes visited her daughter at the hospital every day, keeping her up-to-date with her family, bringing her favorite foods, and gently rubbing soothing cream on my mother's swollen abdomen. Mercedes suffered deeply with her daughter's physical and spiritual plight. It had been more than a year since my mother had received Communion, which greatly troubled my grandmother. Mercedes was very involved with her church and was fond of her parish priest, Padre Antonio, who had become a close family friend. My grandmother shared my mother's distress with Padre Antonio and arranged for the priest to visit my mother at the hospital one afternoon. She reluctantly agreed, mostly to appease my grandmother. To her surprise, Padre Antonio told her that he believed her circumstances warranted justification for practicing the rhythm method.

The following day, Padre Antonio brought Communion to my mother at the hospital. He stood by her bedside, and kissing his stole, he draped it around his neck. He held up the host and solemnly said, *"Corpus Dómini nostri, Jesu Christi, custódiat ánimam tuam in vitam aetérnam*—The body of Our Lord, Jesus Christ, preserve thy soul unto life everlasting."

My mother responded "Amen" and looked at the holy wafer. Then she closed her eyes and opened her mouth to again receive Communion with Christ.

The fraternal twins were born on September 24, 1952, the feast day of Our Lady of Mercy. "La Virgencita's answer to our prayers," Mercedes told my mother at the hospital. Throughout her daughter's perilous pregnancy, Mercedes prayed diligently to the statue of the Blessed Mother, which, after Sofía's death, was now in her care.

My mother easily delivered 16 pounds of babies, in spite of her troublesome pregnancy. María Magdalena de las Mercedes, whom my father nicknamed Madeleine, another French name, weighed 8.5 pounds, and Jorge Ignacio followed at 7.5 pounds.

At nine and four years old, María Elena and I were anxiously awaiting our siblings' arrival with Consuelo and the new live-in *tata*, Caridad, who was hired to help with the five children. My father was unaffected by the twins' births. He seemed dazed the day he brought them and my mother home from the hospital. Carrying an infant on each arm, he said to them without feeling, "Welcome home, *bebés*." Then he handed them over to the nannies and went up to his room.

My father was healthy just long enough to see the completion of the two-story house for his family. My parents named our new home La Coronela. It was ample and cool, its property surrounded by a variety of tropical fruit trees, palm trees, and willowy framboyáns. Our mango tree yielded its sweet juicy fruit and was conveniently planted by our large back porch. A huge ceiba tree grew wild orchids from its trunks. My sister and I used the tree's rope-like vines for our Jane and Tarzan swings.

We moved to La Coronela in December 1952 and prepared to celebrate a happy Christmas. Decorating *el arbolito*, the Christmas tree, was a traditional family event in our home, and everyone was involved. While my father was stringing up the last of the colored lights, María Elena and I eagerly helped my mother open the boxes of decorations.

"Papi, I can't find a branch to hang my star," I said as

I circled the tree, leaving a trail of glitter from my homemade ornament behind me.

"How about way up here, right next to Baby Jesus?" he suggested, lifting me up to reach the tiny glass nativity. "Perfect!" he said as I hooked the glittery mess on the thick branch. My mother was sitting on the couch separating the garlands and tinsel packets. My father walked over and sat next to her while we continued decorating the tree.

"It's a pretty tree, Rolando," she exclaimed. "You did a fine job with the lights." Papi kicked off his shoes, stretched back on the couch, and put his arm around my mother.

"*Gracias, cariño.* The kids are having fun trimming it," he said as he watched me load up another branch with ornaments. "You smell good," he told my mother, nuzzling her neck. "Is that a new perfume you're wearing?"

"It's the French perfume you gave me for my birthday," she answered inattentively, separating the tinsel.

"That's why it smells so sexy," he teased her, kissing her neck. "*Es Francés.*"

"Rolando, there's something I need to talk to you about." My mother's tone grew serious as my father looked at her, concerned. "Remember when I told you I was expecting the twins?" she said hesitantly. He nodded, frowning. "The snide comment you made broke my heart." She looked down at the box of tinsel on her lap and fiddled with a dangling piece. "How could you be so cruel to me?"

My father was startled. "What are you talking about, Ninina?" He stared at her. "What did I say?"

She read his face in disbelief, realizing he did not have a clue. "You insinuated they might not be yours. It's hounded me since then." She paused, cautious. "Did you really mean that?"

"¡*Ay, mentira*!" my father cried out. "I don't remember saying that to you, I swear!" His eyes were brimming with tears as he drew her nearer to him. "I'm sorry. You know I don't mean the sick things I say sometimes." He angled his forehead to touch hers, side by side. "It's as if there is someone else living inside me," he said ruefully. "When he takes over, I feel lost and powerless." He was distant for a moment, and my mother held his hand. "Don't give up on me," he pleaded. "Always remember how much I love you, no matter what this illness does to me." He gave her a tender kiss. "You are my life, *muñequita linda*."

Consuelo came to retrieve us for our *merienda*. As she, my sister, and I sang a raucous rendition of "Cascabel" on our way out of the living room, I turned to look at my parents. They sat quietly, facing the tree as its colored lights shimmered in the darkening room.

* * *

My grandfather Gustavo, successful in his position as vice-treasurer of Havana's sugar industry, invested the majority of his wealth in Cuban real estate. Bibi, as his grandchildren nicknamed him, owned properties in a countryside suburb of Havana and in Varadero Beach, in Matanzas province, on the northern coast of Cuba's Hicacos Peninsula.

Bibi made his home in a stately mansion in Marianao, Havana, and spent his weekends with his family relaxing at his country estate in Guatao, a rural area on the outskirts of Havana. This plantation home was the fulfillment of the promise Bibi had made my grandmother Mercedes, whom the grandchildren called Mama, when her family's *finca*, El Jardín, was sold.

"Now we have our own *finca*, Bebita," Bibi proudly told her the day Rancho Perea was completed, in the fall of 1952. My grandfather created this peaceful country haven with his extended family in mind. He and Mama gathered there every weekend, rain or shine, with their children and their spouses, grandchildren and *tatas*, friends and relatives. All birthdays, anniversaries, and holiday events were celebrated there.

My grandparents' *finca* was nestled amid acres of verdant Cuban countryside dotted with sleek royal palms. The grounds were abundant with exotic tropical plants, sapodilla and sacaranda trees, and flowers, especially the *mar pacífico*, a variety of hibiscus blooming in brilliant colors. The long driveway leading to the ranch-style home was lined with feathery areca palms and dense, shady trees. The heart and soul of the house was *el portal*, a spacious, tile-floored veranda that hugged its front and side. The flagstone steps were shaded on either side by scarlet hibiscus and pink oleanders. Alongside were *tinajas*, large earthen jars filled with fragrant heliotrope.

The kids' favorite hangout was a kidney-shaped pool, sparkling under the hot Cuban sun. Beyond the pool area, Bibi reserved several acres for an orchard of fruit trees: lemon, orange, lime, cherry, anon, mango, mamoncillo, and tamarindo, whose tart fruit lay hidden inside brown pods. Roaming free throughout the *finca* were peacocks, geese, and ducks, the latter always close to a small man-made pond near the orchard.

My grandparents built an elaborate playground for their grandchildren, complete with huge slides that ended in deep sandboxes. We slid down fast after one another, causing a pileup at the bottom, laughing wildly until our stomachs hurt. We kicked off our shoes in every direction and buried our socks in the sand, just to drive our *tatas* crazy. There were seesaws, merry-go-rounds, swings, rings, and teeter-totters. Nature provided my favorite plaything: bent palm trees, ideal for climbing to try to reach their delicious coconuts (much to the dismay of our worrywart *tatas*).

The family *finca* and my maternal grandparents are inseparable in my memories. Bibi, wearing *pantalones mecánicos*, his plaid shirt, and leather boots, sitting poolside with *un cigarrito con un traguito*—a little smoke with a little drink—and watching his grandchildren playing. "¡*Al agua patos*!" he would yell, giving us the go-ahead to jump in the water after an interminable three-hour wait post-meals.

Together, my grandparents formed a well of strength, love, and faith from which our family drew. It was my grandfather's love that got us through the worst of times, keeping us ever close under his protective wing. Bibi was a tremendously important part of my life; he filled the painful void created by my father's illness. To me, he was bigger than life. He walked around his *finca* with his Bebita, enjoying the beauty of his country and his family; he was fiercely loyal and devoted to both.

I remember Rancho Perea with an eerie precision, as if my mind, in its frequent yearning for it, will never let me forget. The core of all my fondest memories of Cuba was my maternal grandparents' beloved *finca*. Gathering at Rancho Perea preserved our family continuity. There I spent my early childhood in Cuba playing, sharing, and bickering with my cousins. There I learned how to swim, dive, climb trees, and ride my bike.

I remember all the activity: bikes, tricycles, and *carriolas* (scooters) whizzing up and down the long, winding driveway. The frantic *tatas* chasing after the little ones. The cooks prattling in the kitchen as they made lunch, its delicious aroma wafting in the breeze. The chauffeurs sitting under a shady framboyán tree by the kitchen, enjoying a fruit *batido* while they flirted with the maids.

I remember the laughter, grownups dancing to Cuban music on the rambling front porch, the bright hot sun shimmering through the royal palms. The occasional tears as we cousins quarreled, fell, and skinned our knees. But most of all, I recall the enjoyment and love of family, always visible and heartfelt.

Rancho Perea was our bastion. We felt safe in its enveloping privacy. The world and its problems remained outside the *finca's* huge wooden gates. As a child I thought it would be that way forever.

Chapter Four

El Guerrillero

The warm, foamy water inched closer to my sandcastle as the tide crawled in. Nearby under a thatched-roof umbrella, Caridad and Consuelo were tending the twins while my three-year-old brother and I played along the shore. It was August 1953, and we were enjoying the last day of our vacation in Kawama Beach.

"*El guerrillero* will return, Consuelo." Caridad absentmindedly handed my sister a pail and shovel. "That rebel, he won't give up. Next time he and his *barbudos* will come from the mountains and whip Batista," she told the *tata* confidently.

"*¿Ah, sí?* And what will happen then?" Consuelo asked, intrigued.

"He'll save us from this dictatorship, that's what," Caridad said knowingly.

I listened to the *tatas'* conversation from my sandy dugout until my brother waddled over and sat on my castle, giggling.

"¡*No, chibón*!" I wailed as he picked up a clump of my creation and whirled it at me. Consuelo stopped me before I poured a pail of water on him.

"Gloria, *él es un bebé*" she hissed at me, holding him

protectively. Consuelo had been showing an obvious partiality to my three-year-old brother.

"He's *not* a baby!" I protested, kicking sand over my wrecked castle. "He knew what he was doing and he's a brat!" I tossed my shovel on the wet sand. "I'm going inside," I announced to the *tatas* and trudged up the sandy path that connected our cottage to the beach. My mother was preparing lunch, and the sight of *empanaditas de carne*, her delicious meat turnovers, made me forget about my brother.

"Mami, who is *el guerrillero*?" I hopped on a stool by the kitchen counter.

"Where did you hear that name?" A frown came over her face.

"Caridad says that he will come again from the mountains with bearded soldiers and guns to save us from Batista." I watched my mother nervously wipe her hands on her apron. "What does that mean, Mami?"

"He's a man who doesn't like the way things are in Cuba." She paused, offering me a turnover. "And recently he tried to change them by making trouble for our government."

"Did he change them?" I asked with my mouth full.

"No, he was put in jail for breaking the law," Mami answered with a serious expression. I was five years old. That was all she thought I could handle.

"What's his real name?" I pressed on.

"Fidel Castro." My mother closed the subject, opening the porch screen door. "Now let's go out on the beach and call everyone in for lunch."

That summer Fidel Castro had become a household name. The hubbub in Havana was intense with details of the *guerrillero's* July 26 attack on the Moncada barracks in

El Guerrillero

Santiago, a heroic but futile attempt to overthrow the Batista government. Moncada was Cuba's second largest military installation, defended by more than four hundred of Fulgencio Batista's best military troops. Castro's small army of 123 revolutionaries, trained high in the Sierra Maestra Mountains, was no match for Batista's army. Only forty of the rebels survived. The rest were first horribly tortured and then assassinated by Batista's soldiers.

Castro and the few remaining rebels hid deep in the Santiago Mountains. Many of them surrendered as Batista's army approached. Castro was eventually found hiding in a small mountain village and was imprisoned.

¿Quién rayo es Fidel Castro? Fellow Cubans asked themselves that July in 1953. Where did he come from?

In 1887, an orphaned thirteen-year-old boy named Angel Castro arrived in Cuba from his native Spain. After enduring a miserable and abusive young life living with an uncle, he left Spain to live with another uncle in Cuba. Angel worked in his uncle's brick-making business for several years and then left to make it on his own. Uneducated, he worked relentlessly at various odd jobs and saved every penny he earned. Eventually he learned to read and write, and at the age of twenty-five he started his own business as an itinerant peddler.

Angel invested the bulk of his money in land in Mayarí, on the northern coast of Oriente province. Mayarí was a highly fertile agricultural area, excellent for harvesting tobacco and sugar cane. Angel continued his investments and soon became Don Angel Castro, an extremely wealthy landowner in Oriente. He built a grand plantation called the Manacas *finca*, encompassing approximately twenty-six thousand acres. He kept two thousand acres for himself and rented out the rest. Mostly a sugar cane plantation, the *finca* also raised cattle, cultivated fruits, and operated a sawmill where lumber was sold in large quantities.

Don Angel married and had two children. It is not clear whether his wife, María, died soon after delivering her second child or whether he left her. Don Angel later married Lina Ruz González, a maid in the household. Their child was born on August 13, 1926, and they named him Fidel Alejandro Castro Ruz.

Fidel enjoyed a privileged childhood. His early education was in Santiago, where he studied at La Salle School, a private boys' school run by the Marist Brothers. He was a rebellious student. Once, after being severely reprimanded by a priest, Fidel hit and bit him. His father took him out of school and put his son to work at Manacas *finca*. When Fidel's pleas to return to school were refused, he threatened to burn down the house. His petrified parents gave in.

When he was nine years old, Fidel began study with the Jesuit priests, known for their tough discipline and military-like school atmosphere. He grew into an excellent student, one who loved history, possessed a phenomenal memory, and enjoyed a good debate, claiming it built up his courage.

Fidel attended Belén, the exclusive Jesuit school in Havana. During his four years there, he was a formidable athlete. He bragged that he could succeed at anything he set out to do and overcome any weaknesses. Graduating in the top ten percent of his class, Fidel was respected and admired by his fellow students and professors. When he was handed his diploma, he received the longest standing ovation ever given to a student.

After graduating from Belén in 1945, Fidel Castro studied law at Havana University, and it was there that he became politically involved. In 1948, during his third year at the university, Castro became interested in the ideas of Lenin, Marx, and Engels and was lured by the concept of communism. He resented the United States and its foreign policies, claiming that he became a communist after studying the capitalist political economy. At this time, Cuba was disintegrating socially and politically. The island's population was divided between a small minority of the very wealthy and a large class of poor peasants.

That same year Fidel married Mirta Díaz-Balart, also from a wealthy Oriente family. They honeymooned in the United States and had a son the following year. In 1950, he graduated from the University of Havana with a doctorate degree in law, social sciences, and diplomatic law.

Castro worshipped José Martí and felt a personal link to the hailed Cuban apostle of independence. They were both sons of Spaniards, and Castro's home was near the Dos Ríos battlefield, the site where Martí was killed in 1895. Castro vowed to imitate Martí's life and follow his liberation ideals. He entered law practice with two other lawyers, working primarily to help the poor. In 1953, Fidel Castro became consumed by his dream of a revolution to depose the decaying Batista dictatorship. His marriage failed as a result of his burgeoning obsession. He formed a movement composed of bold revolutionaries, but they needed arms for their struggle. Not having money, they planned to attack the Moncada government barracks in

Santiago to seize the necessary arms and establish a headquarters for their movement.

Fidel Castro's revolution was born on July 26, 1953, the day he and his *guerrilleros* raided Moncada. In spite of being a failed attack, it was a great political success for Castro, introducing him to the Cuban people. He made a public vow: "Today we lost, but we will return." Those words reverberated around the island as Cubans waited and wondered what would happen next.

Fidel Castro acted as his own lawyer during his trial in September 1953 and defended himself eloquently. He claimed the rebels were justified in attacking Moncada because Batista had taken over Cuba through a military *coup* and violated the Constitution. He urged the Cuban people to fight the corrupt Batista government and ended his defense with passionate words: "Condemn me, it does not matter. History will absolve me."

Castro was sentenced to a fifteen-year prison term in Boniato prison, on Isla de Pinos south of the mainland. He used every moment to study, read, analyze, strategize, and continue to prepare his imprisoned men for the uprising. By age twenty-eight, despite his incarceration, Fidel Castro had gained notoriety as a major political leader.

Chapter Five

Hope in America

Little pieces of crumpled paper began appearing throughout the house again. *They're tapping our phones. Closing in on me. I'm a dead man...* my father scribbled after the phone repairman left. By November 1953, our family contentment in La Coronela came to a screeching halt.

Papi's fears of food poisoning and persecution were back with a vengeance. He was extremely sensitive to the maids' and *tatas'* conduct and became upset if they walked by him, looked at him, or, worst of all, coughed or sneezed near him. At times he seemed languid and confused, not making sense when he spoke. I recall how quiet he would be sometimes while I chattered away at him. He stared at me, his face impassive and cold. Yet there was a gentleness about my father that drew me to him, allowing me to love him despite his emotional deterioration.

By the time I started kindergarten, calm moments with Papi ebbed and flowed like the tides of the Caribbean as his illness claimed him again. From that point on, my mother became the sole parental figure in my life.

My father grew progressively worse. He claimed that my grandfather was having him watched at work, intending to kill him. He was suspicious of everyone and everything.

He refused to leave the house and did not allow anyone to visit our home. For three days he remained in bed, without changing his clothes and barely eating. Papi was hospitalized again. For the next two months, he stayed in a private mental clinic, and he was not well enough to come home for Christmas 1953.

Following another intensive round of drugs and hypnosis, my father's prognosis remained poor. The discouraged psychiatrist told my mother there was nothing more he could do. He suggested that my father be declared incompetent and institutionalized for the rest of his life. Again, my mother vehemently objected. She would not give up hope that somewhere, someone could help her husband.

In awe of her determination, the doctor researched a schizophrenia treatment by a psychiatrist named Jacob Naten in the United States. My mother enthusiastically urged that he contact him. After several phone conversations, the American psychiatrist agreed to handle my father's case.

In January 1954, my parents, paternal grandparents, and my father's psychiatrist boarded a plane to Philadelphia to meet with Dr. Naten. Following an initial evaluation session with my father alone, the psychiatrist quipped to my mother, "So, I hear you are Batista's mistress?"

"I guess that's who I am today," my mother replied. My father also told the doctor that his father was having him followed and that the Havana police were after him.

At that very first meeting, Dr. Naten assured my mother that after seven months of psychoanalysis treatment, without medication if at all possible, my father would be cured. He charged $7,000 a month plus all travel expenses.

Dr. Naten believed that patients would make better

social recoveries when treated in a home environment instead of in psychiatric hospitals, which involved lengthy stays, powerful drugs, and electric convulsive treatments, all of which usually had negative effects. The treatment homes were located in a picturesque farming community near the doctor's home in Plumsteadville, Pennsylvania. Papi would be living with Dr. Naten's medical assistant, David, and his wife, along with two other patients. David's large country home was set back in a secluded wooded area of the town of New Hope, in Bucks County. The residence was a peaceful place, with nature trails and a brook running through the property.

My father's treatment would entail conversational sessions with Dr. Naten, whose supposed insight into schizophrenia would hopefully enable him to communicate with Papi in a way that would persuade him to alter his behavior. Part of this treatment included recreational activities, always accompanied by a medical assistant, with the purpose of gradually exposing my father to the realities of the outside world, which would help him to better cope with life. Medication was used only when absolutely necessary.

Dr. Naten conducted his treatments in the homes where the patients resided, alternating with his own home in the countryside. He would be seeing my father two to three days a week. The remainder of the time, Papi would be under the constant care of David, who would supervise the recreational part of his treatment.

Following the lengthy meeting with Dr. Naten, the group stayed overnight at a Philadelphia hotel. The next day they drove my father to Bucks County to begin his treatment.

Heartbroken, yet full of hope, my mother returned to Cuba to care for her children.

For the next seven months, Mami traveled to Pennsylvania faithfully one week every month to be with my father. She stayed in a little hotel and visited him daily. My father was lucid most times, since medication was minimally administered. My mother never knew what to expect when she saw him. Sometimes he was thrilled to see her, attentive and affectionate. Other times he was irritable and withdrawn. He lost weight. Since he did not have anyone who would taste his food like my mother had done for him in Cuba, he ate little. Once an occasional cigarette smoker, he now smoked incessantly and often looked unkempt.

Doubt weighed heavy in my mother's heart each time she saw him. Month after month, no improvement was apparent. Each return trip to Cuba was more disheartening than the previous one. When the treatment ended in August 1954, my father was the same, if not worse.

"Señora Ninina, *teléfono*," Caridad called out to my mother in the backyard, where she was gardening while we children played. "It's the doctor from America returning your call." My mother was anxious to discuss the status of my father's treatment. Dr. Naten claimed that there was a communication problem with my father because of the language barrier.

My mother countered the doctor's statement with the fact that my father had been educated in the United States for ten years and had mastered the English language. Her confidence in the treatments began to waver.

Dr. Naten suggested another seven months of psychoanalysis. Reluctantly, my mother consented, on the condition that this time she and the children would go to America and live with Papi for the duration of the treatment. The separation had been hard on everyone, and Mami felt that having his family with him would help Papi. She also felt it necessary to supervise what the doctor was doing and ensure that my father was being cared for properly. Dr. Naten agreed and lowered the price to $3,500 a month since my father would be living with us instead of with the assistant.

My mother began preparations for our family to leave Cuba as soon as possible. She wanted my sister and me to start our next school year in America. Not wanting to leave La Coronela vacant for such a long period of time, she asked her brother, Gustavo, who was living in a rented apartment with his wife and five children, to stay in our home while we were abroad.

My uncle would rent our home for a minimal amount in return for taking care of its maintenance. When we returned to Cuba in approximately ten months, we would move back in. She would give him advance notice of the exact date so that he and his family could leave La Coronela prior to our arrival.

Consuelo was somber when she heard we were leaving for almost a year. Two weeks before our trip, my mother asked her if she would like to go to America with us. The *tata's* face beamed with surprise.

"*¿Yo, a Norte America?*" She looked at Mami open-mouthed, her hands on her cheeks.

"Well, what do you think?" my mother asked brightly.

"Your companionship and help would mean a lot to me."

"¡*Ay, sí*, Señora Nini! I'll come with you," Consuelo enthused. "I've been so worried about how you would manage with *el caballero* and taking care of *los niños*." My mother smiled, relieved that she had accepted her offer.

"*Gracias*, Consuelo."

The morning of our trip, Consuelo was unusually chatty, especially about flying in an airplane to another country. As she brushed my hair, I watched her in the dresser mirror. I thought Consuelo was beautiful. Her smooth complexion, the color of my *café con leche*, seemed to glow that morning. She tied the bow on my ponytail ribbon harder than usual.

"*Ya, vamos,*" she said excitedly, smiling at me in the mirror. "We're going on an adventure." Her almond-shaped, green eyes appeared almost translucent in the sunny room. I sprang to my feet.

"And I can't wait to see Papi."

Our plane landed at the Philadelphia airport late that night, and we were greeted by my anxious father and David, Dr. Naten's assistant. David drove us to the furnished three-story Victorian home Dr. Naten had rented for us in Lumberville, in southeastern Pennsylvania. The house was conveniently located near Dr. Naten's home and David's home in New Hope. This was crucial, since David would continue to be in charge of my father. He would also be our primary means of transportation, driving us wherever we needed to go. My father's condition prohibited him from driving, and my mother had never learned how to drive. As a child, she had been in a horrific car accident with her parents and siblings. A truck crashed into their car, causing it to spin and lodge itself underneath the truck sideways. The family was trapped there for more than an hour. They escaped major injuries, but the accident traumatized my mother for life. In Cuba she had attempted driving lessons twice, but was unable to overcome the terror she felt behind the wheel. Consuelo did not drive, either; in Cuba there had been no reason for her to learn.

We arrived at our new home at four o'clock in the morning, sleepy and exhausted. A couple of hours later, I stumbled out of my bottom bunk bed while María Elena slept above me. My bare feet, accustomed to walking on cool, tiled floors, were cushioned by a thick braided rug. Tiptoeing to our bedroom window, I pulled the curtains apart. I was surprised to see a windowpane and screen. *The windows here aren't wide open with wooden shutters and wrought-iron bars*, I wondered, gazing through the glass. My eyes caught a quick movement at the base of a towering oak tree. The first squirrel I had ever seen scampered off, its bushy tail seeming to wave goodbye. *I bet there are no lizards here either,* I thought. To my amazement, our backyard was a mountainous wooded incline, rising toward the gray early-morning sky. *No palm trees, no sun shining hot and bright…the house next door is dark, tall and gloomy…*nothing looked familiar.

My sister stirred. "What's it like out there?" she mumbled. I drew the curtains closed and headed back to bed.

"Strange."

Chapter Six

Lumberville

"Rise and shine, you sleepyheads!" My father's cheery voice filled our room. "I'm making pancakes, your first American breakfast."

"What's pancakes, Papi?" I asked as I watched him throw open the curtains.

"Follow me to the kitchen and you'll find out." His voice trailed down the hallway. Sunlight bathed our bedroom and for the first time, I looked at my new surroundings. The room I would be sharing with my sister was big, with dark wood furniture instead of the white wicker and mahogany of our bedroom at home. In the corner alcove, a desk, lamp, and chair faced a window to our backyard. I took in the backyard view again. *Lumberville*. Papi told us it meant a village of wood. We were totally surrounded by woods. I shuffled out of the room and followed my sister to the kitchen downstairs. The narrow boards creaked as I stepped on the worn carpeted staircase.

I liked the kitchen. The large room welcomed me with deep windows that almost reached the floor. In the center was a rectangular wooden table with padded deacon benches. From all the windows I saw woods. All around me woods.

My father was whistling as he pulled the pancake mix and measuring cups out of the cupboards. This was the first time I had ever seen Papi preparing a meal. Consuelo stood by looking confused while Mami helped the little ones onto their seats.

"You just watch me, Consuelo. It's a cinch making pancakes," Papi said. He cracked the eggs expertly.

"*¿Pang kays, caballero?*"

"*Sí,* pancakes," he enunciated, chuckling. He poured the batter on the griddle in small amounts. "Now, watch this, everyone." My father flipped the pancake high in the air, and we sighed in amazement when it landed back in the pan. "*Voilá!*" he said enthusiastically.

"*¡Pero mira 'pa eso!*" Consuelo exclaimed, obviously impressed. "*Bueno, caballero,* looks like you will be making breakfast then, *sí?*"

My father handed her the spatula. "Now you try one, Consuelo. Just flip it over gently, you don't have to throw it up in the air."

"*Ay, caballero, yo no sé,*" Consuelo said, fumbling with the batter. But within minutes, the two of them had made breakfast together. Our nanny beamed as she served my mother. "*Pang kays,* Señora Nini, *que le aproveche.*"

"*Gracias,* Consuelo. Now you sit here and join us for breakfast," my mother told her, scooting over on the bench to make room.

"*Ay, no,* Señora." Consuelo was taken aback. "I'll eat when you are all finished, like always."

"Consuelo, we are in America now," my father said, pouring syrup on my little brother's pancakes. "We want you to have your meals with us." Consuelo's eyes were bright as she smiled and awkwardly sat next to my mother. Consuelo sensed the importance of my father's welcoming expression—a rare moment when his illness seemed to have disappeared.

"I'm so glad to have my family with me," my father said, looking at all of us and fixing his gaze on my mother. A beautiful smile illuminated his handsome face. *So this is what a father acts like,* I thought. *He is happy and loving like my uncles are with my cousins.* I felt at ease, free to laugh loudly and be silly without worrying about disturbing him. *Why can't it be like this always?* I wondered, watching Papi's relaxed interaction with our family. I knew at any moment it could change, dissolve as if it never happened, and Papi would retreat for days into his isolated world, which none of us could enter. I took that scene and stored it in my mind's file of cherished moments with my father. I feared they would be few and far between.

"I love *pang kays,* Papi," I said, licking the syrup off my finger and giggling with glee.

After breakfast Papi rounded us up for a walk to explore our new neighborhood. Our house was one of several lining the narrow, winding River Road, bordered on both sides with enormous evergreen, oak, and walnut trees. Behind the homes were dense, mountainous woods. Facing the houses on the other side of the serpentine road was the mighty Delaware River, steel gray, so unlike the familiar crystal-clear blue Caribbean.

Tucked between River Road and the river was the historic Delaware Canal, a major travel route for both people and commerce between Philadelphia and Bethlehem,

Pennsylvania, during the 1800s. Papi told us that this canal was one of the few preserved in the country, still used today by canoeists and barges, which were pulled along by mules on either side of the waterway.

We strolled along the picturesque roadside leading into Lumberville, a village in the heart of Bucks County, a notably historical area of Pennsylvania. My father had a passion for history and considered himself an American history buff.

"There's the famous Black Bass Hotel," he announced, pointing to a colonial inn on the shores of the river. Past the stretch of homes, we reached a small general store with an adjacent tiny post office. Papi opened the wooden door, and two small bells jingled as we filed in. The time-worn floor creaked with each step we took. The smell of pipe tobacco and perked coffee hung in the room. In the corner, a calico cat dozed in a warm pool of sunlight next to a pot-bellied stove.

"'Ello!" A cheerful voice behind the counter greeted us. A thin, stooped man with bushy gray eyebrows peered at us over his reading glasses. "You must be the new folks from *Kee-u-ba*, is it?" he asked my father, holding his pipe.

"Yes, we are." Papi smiled, picking up a newspaper. "News travels fast around here."

"'Deed it does." The old man grinned, nodding. While Mami and Consuelo shopped, I stood in front of a row of glass jars filled with colorful candy sticks, chocolates, lollipops, licorice sticks, and every imaginable confection.

"Which one would you like, missy?" the man asked, peeking at me over the jars. He had kind blue eyes in his pale, wrinkled face, but I didn't understand what he was saying. Papi translated and told the man we didn't speak English yet. I pointed to a gooey chocolate concoction on a stick.

"*Este, pliss.*"

"Welcome to our hamlet. My treat," he said, handing each of us children a piece of our choice candy.

"*Zenk kew*," I told the smiling old man, using my limited English. My father put his hand on my shoulder and gave it a little squeeze.

"*¡Qué divino*! Free candy!" María Elena whispered to me while chomping on her taffy. "I'm going to like living here." In spite of the storeowner's generosity, I did not share her enthusiasm. The cat stirred and gave a wide yawn. I walked over to pet him.

"This is your school bus stop, girls," my father announced as we stepped outside the general store. *School!* I felt like a rock landed in my stomach. *How will I talk to people?* A wave of panic washed over the rock. *I can't speak English!* I was starting first grade, and María Elena would be in sixth. She had learned English in school in Cuba and at least had a basic understanding. But in kindergarten, I had not yet been taught the language. "Please," "thank you," and "pancakes" were the only English words I knew. I tugged at my mother's skirt, hard.

"Mami, I can't go to school," I said with resolve.

"What on earth do you mean, Gloria?" She hoisted my little sister onto her hip.

"I won't understand anyone," I said, pressing close to her and draping my arm around her waist as we walked. "I can stay home and help you and Consuelo and I'll go to school when we return to Cuba, okay?" María Elena covered her mouth to stifle a chuckle. "What's so funny?" I barked at her. "Mami, tell her to stop making fun of me."

"María Elena, *por favor-r-r.*" Whenever my mother trilled her *r*'s and spoke under her breath with clenched teeth, we knew she was mad. She gave my sister the "knock it off" stare and turned to me. "You have to go to school." I pulled away from my mother and stomped along next to her, kicking a hickory nut out of my way. "It will be a little hard at first, but you're a smart girl. You'll learn to speak English right away, you'll see."

"*Sí*, Gloria, it's easy to learn English," María Elena said in a superior tone. "Besides, aren't you excited about riding a school bus for the first time? ¡*Qué divertido!*" she said, skipping off to walk ahead with Papi and the boys. *How can she be so excited when I'm so miserably scared?* I wondered. *What's so fun about riding a school bus full of strangers?*

"Mami, I can't do it," I said, my mind made up.

"*Tú sí puedes*," my mother replied firmly. "Yes you can. Think of the new friends you will make!"

Who cares, I thought, looking for another nut to kick. The early afternoon air felt chilly. A few leaves fluttered down from the towering trees above us.

"Fall is in the air," Papi said, waiting up for us. He put his arm around Mami as our small caravan headed for home. "I love fall in America." He took a deep breath, looking at our surroundings. "There's a scent of history in the air, too. Just think. This road we're walking on dates back more than two hundred years to the early colonial days."

"'*Magínate tú.*" My mother made a smart remark. Papi gave her a squeeze.

"¡*De veras que sí!*" The storekeeper told me some interesting facts about the Black Bass Hotel, how dangerous this part of the country was back in the 1740s, with the hostile Indian bands roaming these forests." My ears perked. *Indians!*

"You mean, like the Indians who fought with cowboys in that movie we saw?" I asked my father, suddenly forgetting about school.

"*Sí*, real Indians, right in these woods we're walking by." I gawked at the dark, haunting forest as my father continued his storytelling.

The Black Bass had always been an inn, even during the Revolutionary War. It had welcomed river travelers and pilgrims along the road through the colonies. Early traders, boatmen, and rafters had made the inn their home.

"It has a tavern right at canal level," Papi said enthusiastically. He explained how in the early 1800s, the area was so rugged and perilous that by having a tavern off the water, the boatmen did not have to set foot on land. "Isn't that interesting?" Papi turned to look at the inn behind us.

"I'd like to see that." I was still thinking about Indians.

"When your parents come to visit and stay at the inn, we can see it then," my mother commented.

"*Sí*, I told the man that's where Mamá and Papá would be staying." Papi put in. "He told me they're in for a treat. Good food, comfy beds, and a friendly ghost or two."

We turned and walked up the short driveway to our dark gray house, looming over us from an embankment. I stared at the dense, silent woods beyond it. *Indians and ghosts!* A cool gust of wind made me shiver, and I missed my Caribbean island in the sun.

I decided I didn't like remote and spooky Lumberville.

My big sister, on the other hand, loved it.

"I can't wait to explore those woods," she said breathlessly, looking up at the steep wooded incline. "Maybe I'll find some arrowheads." María Elena was convinced there were Indian artifacts waiting to be discovered in our backyard. She and I were nothing alike. She was a rough-and-tumble tomboy, quiet and studious. I was an imaginative chatter bug, with a love for animals, books, baby dolls, and all things pretty. Yet I was aware of a bond that wove us together tightly.

On our first day of school at New Hope Solebury Elementary, Papi walked María Elena and me to the bus stop. As the huge yellow bus approached I squeezed my father's hand tighter.

"Papi-i-i, I don't want to go," I said, pleadingly. My father bent down and buttoned the top of my sweater. His mustache twitched as he smiled.

"Hey, Yoyi, you're going to love school." Papi addressed me by my nickname. "Just think of all the new things you're going to learn. You're a big first grader now," he said proudly. "You'll be rattling English in no time, I promise." I wanted to stay in his hug forever, but he handed me over to my sister.

"You ready, María Elena?" He hugged her sideways. "You take care of your little sister."

"Yep," she replied, grabbing her school bag firmly in one hand and my hand in the other. My sister looked prepared, but I suspected she too was nervous. The bus opened its doors as if to swallow us up.

"C'mon Gloria, stop being a baby. Let's go, get in," my

sister said gruffly, giving me a yank. A sea of alien faces looked up at us as we climbed aboard the bus.
"Mornin' girls!" the bus driver greeted us. He was heavyset, with a gray beard and brown cap. His bulky green sweater had a hole on the elbow. The bus lurched with a rumble as María Elena led me toward the back, where she'd spotted two seats together. The children kept staring, turning their heads toward us as we wobbled past. I felt I was walking a gauntlet.

Sitting in the aisle seat, I watched my feet dangle. Someone hissed, "Pssst." I looked up. The boy sitting in front of me had turned around to take a closer look. He had white-blond hair, beady blue eyes, and green mucous streaming out his nose. He stuck out his tongue in a grimace and licked the green gunk. His gaze suddenly shifted to my sister. He frowned as his lips tightened and the corners of his mouth drooped. María Elena was staring him down steely-eyed without blinking. The boy spun around and crouched in his seat.

"¡*Estúpido!*" she muttered, then looked out the window. Thankfully, it was a short ride to school. As the bus drove in the parking lot, I looked at the girl sitting across the aisle from me. I had never seen anyone with such bright orange-colored hair. Even the eyelashes over her green eyes were reddish. Her thick braids dangled halfway down her chest, and she had so many freckles her face looked partially tanned. She smiled at me as we got off the bus.

I bravely walked into school armed with two important pieces of paper. *May I please go to the bathroom?* my mother had written on one and *May I please have sugar for my milk?* on the other. María Elena walked me to the first-grade classroom.

"See you after school," she said quickly and left. I gulped, watching her disappear down the crowded hallway. I stood by the classroom doorway, my legs refusing to go any farther.

"*Bee-ain-vay-nee-dah!*" my teacher said, putting down the chalk on the blackboard rim and coming toward me. She had chestnut eyes, bobbed brown hair, and perfectly painted red lips.

¡*Qué fenómeno!* I thought, relieved. *She speaks Spanish.* "*Buenos días.*" I answered. "*Me llamo Gloria Mar…*"

"Oh, no, honey," my teacher interrupted me, laughing. "That's all I know. I'm afraid I don't speak Spanish." My understanding of English was better than my conversational skills. NO SPANISH. I quickly understood that. She reached over, took my hand, and led me to the front of the room.

"Good morning, children," she addressed the class with her soft, musical voice. She stood behind me with both hands resting on my shoulders. "We have a new student this year. Her name is Gloria Fernández, and she comes to us from Cuba." *Why did she change my name?* I wondered. *My name is Gloria María Fernández Perea.* (In Cuba, we used our middle name and mother's maiden name.)

"Do any of you know where Cuba is?" she asked the attentive class. Silence, except for my thumping heart. "It's an island in the Caribbean Ocean," she said, tapping my shoulders excitedly. There was some tittering and muffled laughter. I wanted to go home. But then I saw a familiar face. The little girl with the carrot-colored braids from the bus was smiling at me again. I smiled back, and she gave me a little wave.

"Now children, I want all of you to be especially nice and helpful to Gloria." The teacher paused, looking at the children individually. "She doesn't speak our language, only Spanish. And it's up to us to teach her how to speak English."

At that moment I became a celebrity. The children were fascinated with the little Cuban girl with such dark hair and eyes who could not speak English. I was bewildered by so many blue-eyed, blond, redheaded, and freckled children.

"Hi, I'm Sally." The girl with the red braids introduced herself after working her way through the kids crowding around me.

"*Hola, aim* Gloria," I said, making an attempt. From then on Sally became my personal tutor, making me repeat everything like a parrot until I said it right. At the end of my first day at school, she and I walked hand in hand to board our bus home.

One afternoon our teacher put a record on the phonograph and the children formed a circle and started to sing along. Sally quickly grabbed my hand and showed me where to stand.

"*Did you ever see a lassie?*" she sang to me.

"No, I *haben't*," I answered in my best English.

"No, silly," she giggled. "Didn't you ever hear this song?" The children immediately joined Sally, eager to show off and teach me something new.

Go this way and that way, go this way and that way. They

sang, giggled, swayed and spun around to the music, while I imitated them. *Did you ever see a lassie, go this way and that.* I sang along with them, suddenly without an accent.

"Hey, children. I think Gloria's got it," my teacher sang out while the children clapped and cheered loudly. It was a victorious feeling that day when I broke the barrier of communication and melted into the group of children. On the bus ride home I kept singing "Lassie".

"I'm trying to read here." María Elena looked up from her book.

"*Go this way and that way,*" I sang, poking her in the arm. She couldn't help but smile as she went back to her reading.

"*Boba,*" she smirked, shaking her head.

* * *

By early fall 1954, my father's moods had become unpredictable again. He was quiet most of the time and wandered impatiently throughout the house, looking for my mother to check what she was doing. Other times he sat on the back porch for hours, smoking while staring at the woods. One evening, Mami could not find him. She walked up and down River Road searching for Papi. While scouring the backyard one last time before calling the doctor, she spotted the orange glow of his lit cigarette. My father was smoking, crouched against a huge tree at the edge of the deep forest.

My mother was constantly on guard and could relax only when my father was at the doctor's for his therapy or when he slept. Dr. Naten reassured her that the treatment was going well and urged her to be patient.

Living in a secluded country village in Pennsylvania and coping with an emotionally crippled husband, five young children, a loyal but dependent nanny, and no means of transportation except from Dr. Naten's assistants was beginning to take its toll on Mami. Her English was minimal, and my father was the only one who spoke the language fluently. She was becoming increasingly homesick for Cuba and our extended family.

My mother felt the sacrifice was well worth it if it helped my father, but as the months passed she saw no improvement and was heartsick as Papi's erratic behavioral deterioration continued. She tried to remain optimistic and maintain a normalcy in our family life when she knew there was none.

* * *

"¡*Miren, miren todos por la ventana!*" Consuelo ran around the house calling us and pointing at the windows. "*¡Está nevando. Mira la nieve que linda!*" she sighed in awe, looking out the kitchen window at the swirling snowflakes.

I took Nancy, my new doll I had gotten for my recent sixth birthday, and sat on the living room bay-window seat. We had a panoramic view of the Delaware River through the sparse trees lining the other side of the road.

"Look, Nancy, look—¡*mira la nieve!*" I said with wonder, holding her up close to the windowpane. I turned her face toward the gray sky and made sure her eyes were open. I was fascinated with her crystalline blue eyes, which opened and closed.

There was an eerie silence outside as the snow fell

softly, rhythmically, like little pieces of cotton floating down from the sky. The ground was covered with an immaculate mantle of white. Papi came over and sat on the wide sill beside me.

"Can you see the little sailboats on the river?" he asked me, pointing ahead. I looked everywhere but could not see any.

"Where, Papi? I don't see any sailboats." I pressed my nose on the cold pane. "Where are they?" My father inched his head close to mine and pointed again.

"See those floating pieces of ice with big clumps of snow? They look like little sailboats racing down the river." The snowflakes kept falling steadily, peacefully.

"Oh Papi! You mean pretend sailboats." I leaned into him.

In the foyer, Consuelo and Mami were bundling up the kids to go outside. María Elena was already out making snowballs.

"Well, what are we waiting for?" my father's voice piped up. "Let's get out in that snow!" My Cuban blood rebelled against the cold as I burst out into the icy snowfall and tried to catch my frozen breath. But the thud of a snowball exploding on my knit cap snapped me out of it. I bent down and with both hands scooped up the fluffy snow and threw it toward María Elena. Then I stood mesmerized, looking up. The sky was a quiet gray, and the snow seemed to come out of nowhere. I stuck out my tongue and caught a snowflake. We all gazed up at the sky, smiling. The neighbors must have thought we were zombies waiting for our spaceship to arrive.

Next to me, Consuelo was holding my brother Roly.

Big marble-like tears rolled down her smiling cheeks as she picked up some snow and put it on his mittens. She turned to my mother standing nearby with the twins.

"Señora Nini, will my tears freeze?"

The next day I was playing with my dolls in the living room when Dr. Naten stopped by with an assistant to pick up my father for a session at his home. Papi's psychiatrist had piercing eyes, a ruddy complexion, and snow-white hair, and he was loud.

"Well Ninina, what do you think of your first snow?" he asked my mother as he and the young man ambled into the living room.

"I feel like I'm in a cemetery," she replied in a flat tone. "That's what our cemeteries in Cuba look like: quiet and totally white."

"That's because you're depressed," he told her casually, taking off his coat. My mother gave him a look of total dislike.

"I think I have reason to be, Doctor." Not expecting an answer, she extended her hand out to me. "*Vamos* Gloria, let's go get Papi." I reached for my mother's hand as she turned to leave the room. I glanced at Dr. Naten. He gave Mami a wry grin as he slumped into the armchair. I wished he would go away.

That December in 1954, my father began staying up late at night, meandering around the house while we slept, writing notes, looking out the windows, and sometimes wandering outside for a moonlight walk. Once Mami found him standing over my little brother's bed watching him sleep in the dark. My mother knew no peace, constantly worrying about what he was up to. She was unable to sleep much. Consuelo feared that my mother was becoming physically and emotionally exhausted.

The winter of 1955 made us all homesick for Cuba: freezing cold temperatures, blustery winds, and frequent snowstorms. The Delaware River froze over, and school was cancelled often. On one such late morning, the snow had taken a break and the sun brightened the dull gray wintry skies. River Road was buried under twelve inches of snow. The solitary tire tracks of our neighbor's truck lined the narrow roadway, resembling two wiggling snakes.

Despite the cold, my father was eager to get us out in the fresh air and show us something new. My mother welcomed a relief from our bad case of cabin fever. Bundled from head to toe with extra layers of clothing and two pairs of socks and mittens each, a large group of us trudged through the snow to the canal across the street.

Leading the group were my father and our neighbor Mr. Dawson, each carrying a snow shovel on their shoulders. Mami, Mrs. Dawson, Consuelo, we children, and the Dawsons' children trailed behind them. We reached a clearing by the frozen canal and perched ourselves on the embankment, watching Papi and Mr. Dawson shovel snow. By the time the Dawson children had their ice skates on, the area had been converted into our own private little skating rink.

The Dawsons' twelve-year-old son had an extra pair of skates for María Elena. I made do with my snow boots. Mr. Dawson skated around the ice to make sure there were no cracks.

"Go to it, kids," he yelled. Peals of laughter filled the

cold air as the Dawson children got on the ice. They glided effortlessly on the frozen surface. Papi helped María Elena as she waddled onto the ice. After a couple of falls, she sailed off with the kids as if she had been skating all her life.

"It's just like roller skating," she cried out happily.

My younger siblings played in the snow while Consuelo, Mami, and Mrs. Dawson sat on a log watching us, talking and sipping hot chocolate from the thermoses they had brought along.

I took three steps on the ice and landed on my derriere. Behind me, two strong hands under my arms lifted me up and I was back on the ice.

"Good thing you're well padded, right?" Papi stood facing me and, holding both my hands, pulled me along on our makeshift rink. As I looked up at him, smiling, a few snowflakes began to fall. Another fleeting, picture-perfect moment with my father.

※ ※ ※

One night the howling wind woke me up. My active imagination convinced me there were wolves in our backyard. Through the partially open curtains, I could see the trees in the moonlight, their bare branches bending and flailing in the freezing winds.

With the sheet half-covering my face, I shivered and knew I had to pee. I dreaded walking to the bathroom at the end of the dark hallway on such a spooky night.

"María Elena, are you awake?" I whispered to my sister on the bunk above me. Silence. *It wouldn't be as scary if she was awake*, I reasoned. Taking Nancy with me, I crept out of my warm bed. As I turned to leave the room I gasped, clutching my doll to my chest. The moonlight streaming in our bay window outlined a shadowy silhouette sitting at our desk. A glowing orange dot slowly moved up, paused, and floated down. I would have to walk by it to leave the room. I stood frozen for an instant. Again, the orange dot moved. The wind howled louder. *The wolves!* I let out a blood-curdling scream. Within seconds two hands were on my shoulders behind me.

"Gloria, Gloria, wake up! You're dreaming!" I heard the voice say, but I screamed louder. The lights came on and my mother rushed toward me.

"*¿Qué pasa?*" Mami asked, looking me over to make sure I was all right. She followed my gaze to the alcove in our room. There sat my father, staring at us, immovable as in a daze, smoking a cigarette. The hands on my shoulders clutched me a little tighter.

"Rolando, *por Dios*, what are you doing here?" My mother's voice was high-pitched, like she was ready to cry.

"I'm keeping watch over my children, making sure they're safe," he said serenely, his voice low and raspy from smoking. "They're coming to deport us, you know."

I turned and buried my face in my sister's flannel pajamas. I felt her arms around me as my mother led our somnambulist father out of our room and back to their bed.

After that fearful episode I was on the lookout for my father's odd behavior. He seemed withdrawn more often and acted nervous and tense around us. Each time I woke during the night, my eyes immediately focused on the alcove, searching for my father's shadowy silhouette. *Why was*

Papi behaving like this? I thought, trying to go back to sleep. More and more I saw his role as my father diminish as Mami was forced to manage our family matters alone. It was distressing to witness his lack of emotional responsiveness. I missed his smile. It was as if a stranger lived with us, and we never knew if or when we would have our father back.

Gradually, we learned the signals that told us when to enjoy his company and when to stay away. More and more we heard Mami say to Consuelo, "*Los niños, por favor.*" That was the cue for our *tata* to take us outside or out of the room because Papi was behaving erratically.

My father's bizarre nightly wanderings continued to the point where my mother was afraid to fall asleep. For twenty-one consecutive nights, she sat at the top of the stairs by the master bedroom while Papi slept. She kept vigil, making sure he would not wander off outside or go into our bedrooms while we slept. The unpredictability of my father's behavior, especially toward us children, was a major concern for my mother. She began to wonder if we were being exposed to danger. Could her husband, in his often delusive state of mind, ever harm his own children?

Early one morning Consuelo found Mami asleep, leaning against the railing. "Señora Nini, wake up, Señora," Consuelo said, her voice catching, as she touched my mother's shoulder. "¡Señora, *no más*! You cannot go on like this. If you do you are going to die, and I'm not going to watch that happen, *me oye?*" Consuelo's eyes were blinded with tears. "I am going to call Cuba and tell your parents what is going on here. *No más*, Señora, *por favor.*"

"No, Consuelo, you don't have to do that," Mami told her calmly. "We're going home to Cuba in two months, as soon as the girls finish the school year."

"¡*Ay, gracias, Dios mío!*" Consuelo rejoiced, helping my mother to her feet.

At our nanny's insistence, Mami would sleep for a few hours while my father was at Dr. Naten's for his sessions. But on the days he stayed home all day she hardly slept. My mother had very little time for us. Every waking moment was spent guarding my father, talking to him and calming him down when he became irrational and agitated, while Consuelo watched over us.

When my mother told Dr. Naten how bad things were, he replied, "That's what you're there for, Ninina. You're part of his treatment. Think of yourself as one of his assistants."

Mami realized then that things were not working out in Lumberville. There was no structure to Dr. Naten's treatment of my father. Most of the time, Papi was home all day long. Sometimes he would see the psychiatrist three times a week for a few hours at his home, other times only once a week, with the assistants taking Papi on frequent outings to observe his behavior. Quite often, Dr. Naten saw my father in our home. He always came with an assistant and had the sessions in our living room. This greatly concerned my mother, not knowing how my father would react while we children were home.

One afternoon Mami and I returned from the general store while my father was in a home session. As we walked down the hallway past the living room, Papi looked at my mother, then at the assistant.

"You like Cuban women, don't you?" Papi addressed the startled man. "Well, you're not having your way with mine, *hijo de puta*—you bastard," he yelled out, raging with passion, and charged at the assistant with clenched fists. "¡*Ay, no,* Rolando!" Mami screamed behind me. As Dr. Naten grabbed my father, he yelled at her, "Run, Ninina, he's going to rape you!" Papi looked flushed, emanating a manic energy. "For God's sake, get out of here." It all happened so quickly, yet time seemed to stand frozen in that horrible moment. My insides trembled as I stared at my sick father. Mami pushed me toward the kitchen, but I turned around in time to see Papi wrapped up in a tight white jacket, screaming at the assistant as he and the doctor dragged him out our front door.

When my father returned home two days later, my mother told Dr. Naten there would be no more sessions at our house.

Almost a year had gone by and my father's condition had not improved. Dr. Naten told Mami that Papi's case was baffling. He could not predict when my father would be cured but felt strongly that in time he would be. He recommended that Papi continue the treatment regardless of how long it took. My mother was torn between doing everything possible to help her husband and her growing doubts about the psychiatrist's methods and competence. The cost of the treatment was exorbitant, and seeing no improvement in Papi increased Mami's distrust of Dr. Naten.

My mother had made up her mind to return to Cuba. She felt that the isolation, lack of transportation, and being away from our home and extended family was affecting us all negatively. After a painstaking discussion with Dr.

Naten, Mami agreed with his recommendation that Papi remain in Pennsylvania to continue treatment.

María Elena was sad to leave Lumberville. She had made friends and loved our backyard's mountainous forest, which she often explored with them. But I was ecstatic when Mami told me I would be celebrating my seventh birthday in Cuba. I was not going to miss the somber, remote "village of wood" that had been our home for almost a year. Yet I was distraught about leaving Papi behind. I did not understand why he would not be coming home with us. Mami explained that my father was sick and needed to stay with Dr. Naten so that he could make him well. We had to make this sacrifice of being apart temporarily, and we would see him again as soon as he was better.

My father became extremely emotional and had to be sedated the day we left for Cuba in June 1955. He was not able to see us off at the airport. We said our goodbyes in Lumberville. I looked out the assistant's car window to wave at Papi, standing on the porch with David, with whom he would be living. My father's face drooped with sadness; his arms hung limp at his sides.

As the car pulled away I searched his face for that beautiful smile, the one that lit up our hearts that morning we ate our first pancakes. But all I could see was the dark woods looming over the house and over my father.

Chapter Seven

NO PLACE TO CALL HOME

I had finally gotten my turn at the window seat. While the stewardesses checked our seatbelts in preparation for landing, I pressed my forehead against the windowpane and looked down at the marshmallow clouds in a brilliant cobalt-blue sky. The sun smiled down at me, its bright rays forcing me to squint. Sitting in a seat-patch of sunlight, I felt Cuba beneath me. Suddenly, the plane broke through the clouds. Emerald fields scattered with tall palm trees and *bohíos* welcomed me home. I lifted my doll's face up to the window. *"Mira*, Nancy. Cuba."

At Rancho Boyeros airport a large group of relatives awaited our arrival. Mama and Bibi were the first to greet us at the gate. Mami rushed to her father's open arms. They clasped each other in a tight embrace. Her shoulders quivered slightly. Slowly pulling away, she wiped her cheek and gave Bibi a kiss. I wove my way through relatives' hugs, kisses, and their *"mira que grande están los niños"* comments until I reached my grandfather. I wrapped my arms around his waist, pressing my cheek against his crisp *guayabera*—a linen shirt. "Bibi, I missed you so much."

His hand rested across my shoulders. "Yoyi, *deja verte.*" His hazel eyes were brimming, smiling as he looked at me. "How you've grown!" He bent down and kissed my forehead. I was home again.

I couldn't wait to go home to La Coronela. But because my uncle and his family were still living in our house, we had to stay with our grandparents in Marianao. *What is going on?* I wondered. *I want to be in my own bedroom and play in our backyard.* But we were not going to live in our home; we had come back to Cuba for only an extended visit. We would most likely return to America the following summer, depending on my father's treatment. Because of the uncertainty of our situation, my mother agreed to let my uncle remain in La Coronela until we were back in Cuba for good. I felt cheated, unsettled with our new living arrangements. It was the first yank of my childhood uprooting.

The following month, in July 1955, we moved to a large second-floor apartment across the street from Mama and Bibi. If we could not be in La Coronela, living close to my grandparents greatly eased my disappointment.

I loved my new neighborhood. The homes varied from baroque/neoclassical styles to turn-of-the-century Spanish architecture, from white-walled houses with terra cotta roofs to grand mansions with stucco balustrades, mahogany front doors, and flagstone terraces. The quiet street was bordered with sidewalks, tall flowering hedges, and thick areca palms.

Our apartment had four bedrooms, high ceilings, and colorful stained glass and iron-grilled windows. A roofed balcony porch with a granite balustrade graced the front of the building, overlooking the street. I liked waving to my grandparents from our balcony.

We did not have a yard, but a splendid park across the

street more than made up for it. The landscaped grounds included an immense fenced-in playground, a *glorieta*—roundabout—in the center surrounded by wrought-iron benches, and small courtyards with fountains. The entire park's perimeter was ringed by ten-foot-wide sidewalks, which provided an area for bicycling, strolling, and roller-skating under tall royal palms.

One block from the park was the highlight of our *vecindario*, the Tropicana Night Club. It was Havana's hottest entertainment spot, famous for its opulence and throbbing Cuban music. During its nightly entertainment, the club's dense tropical landscaping was illuminated with the show's high-intensity colored lights. The lively music could be heard throughout our neighborhood as musicians played the *mambo, cha-chas,* and *guarachas* for the evening's show.

Street vendors' *pregones,* their enticing selling cries, were welcome sounds in our neighborhood. Among the favorites were *el manicero,* selling his *cucuruchos de maní,* warm roasted peanuts in brown paper cones, and *el pirulero,* whose colorful *pirulís,* taffies, and lollipops came in a variety of delicious flavors. Sellers of fresh fruit, vegetables, and *tamales* also pushed their rickety wooden carts door to door, while women on their balconies gossiped with neighbors on the sidewalk.

But most important, many children lived on Calle 43 in Marianao. Cheerful, laughing voices that called to one another in excited squeals of uncontrollable energy filled the park playground. Children rode bikes and roller-skated under the watchful eyes of their *tatas* sitting on park benches. After the solitude of Lumberville, I welcomed the pulsating life of our Cuban neighborhood.

My mother hired Cuca, Consuelo's cousin, to cook for us and help Consuelo with the housekeeping. Cuca was a spirited mulatta who loved to sing while she clanked around in the kitchen. She wore *chancletas*—backless sandals—did her hair up in several tight braids, and one of her front teeth was missing. Cuca's happy-go-lucky personality and culinary prowess won us over immediately.

One afternoon I walked in the kitchen to ask Consuelo for my *merienda*.

"*¿Oye,* Consuelo, *te enterastes de la última?*" Cuca was asking her cousin while she chopped an onion. "Fidel Castro is out of jail." Cuca chopped a little faster. "That *cochino* Batista freed him in May in honor of Mother's Day."

"*¿Pero, y eso?*" Consuelo almost dropped my *fanguito*, a "mud puddle" of condensed milk with cocoa. "Why did he do that? Did he forget about Fidel's attack on Moncada?"

"*Te digo a tí, mi prima.* Fidel is not going to give up, *no señor.*" Cuca shook her head vigorously while stirring the *sofrito*. "Rumor has it he took off to Mexico and is training an army of rebels to come back and whip Batista's butt, this time for good."

I stopped stirring my *fanguito*. "Cuca, is that *el guerrillero?*" I asked. "Is he coming to kill us?" I glanced uneasily at both women.

"No, no, Glorita," Consuelo answered. She glared at Cuca, her eyes widened in warning. "Nothing is going to happen. It's just gossip."

As I left the kitchen I heard Cuca resume their conversation. "*Sí,* Consuelo, *una revolución.* That's what Cuba needs to make life better for you and me."

Fidel Castro had indeed fled to Mexico before Batista could regret his fateful decision. He openly opposed Batista's dictatorship, relentlessly recruiting and training men for guerilla warfare while raising funds to buy arms and ammunition. Castro was obsessed with planning another invasion to overthrow Batista, liberate Cuba, and install a revolutionary government. *Revolución* became a new word in my vocabulary.

We settled easily into our Cuban life that summer in 1955, but still, I missed my father. Papi's treatment in America was not progressing well. His homesickness for his family and country made him morose and uncooperative. My mother visited him for one week every month, as she had done before, staying in the little hotel in nearby Danboro.

In September, during her trip to Pennsylvania with my grandparents, José and Clara, they visited Doylestown, a charming, traditional town in Bucks County. My mother liked its vibrant activity, so different from the isolation of Lumberville. She decided that if we had to return to Pennsylvania to be with my father, we would live in Doylestown.

When my mother returned, I greeted her with my usual questions: "When is Papi coming home? Is he cured yet?" Mami's downhearted expression told me nothing had changed.

"Soon he will come for a visit, *m'ija*," she said, unpacking her suitcase with disinterest. "He misses all of you very much." She forced a subdued smile. "So, are you ready to start school next week?"

"I can't wait." I sat cross-legged on her bed. "Consuelo has my uniform ready and I get to wear a bow tie like Bibi does." Uniforms, no boys, no school bus, a cloistered convent school run by nuns...a startling contrast to my previous school year in Lumberville. Being predominantly Catholic, Cuba's education system was primarily private or parochial. Unlike in America, public schooling was strictly for the poor.

María Elena and I were enrolled in the exclusive convent school of the Sacred Heart in Marianao, Havana's country club district. On our first day of school our chauffeur, Joaquín, drove us. I didn't miss riding Lumberville's big yellow school bus, but I did miss Sally.

"Do *you* miss your American friends?" I asked my sister. María Elena was reading over her textbook list.

"Yeah, I do." She gave me two of her brand-new pencils. "But I also missed my friends at the Sacred Heart." Joaquín was whistling and began to sing:

"Los marcianos llegaron yá, y llegaron bailando el cha-cha-chá. Ricachá, ricachá, ricachá, sí, llegaron bailando el cha-cha-chá."

He smiled at us from the rearview mirror and urged us to sing along. By the time we reached the academy's long, winding driveway, we were all singing *"ricachá"* at the top of our lungs. As we approached the columnar portico where Joaquín dropped us off, the life-size marble statue of the Sacred Heart of Jesus, with his arms outstretched, welcomed me with a peace I had never known. As we walked up the wide steps toward the main double door entrance, a young *madre*, dressed in her floor-length black habit, greeted us.

"*Buenos días, mis niñas,*" she smiled warmly. Her fluted white bonnet, worn snugly around her face, crinkled as she spoke.

"*Buenos días, Madre,*" we replied in angelic unison.

"See you later," my sister said to me. She straightened my bow tie as she turned to go her way. "Good luck."

"You too." This time I wasn't nervous. I gripped my schoolbag handle a little tighter and hurried down the familiar marble-floored corridor to my classroom. Once again, I felt at home.

My father was coming to visit for Christmas. Dr. Naten felt a trip to Cuba to see his family would be advantageous to the treatment. So Papi came for a week, accompanied by Dr. Naten and his wife, and two of Dr. Naten's assistants, who were in charge of my father.

The afternoon of Papi's arrival, I sat on a porch rocker with my doll Nancy. I had a bird's eye view of the highway where it branched onto our street.

"*¿Donde estás*, Joaquín?" I mumbled, willing our chauffeur to appear with my parents. I kicked off my sandals and rocked a little faster. Finally, the car turned the corner and parked in front of our building. My heart thudded wildly as I jumped to my feet and peered over the balcony. Joaquín opened the car door and my father stumbled out.

"¡Papi, *hola* Papi!" I shrieked, waving. He looked up at me impassively. Slowly, a grin unfurled his lips as he waved back. I hardly recognized my father. He had lost weight and looked haggard and disoriented. My Papi was a shell of the robust, handsome father I knew.

Lackadaisically, he followed my mother up the front steps to our apartment. I hugged him, but his body felt rigid. His hair was unkempt, and he smelled of stale cigarette smoke. I missed the scent of Guerlain, the fine cologne he always wore. Papi hardly spoke to me and showed no affection. I feared he did not love me anymore. *Why is he acting like this if he missed us so much? Where is my father?* During the holiday festivities at Rancho Perea, Papi kept to himself, staring nervously at everyone. He was constantly by Mami's side.

"What's wrong with your father?" my cousin asked me with her usual outspoken attitude. We were water and oil. To make matters worse, she was living in our home, La Coronela, and sleeping in my bedroom.

"Nothing. He's tired, that's all," I said defensively and walked off. I felt conscious that Papi was different from other fathers, that there was something very obviously wrong with him, obvious to the whole world.

My father's visit left us unsettled. I had waited so long to see him, only to be disappointed and hurt. Yet despite my father's display of indifference, my mother clung to the hope that Dr. Naten's treatment would cure him in time. In the ongoing time of thousands of dollars wasted.

In early January 1956, Dr. Naten called my mother and strongly advised that she return to Pennsylvania with the children to live with my father as a family, or the treatment would be in vain. Papi was being uncooperative, demanding to have his family with him, and eating minimally. Mami agreed to the move, with the condition that this time we would live in Doylestown. My father was buoyed by the news, and he began to respond positively to his psychoanalysis.

The year we spent in Cuba after Lumberville was a respite from the instability of our family life. As summer ended, my mother prepared us for another trip to America.

"Are we going to live in Lumberville again?" I asked Mami. We were visiting with Mama and Bibi on their front porch.

"No, this time we'll be living in a little town called Doylestown." Mami tried to sound upbeat.

The small red rubber ball bounced off my hand and I missed scooping up the jacks. I sat on the cool tile floor and watched the ball roll away and drop onto the flowerbed.

"I don't want to leave Cuba," I said. I inched closer to Bibi's rocker and leaned against it. "I don't want to go to another school." My voice caught, but I continued. "I love my school, my friends, Rancho Perea…" I paused and glanced at my grandparents, then looked down at my sprawled jacks. *"No quiero ir."*

Mama stopped her rocking and fanned herself a little faster. Bibi gave my ponytail a little tug.

"Oye, Yoyi.*"* My grandfather's smile and his voice were as gentle as could be. "It's just for a school year, and then you will come home to Cuba just as you did before." He gave my mother a glimpse. She met his gaze. "Hopefully for good."

"Papi misses us," Mami put in. "The doctor says if we are together it will help him get better sooner." The front door was flung open as my five-year-old brother ran out with the four-year-old twins behind him. Consuelo hurried out after them.

"Nos vamos al parque, Señora Nini,*"* she announced.

"Are you coming, Gloria?" María Elena rushed by and grabbed her roller skates.

"Sí," I muttered, getting up, and slowly trailed my sister down the sidewalk to the park. My skates felt heavier than

usual as I dragged them by their worn leather straps. The warmth of the hot Cuban sun enveloped me. A brownish chameleon scampered across the pavement and pounced onto an areca palm. Its skin slowly transformed to a brilliant green as it lounged on the thick fronds. I paused to get a closer look. "I don't want to leave you, either," I said. The lizard cocked its head and puffed out a crimson-skinned fan under its chin.

Chapter Eight

DOYLESTOWN

"*Mira, ahí está* Papi," I spotted our father as María Elena and I hurried down the plane's stairway onto the noisy tarmac at the Philadelphia airport. We raced to our father's open arms. My sister and I exchanged contented smiles as he embraced both of us at the same time. Papi's shirt felt crisp and clean with the scent of Guerlain. He had regained his weight and his smile was resplendent. *My Papi is back,* I rejoiced to myself.

"You're finally here!" he said, giving our foreheads a kiss. His eyes were swimming in tears. Next to him stood two of Dr. Naten's assistants, who had driven Papi to the airport and would be taking us to Doylestown. One of them held a bag with gifts and the other, a bouquet of spectacular stargazer lilies, freesias, black-eyed Susies, lavender, and hot pink and white mini carnations. Papi handed out little trucks to the boys, a rag dolly to Madeleine, a book to María Elena, and a floppy-eared stuffed puppy to me.

"This will have to do until you get the real thing, Yoyi." He winked at me. In my letters I constantly told him how much I wanted a dog.

"I didn't forget you, Consuelo." He smiled mischievously at our nanny and gave her a box of candy. "*Y para tí, mi vida."* He presented my mother with the flowers, held her to him and kissed her. Mami's smile softened her expression. *Maybe this is it.* I floated in hope. *Maybe now Papi will really be cured.*

I was leery about Doylestown. I recalled our first trip to America and the lonely year we lived in Lumberville. During the 45-minute drive from the airport, Consuelo kept praying to herself that our home would not be in the woods.

"*Oiga, caballero,* what a pretty little town this is," she sighed, relieved, when we drove down the busy Main Street through the heart of Doylestown.

"*Sí,* Consuelo, this is a typical American town," my father boasted, showing us the pointed stone spires of the old courthouse. Victorian gingerbread houses with wraparound latticework porches lined the pretty streets. There were fancy wrought-iron benches underneath colorful flower-boxed windows, and every corner was marked by old-fashioned gaslight streetlights.

We drove by an imposing red brick building on the corner of the town's main intersection. A sign above the wide front door read "Weisbard's Drug Store."

"And that's the Lenape Building," Papi said, pointing to it. "It was built as the town's second inn in 1774 and called The Ship's Tavern."

"*Mira,* Rolando," my mother exclaimed. "There's the Doylestown Inn, where your parents stayed when they visited you." My father continued sharing his knowledge of the town's history, telling us that the historic hotel in the center of Doylestown had changed little since 1902, when it first opened its doors as an inn. He particularly liked its renowned "witch's hat" turret.

"It's Victorian splendor at its best," he concluded. *Whatever that means*, I wondered, looking up at the turret and imagining a witch's face under it. But I instantly liked Doylestown. It was colorful, and buzzing with activity, so different from the sleepy quietness of Lumberville.

Our rented home was a three-story duplex on the corner of West State Street. It was not furnished, so my mother had bought all the necessary furniture during her last visit and arranged with the realtor to receive the delivery days before we arrived. The house had a big fenced-in backyard with gigantic maple trees and was ideally located near the center of town within walking distance to most everything. As in Lumberville, we did not have any means of transportation.

María Elena and I were students at Our Lady of Mount Carmel parochial school. Our adjustment was much easier this time, having fluent English under our belts. I became fast friends with a classmate named Kathy. Outgoing and funny, she loved hearing my stories about Cuba. We were inseparable at school, and living close to one another, we walked the long eight blocks to and from school together with my sister and looked forward to our daily stops at Hornberger's Bakery. Combining our leftover lunch pennies, we splurged on freshly baked cookies or cupcakes with thick gooey icing and colorful sprinkles.

My sister, now a teenager at thirteen, liked everything about being in America: the weather, lifestyle, food, music, and people—especially boys. She gabbed on the phone constantly and loved rock and roll.

My mother secretly swooned over Perry Como, and

Consuelo was crazy about Fats Domino when she saw him on the *Ed Sullivan Show*.

"I foun my trill," she sang while cooking, swaying her hips, "ong blu-bah-ry heel."

My father did well during our first three months in Doylestown. He was calm and affectionate and enjoyed taking us on long rambles through town, especially to Saturday matinees at the County Theatre. But late in November 1956, his moods fluctuated again. He became remote and quiet, feverishly writing notes about nothing in particular. He slept fitfully and often napped during the day. We stopped going for walks and to the movies.

My mother expressed to Dr. Naten her concerns over signs of aggression in my father's behavior and his uncharacteristic use of foul language. The doctor reassured her that my father was asserting himself, a good sign, and it was part of what he was learning in his treatment.

During the sessions of psychotherapy, Dr. Naten constantly assured my father that as soon as he showed signs of independence and self-assuredness and proved that he could take care of himself, Papi would be given more control of his life and soon after, be released from constant psychiatric vigilance. But my mother feared a negative change overcoming my father. We were in alert mode again.

Despite his illness, Papi had occasional lucid periods when he enjoyed reading, listening to jazz, and especially pursuing his passion for history and politics. My father had been closely following Fidel Castro's activities. At dinner one night in early December, he told my mother that Castro was back in Cuba.

Fidel Castro had landed in Oriente province on December 2 on a dilapidated yacht called *The Granma,* overloaded with eighty-two men aboard. The rugged *guerrilleros,* among them an Argentine revolutionary named Ernesto "Che" Guevara, headed for the Sierra Maestra Mountains, a rough, impenetrable territory ideal for guerilla warfare training. Peasants aided the rebels by providing shelter and food, knowing that Batista's soldiers arrested and brutally murdered anyone who helped Castro and his men. Days later, Batista's army ambushed and destroyed the small rebel army. Only sixteen of the eighty-two men survived. Among them were Fidel and his future revolutionary leaders.

A few days later I was sitting at the kitchen table enjoying my new coloring book. Consuelo was reading a letter while stirring the *potaje.* The thick soup started to bubble and sputter. Flustered, she quickly set the letter on the counter and tended the pot.

"What are you reading, Consuelo?" I asked while deciding which crayon to use next.

"Oh, a letter from Cuca." Consuelo's tone was edgy as she wiped some soup off the range.

"Do you miss Cuca?" I tilted my head side to side admiring the cornflower blue I was using.

"*Sí,* I can't wait to see her soon." She was reading the letter again, and without looking up she walked over and sat at the table across from me. My mother walked in and grabbed her apron hanging by the door.

"*¿Qué cuenta* Cuca?" She asked Consuelo what her cousin had to say, seeing her poring over the letter. Mami had been curious ever since she gave Consuelo her mail. Our startled nanny looked up and fidgeted with the papers.

"She says Fidel Castro is back in Cuba."

"*¿Ah, sí?*" My mother sat down next to me, watching Consuelo intently. She wanted to know what Cuca had to say before discussing it with Consuelo.

Consuelo's eyes skimmed the onionskin. She looked at Mami for a moment, then read parts of the letter out loud.

"*Los guerrilleros* are hiding in the Sierra Maestra Mountains, and when they are strong and ready they will revolt against Batista."

I stopped coloring and looked at Consuelo. "Is that the same *guerrillero* that made trouble before?" My mother tapped my arm.

"Sh-h-h, don't interrupt. Yes, that's the same person," she told me, her attention totally on Consuelo.

"Cuca says the latest word in Havana is that Castro is training his rebels and gathering followers, mostly *guajiros*, who are fired up for a revolution."

"A revolution?" my mother asked, incredulous. Consuelo's eyes fixed on Mami.

"*Sí*, Señora. Castro has promised our peasants that when he overthrows Batista, they will work for themselves instead of working for their landowners." Her luminous green eyes were blazing. "Then the land they are now working will be theirs." Her eyes shifted back to her cousin's letter. "Cuca says our liberation has begun."

"What liberation?" My mother sounded alarmed.

Consuelo nervously folded the letter and put it in her apron pocket as she got up to help my mother with dinner. "Soon things are going to change in Cuba, Señora," she said in a stiff voice.

"What do you mean by that, Consuelo?"

"Nothing, nothing, Señora." Consuelo accidentally banged the saucepan on the burner. "It's just a feeling I have." My mother was visibly uneasy, detecting an air of defiance in her childhood friend. Abruptly standing, she gave her apron a sharp tug in the back as she fastened it.

"I wouldn't get my hopes up too high with this talk of revolution," Mami said firmly. "*Eso no llegará a nada.* Batista will take care of these troublemakers and all this will amount to nothing." I had stopped coloring my picture while Consuelo and Mami were talking. Instead, I wrote in big letters "I miss Cuba" at the bottom of the page. The crayon I used was crimson red.

* * *

December's weather was a bear. We were socked with another Pennsylvania winter of heavy snowstorms, blustery winds, and freezing temperatures. On days off from school we made snowmen, went sledding, and had rousing fights from behind our snow forts. Consuelo loved snow, but she minded the cold and hated going outside. Our *tata* watched us playing in the yard from the kitchen window, occasionally looking up at the snowfall in childlike wonderment. Sitting by the radiator with a cup of hot chocolate, she grimaced and diligently motioned us to behave each time we threw unexpected snowballs at each other. But seeing her runaway smile, we knew she was enjoying our snow fights.

Throughout the winter and spring of 1957, Papi's behavioral problems spiraled. During his sleepless nights he roamed the house, often cooking in the middle of the night. When he did, he usually made a French omelette, his favorite. My bedroom was directly above the kitchen and the floor heater grate was above the stove.

On one of these nights, the clanking of pans and the opening and closing of cupboards awakened me. I crawled out of bed and knelt on the floor, quietly opening the old-fashioned grate. Crouching over, I could see the eggs spreading out on the pan and watched Papi's busy hands adding ingredients. There was something soothing about seeing my father perform such an ordinary task in the quiet of the night. Yet, I felt sad when he removed the pan and all I saw was the blackness of the range. I felt even sadder thinking of him eating all alone while his family slept.

Pieces of crumpled paper with cryptic notes continued to appear around the house. My father hovered over Consuelo while she cooked, asking her to wash her hands frequently. She patiently obliged. Consuelo's resignation with my father's oddities was extraordinary.

Again, Papi had my mother try his food before he ate it. In his agonized mind, noises meant imminent danger, the mailman was an alien out to kidnap us, and the milkman, a private detective hired by his father to watch him.

Papi was forbidden to drink alcohol because of his condition, but he started drinking behind Mami's back. This escalated his aggressive behavior and made him volatile, especially with her. Smelling whisky on his breath one day, she confronted him.

"You can't tell me what to do, *coño*," he yelled, bounding out of the house. "I'll do whatever I damn well please."

My mother called after him. He ignored her and walked faster down the street. Immediately, Mami called the psychiatrist, who sent two assistants after my father and found him walking downtown.

"When he gets home, give him a sedative," Dr. Naten instructed Mami. "He'll be fine after he sleeps it off."

"I'm concerned about the amount of sedatives Rolando is taking, Doctor, especially when he drinks."

"Trust me, Ninina," the doctor said casually. "He'll be fine. Just keep him away from alcohol." My mother set the phone firmly on the cradle.

"I've had it with this American doctor," she said to Consuelo. "Sedatives and more sedatives, that's all he's doing for him." To my mother, it seemed tranquilizers were once again becoming the core of my father's treatment. The psychoanalysis sessions were few and far between, and Papi's condition was getting worse. She was especially concerned with his increasingly aggressive behavior, especially around the children.

With Consuelo's help, Mami searched the house for hidden alcohol. She found a half-empty bottle of whisky stashed behind Papi's sweaters on a closet shelf, and Consuelo discovered an unopened bottle of gin inside one of his snow boots. Standing together in front of the kitchen sink, they poured the contents down the drain. Consuelo noticed a slight trembling in Mami's hand. She placed her free hand on my mother's, steadying the bottle.

"It's alright, Señora Nini." She took the bottle from my mother and finished pouring it out herself. "I'll help you."

* * *

"They're here, Mami! Tita Lala and Tito Pepe are here!" my six-year-old brother Roly yelled, running to the kitchen, his red Superman cape trailing behind him. I was sitting at the kitchen table, practicing braiding my doll Nancy's long blond hair as Consuelo had taught me to do. My mother took off her apron and tossed it on the counter as I dashed by her, leaving my dolly behind. By the time Mami and I entered the living room, Consuelo had already answered the door and let my grandparents in.

My paternal grandparents were avid travelers, especially my grandmother Clara, whom her grandchildren called Tita Lala. Whenever possible, José Fernández, Tito Pepe to his grandchildren, indulged his wife in an exotic trip. They had traveled extensively throughout Europe, Asia, the United States, and the Orient. En route to New York on vacation in early June 1957, my grandfather scheduled a couple of days to visit us in Doylestown. We had not seen them for nine months, and Tito Pepe was concerned about his son's treatment with Dr. Naten.

"¿Yoyi, *qué tal, mi amor?*" Tita Lala greeted me. To me, my grandmother was the very essence of elegance. Everything about her was distinctive, almost imperial. Yet behind the regal façade, there was something enchanting about Tita Lala—a kindliness I always sensed. I gave her a hug and buried my face in her cashmere sweater. The scent of her perfume made me homesick for Cuba.

"I'm so glad you're here. How long will you stay?" I fired away at my grandparents.

"Just a couple of days, but we're so happy to see all of you. We've missed you," Tito Pepe said, flashing me a wide grin and wrapping his arm around María Elena.

"*¿Qué tal* Ninina, *como andas?*" my grandfather greeted my mother with a warm hug and kiss. My grandmother lightly brushed her cheek against Mami's while anxiously looking for her son.

"Where is Rolando?" she asked her daughter-in-law. At this moment, my father stumbled down the stairs to greet them. He had been taking a nap and his hair was tousled, his clothes rumpled. Groggy from his medication, he mumbled a greeting to his parents and gave his mother a kiss. He had lost weight again and looked gaunt, his dark eyes prominent in his expressionless face.

"Rolando, how thin you are!" his father told him, alarmed at the change in his son's appearance since he last saw him in Havana.

"The food here is not too good, Papá." My father looked over at Consuelo suspiciously. Consuelo pursed her lips and looked at my mother, clearly upset by the insinuation. My mother shook her head as my father walked past her.

"He thinks we're trying to poison him," she whispered to her startled in-laws.

Everyone moved to the living room to visit. Papi sat quietly in the armchair, staring out the window, tuning everyone out. He began to fidget with a small piece of paper, shredding it and watching as it fell to the floor piece by piece.

The twins woke up from their naps and joined my brother in jumping off the couch, pretending to be flying. "That's enough!" my father hollered at the children. He abruptly got up and scowled at them, but my mother intercepted him.

"Consuelo, *los niños, por favor,*" she signaled to her. On cue, our nanny rounded us children up and herded us through the dining room into the kitchen for a snack. She closed the door behind us. I knew my mother wanted us out of the room because my father was becoming upset. I could sense it in Consuelo's guarded expression, the way she kept looking at the closed kitchen door, as if someone would come into the room at any minute.

"*Vamos, niños,*" she urged us. "It's a beautiful afternoon; let's eat our *merenguitos* outside." The screen door slammed behind my siblings as they ran out to the backyard.

"I have to go to the bathroom," I told Consuelo.

"*Bueno*, but hurry up." She trailed after them with the *merenguitos*. From the hallway upstairs I could hear the conversation in the living room. Something wasn't right in the house. I felt impelled to eavesdrop.

"I need to lie down for awhile. I have a bad headache," my father announced. Hearing his footsteps on the front staircase, I scampered down the back stairs into the kitchen and grabbed Nancy from the table. I took careful, slow steps until I hovered behind the door; I creaked it open and peered through a sliver. My mother was informing my grandparents that she was planning to tell Dr. Naten that she no longer wanted her husband in his care. My father's health was deteriorating and the psychiatrist saw him less and less. After thousands of dollars paid to him, my father was worse than ever. She would take Rolando and her children back home to Cuba as soon as the school year ended. She would find another psychiatrist in Havana who could help my father. Tito Pepe agreed with my mother. He urged her to make the call right then and see her plan through. He also was convinced that the American psychiatric treatments were not working on his son.

"José, *por Dios*, what are you saying?" cried Tita Lala. "What are we going to do with Rolando in Cuba? There's no one else in Havana who can help him. We have already discussed this. He is better off here with Ninina and the children."

"Clara, stay out of this matter," my grandfather said firmly as he walked with my mother toward the phone in the dining room. They were unaware that my father had been eavesdropping on them from the top of the stairs. In his agitated mind, he misinterpreted the conversation, thinking my mother was leaving for Cuba without him. In a rage, he ran down the stairs and yanked the phone away from her, ripping it off the wall.

"Forget it! You're not leaving without me!" he raged at her, spittle flying out of his mouth. "You're not sticking me in another sanatorium, you hear me?" His face was distorted, beet red with anger. The hair on my arms prickled.

"Rolando, *por favor,*" my mother pleaded, but he lunged toward her, grabbing her by the neck and punching her in the face and chest. Blood spurted from my mother's nose as she covered her face with her forearms, crouching in the corner of the room, screaming for him to stop. Tito Pepe, half the size of my father, pounced on him from behind, clinging to him like an animal and holding back his son's pounding fists. My father pushed him off and Tito Pepe landed hard on the floor. My grandmother rushed in from the living room, her eyes widening with surprise. "José, what happened to you?"

"I'm all right," my grandfather assured her while looking at his son.

"Rolando, stop it. Oh my God!" Tita Lala cried, her

hands clasped in supplication, but my father was still attacking my mother. He grabbed a chair and threw it at her. She rolled her body to the side, missing it as it smashed against the door. I closed my eyes and squeezed my dolly to my heaving chest, my breath caught somewhere between my stomach and my lungs. When I opened my eyes, my grandfather was on his feet again and slammed his son hard against the wall. Suddenly my father stopped fighting, leaned his head back against the wall, and closed his eyes. His body gradually relaxed. His clenched fists unfurled and his hands hung still beside him. His eyes slowly opened and revealed his bleeding wife sprawled on the floor.

"Ninina, what happened to you?" His voice was anguished.

"She had an accident, Rolando. She'll be all right," Tito Pepe reassured him, realizing his son's state of confusion while at the same time trying to keep him calm and away from my mother.

Tita Lala helped my mother off the floor, giving her son a tragic look. She walked with Mami toward the kitchen. I ran to the stairway, out of sight, and sat on the bottom step. I peeked out. My mother washed her bloodied face in the kitchen sink. Noticing blood on the front of her white blouse, she buttoned up her sweater to conceal it. Her nose and right ear were still bleeding profusely. She threw her head back, pressing a napkin against her nose. As she lifted her arm, she flinched, grabbing at her side; she seemed to have trouble breathing. Mami pulled her hair over her bloody ear, covering it from sight. Reaching for my father's sedative and a glass of water, she handed them to my grandmother.

"Clara, have José give this to Rolando immediately. It will calm him down. I will call Dr. Naten." My grandmother's face looked anxious, crumpled. Her hand trembled as she reached for the pill.

Consuelo came in for more *merenguitos*. Her brilliant green eyes opened wide in alarm. "Señora, you are hurt. You are bleeding." Our *tata's* eyes welled up with tears. "*¡Ay, por Dios*, Señora!"

"Consuelo, I need you to be strong and help me. The children cannot know what happened to me. Stay in the backyard with them until I come get you. *El caballero* does not feel well."

"*Pero*, Señora..."

My mother squeezed Consuelo's hand. "I'm calling the doctor. Everything will be all right." The kitchen was quiet, except for the hum of the old refrigerator in the corner. I sat stupefied as my mother opened the door to the dining room. Tita Lala sat at the table wringing her hands. My father was sitting on the couch leaning forward, elbows on his knees, holding his head down. Tito Pepe was next to him, vigilant, comforting, waiting for the medication to take effect and help his sick son.

My mother made the call from the kitchen phone. Dr. Naten nonchalantly told her that he had been expecting this to happen. He would be there shortly to pick up my father and take him to his clinic for observation. As she hung up the phone, Mami looked out the window. Consuelo was sitting on the grass under a huge maple watching the children play.

"This can't go on," said my mother in a hushed voice. "I have to think of my children and keep them safe." Her voice broke off. "I can't live with Rolando any longer."

Small clumps of dried blood caked Mami's hair next to her ear. I remained stunned, unable to move.

The ringing of the doorbell startled me. My mother hastily left the kitchen. I crept behind the kitchen door, opening it a crack, just enough to see. I stifled a gasp, clutching my dolly again as I gaped at the broken chair in the dining room and the hole in the wall where the phone jack had been. A stench of fear saturated the silence of the room.

In the living room, Papi lay slumped on the couch, almost asleep. I wanted to warn him somehow of an impending danger I felt for him.

The room exploded with Dr. Naten's laughter when he and his two assistants arrived. "José, *amigo*, how are ya?" he shook my grandfather's hand vigorously. "Clara, good to see you again!" My grandmother gave him a curt smile. Tito Pepe was not smiling.

"Jacob, come in," Tito Pepe said flatly, ushering the doctor and his assistants into the living room. One man carried a small black bag and the other held a white cloth in his hands, its strings dangling like the one I had seen in Lumberville. My mouth went dry.

I longed for the day I never had to lay eyes on Dr. Naten again. Every time I saw him it was a reminder that my father was a sick man, and I saw him much too often. I disliked his booming voice and annoying familiarity.

"I'm not going anywhere," my father roared. "I'm fine, I just need to sleep." The assistants were forcing a white jacket on my struggling father. His arms were tucked inside it like a mummy, and they were tying straps around his body so he couldn't move them.

"Ninina, don't let them do this to me, please," my father's voice turned to a plea.

"Doctor, he's calmer now. Isn't there another way, please?" my mother begged.

"It's for his own good, Ninina. He'll sleep all the way to the clinic. I'll call you when he's settled in." Dr. Naten instructed the men to take my father out to the car.

Still unnoticed, I peeked out further from behind the kitchen door. Blood trickled down the side of my mother's neck as she spoke to the doctor. A paralyzing cold wave bashed inside me. It was as if the reaction to everything I had just seen and heard was coming to a head. *What was happening to my family? Were they taking my father away forever for hurting my mother? How could she not be angry with him?* I was trying to understand Papi's illness, his unpredictability and violent behavior toward Mami, who instead of being angry with him was acting compassionate and loving. The two sides to my father were battling in my mind: the sick, scary one I had just witnessed, which had nothing to do with me, and the caring, affectionate, fatherly one I longingly remembered and sensed was still there. Despite his horrible sickness, I knew it was right to love him. But as an eight-year-old child, all I knew was that things had gone horribly wrong, and I feared that my Papi was being taken away like a prisoner.

My grandmother, her face pale, stood stoically by my grandfather, who was visibly distraught. My mother watched helplessly, rubbing her crossed arms, as the men finished tying up the straitjacket. Papi looked beaten, spent. As they marched him toward the front door, my father stopped and turned, looking in my direction. He saw me behind the half-opened kitchen door. I opened it wider and his beseeching eyes caught mine. I mouthed the word "Papi", but my voice was silent.

Chapter Nine

Papi Se Fué

My father left. He could not live with us anymore. Upon his release from the psychiatric clinic, he went back to living with David, the psychiatrist's assistant, in his home in New Hope. Dr. Naten refused to allow Papi to return to Cuba with us. He claimed the treatment was far from finished and that in my father's unstable condition, he would be safer with him.

My mother disregarded my grandparents' and Consuelo's insistence that she go to the hospital to be checked over, even though her ear throbbed periodically and her ribs pierced her side each time she breathed deeply.

"I can't go to the hospital here," she told them. "I would have to report Rolando, and that will make matters worse for him. I will go see our doctor in Havana as soon as we get there." My mother's plans to return to Cuba were precipitated by my father's violent behavior. Her injuries compounded her resolve to leave Doylestown as quickly as possible.

During our last two weeks of school, Mami and Consuelo dismantled our home. My mother donated all our furnishings, household items, and winter clothes to a needy family in our church.

As much as I liked Doylestown, it wasn't home for me.

Still, there were things I would miss: snow, my best girlfriend, Kathy, who promised to write me often; and the fresh baked cookies we bought at the bakery every day after school. But these couldn't compare to the sparkling turquoise Caribbean, the warm sunshine, my family, school, friends, and guava turnovers. I was ready to go home to Cuba.

"Are we staying in Cuba for good this time, Mami?" I asked one morning at breakfast, pushing my scrambled eggs from one end of the plate to the other.

"*Sí.*" My mother sipped her *café con leche* slowly. "We're going back to Havana to live in La Coronela."

"But Papi won't be with us." I put my fork down.

"No, he won't. He has to stay here with Dr. Naten until he's better." She set her cup on the saucer, holding it tightly with both hands. Her eyes drifted to the dining room.

"How long will that take?"

"I don't know, *m'ija,*" she answered absentmindedly, still looking at the dining room. I took my stuffed puppy and went out to the front yard.

It was a fine June morning. I sat under my favorite maple tree and leaned against it, kicking off my sneakers. The grass felt like cool velvet under my bare feet. I felt my hopes for Papi's cure and for a normal family life float out of my heart. They drifted upward through the tree's spring-drenched branches, toward the blue skies, and disappeared in the clouds.

"I have no father," I said aloud to myself.

I brought my knees up and cradled my puppy on them, resting my chin on his furry head. *What will happen to us now?* I asked myself. *Will I ever see Papi again? Will he watch me grow up? Or will he be too sick to care?* The sounds of laughter invaded my thoughts as a man and a little girl rode by on their bicycles.

"Good job, Katie." The man smiled broadly. "Now, pump hard up this hill."

I watched them ride by, tears stinging my eyes. I buried my face in my puppy and sobbed. A presentiment that my father would never live with us again took the place of hope in my heart. I already missed his smile, his hugs, his love. I wiped my eyes while watching the bikes disappear over the hill. The sun hid behind the clouds as I went in the house to help my mother pack.

We left Doylestown in late June 1957. The day after we arrived in Havana, my mother finally went to see our family doctor. She learned that she had several fractured ribs and the bone behind her ear had been shattered.

Once again, we had to live with Mama and Bibi while waiting for my uncle and his family to move out of our home. My mother had given her brother advance notice that we would be returning to Cuba permanently this time, and that we wanted our home back, but he complained that it was difficult finding the right home for his large family. The injustice of not being able to live in La Coronela rankled.

"Why not, Mami?" I said bitterly. "That's our home."

"Because they have no place to move to yet." My mother answered resolutely. "As soon as they do, we will move to La Coronela. Meanwhile, we will stay with Mama and Bibi." This made no sense to me.

"Why don't *they* move here and live with Mama and Bibi and give us our home back?" I reasoned, watching my mother unpack my things.

"It's not that easy. We have to be patient and wait."

Wait. It seemed that was all we did. Wait for Papi to get well. Wait until our home was ours again. Wait to put down roots so we could be a normal family. I did not want to wait any longer. Yet living with my grandparents in *la casa de Belén*, as the family called it because it was near the Belén School, gave us a security we desperately needed. Their love and emotional support were healing. The familiarity of their neighborhood was welcoming, since we had lived there before. Mama and Bibi's home, like their *finca* Rancho Perea, was a haven to me.

The two-storied, late-nineteenth-century house had wide windows, guarded by heavy wooden shutters and iron grilles. In the front, a low cement wall enclosed a small garden patch. Tall, plumy areca palms encircled the front porch amid croton plants, with their vibrant red, yellow, and green foliage. The tile-floored *portal* had bamboo shades and wooden rockers with cane seats.

An arched mahogany front door had iron hinges and a small barred window that opened from inside. The home was always filled with family, vitality, and the incessant kitchen chattering of the cook, maids, and nannies gossiping while they worked. My grandparents' enormous, dark blue and white tiled bathroom had mirrored walls, a fancy French bidet, and a bathtub on a tiled platform with broad steps leading up to it. A colorful stained-glass window opened above the bathtub.

As I walked on the black and white marble flagstones of the entrance hallway, the music of Puccini's "Nessun Dorma" and Verdi's "La Traviata" frequently lured me into my grandfather's office.

Papi Se Fué

"What are you doing, Bibi?" I asked one day, barging into the cozy room and perching my hand on his shoulder. I could talk to my grandfather as easily as I could breathe. He stopped his paperwork and looked at me over his readers.

"My office homework, that's what." The tenor on the record player reached a gloriously high note. *"Cucha, cucha"* he urged me to listen, closing his eyes and directing the music with his index finger. *"¡Qué maravilla!"* His face was brilliant with delight.

"What's he singing about, Bibi?" I helped myself to a hard candy from his jar.

"About his love for a beautiful princess," he replied in a far-away voice. I would sit entranced for a long time listening to his interpretation of his beloved arias.

My grandparents' bedroom was off that same hallway. There I would often find my grandmother Mama. In the corner was a makeshift altar with lit votive candles and fresh-cut flowers. Her adored Virgencita smiled down at Mama as she prayed her daily rosary.

María Elena and I shared a bedroom facing a courtyard open to the skies. Water trickled from a spout in a granite lion's mouth above an Andalusian-tiled fountain, filling the courtyard with a musical tinkling.

To the right of the courtyard Mama grew roses and gardenias. Sunlight blazed on dense clusters of crimson bougainvillea cascading all along the top of the garden wall. A jasmine vine arched the entrance, its fluted blooms perfuming the air. On warm, balmy days, the floral aroma wafted throughout the house. An eight-foot-high Japanese aviary filled with colorful, chatty parakeets was nestled beneath a flowering orange tree. To the left of the courtyard an open stairway led to the servants' living quarters.

It was at my grandparents' dinner table that I learned to appreciate Cuban food. We had to try everything, at least once. If we fussed, Bibi would ask the cook to serve us a little more. We quickly learned not to complain at mealtimes. Cuban food is delicious, seasoned yet not spicy hot. But to me, there were some exceptions: the dreaded *kimbombó*, a slimy vegetable soup that made me gag, along with the "delicacy" of breaded calves' brains, which I delicately spit out into my napkin and dumped on the floor. (My grandparents' Chihuahua, Toy, loved it!) White rice, plain or in several variations, was a side dish at every meal. *Asemitas* were my grandmother's lunch specialty. A hole, or window, was cut out on the top of a hard roll, then filled with cooked eggs, meat, and peas and topped with *bechamel* sauce. The rolls were then lightly warmed in the oven. *Ropa vieja* was a shredded beef dish served with white rice and fried sweet plantains. Bibi's favorite was *palomilla*, a thin steak seasoned with lime juice, garlic, peppers, and onions, served with *tostones*, fried green plantains. My all-time favorite was *picadillo*, a flavorful beef hash seasoned with green peppers, onions, raisins, green olives, and tomato sauce served on top of white rice.

We had been in Havana barely two weeks when my mother received a phone call from my father.

"Ninina, I'm on the fifth floor of a hotel in New York City." His voice was frantic. "I'm standing in front of an open window above heavy traffic. If you don't promise me that you will come and get me right away and take me to Cuba with you, I'll jump."

"¡*Ay, Sagrado Corazón*!" my mother cried out. "Rolando, please listen to me...Rolando?" His yelling drowned her words.

"I swear I'll jump and on your conscience will be my death. Promise me," he screamed hysterically, "or I'll jump."

"Rolando, I swear on my life, I will bring you home."

"Naten won't release me. I'd rather be dead than be apart from you and the children any longer."

My mother managed to calm Papi down, vowing to bring him home as soon as possible, and got him to give her the hotel's address. She immediately called Dr. Naten, who had been searching for my father since his disappearance from David's home the night before. Mami was furious that Dr. Naten had not called her.

"There was no need to worry you," he told her matter-of-factly. "I knew Rolando would turn up." Three hours later the psychiatrist phoned my mother to tell her Papi was safe and back in Pennsylvania under his care. Dr. Naten told her my father had saved up the money he was allotted weekly for his incidentals and took a taxi to New York as far as he could afford. He then hitchhiked the remaining short distance into the city and checked into the hotel where Dr. Naten stayed when he traveled to New York on business. Knowing that the psychiatrist had an account there, Papi charged the room to his name.

After that incident, my mother was determined to bring my father to Cuba. Even though she could no longer live with him, she had to make sure he was safe. She met with her in-laws, and Tito Pepe arranged for my uncles to fly to Pennsylvania the following day and bring my father to Cuba.

Once safely in Havana, my father was again hospitalized in a private clinic under the care of the resident psychiatrist. The best doctors in Havana had not been able to help him, but at least he was home, where his family could visit him often and his care could be closely monitored. My mother made the long overdue phone call to Dr. Naten and ended my father's psychiatric treatment with him.

I was almost nine years old the first time I visited my father in the sanatorium, in early July 1957.

Everything was white: the walls, floors, waiting-room seats, bedcovers. The nurses, doctors, and assistants wore white. The only splash of color came from landscape oil paintings on the walls and flower arrangements in the nurses' stations.

We walked past a large recreation area filled with patients alone or with an attendant. Some watched TV, others played table games, and a few socialized quietly.

I slowed down and trailed behind my mother as she walked ahead with my siblings. My eyes were riveted toward a woman talking to herself while nervously grabbing at the air in front of her, as if someone was throwing something at her. In one corner of the room a man stood against the wall repeating the same words over and over again: "You can't make me do it, go away! You can't make me do it, go away!" He seemed terrified when he saw me looking at him.

Sitting by a small table next to a window, a beautiful young woman held out strands of her long brown hair in front of her face, scrutinized them, then shook her head vigorously.

Some patients seemed calm and normal to me; others rocked back and forth on their chairs or yelled at other patients for no reason, then kicked and bit the assistants as they tried to calm them down. How could my Papi get well living in a place like this?

My father was waiting for us outside, in the peaceful gardens. I was relieved that we did not have to visit with him inside his sterile prison. Still, I was apprehensive; I had not seen Papi since that horrible day in Doylestown, almost a month ago.

I could tell by his smile when he saw us coming that my father was having a good day. He was in a sunny mood, and he could not get enough of us. Papi wanted to know the latest neighborhood news and all about the upcoming start of school. Looking back and forth between my parents' faces, I could see no trace of animosity over what had happened in Doylestown.

"Papi, the Gutierrez dog next door is having puppies any day," I gibbered away, sitting on the arm of his lounge chair underneath a framboyán tree. He patted my back affectionately.

"Well, maybe one of those *cachorros* can be yours," he said, glancing at my mother.

"*Ay*, Mami, please, please, pleee-ase…" I begged. "I'll take care of him myself, I promise."

"We'll see," my mother said. I had wanted a puppy for so long. All the way home that was all I talked about. Two days later, five handsome puppies were born to Chati. My mother took us to see them, and I sat with the puppies the entire visit.

"Well, did you pick the one you want?" my mother asked

when it was time to leave. I looked at her, dropping my jaw. The runt of the litter, a male, clung to me for dear life. He was brindle, with a white collar and paws. His cloudy blue eyes looked up at me. I loved the smell of his puppy breath.

"*Este,*" I said to the puppy. "When you're ready, you're coming home with me."

"You have your father to thank for that puppy," my mother told me as we walked home. "He wants you to have a dog, but you have to take care of him and..." I tuned her out. At that moment I thought only of Papi and how much I loved him.

"Popsy," I declared aloud. "I will call my dog Popsy."

* * *

Juana made me uncomfortable. My grandparents' cook had turned their large, bright kitchen into her domain, regarding everyone who entered it with a provocative, fiery expression.

A haughty mulatta with piercing dark eyes, she wore her coal-black hair with streaks of smoky gray tied back in a bun. None of the household staff got along with Juana. They called her a *busca pleito*—a troublemaker. But she was an excellent cook, so my grandmother dismissed their complaints as nonsense. I never saw Juana smile at anyone but my grandmother and the gardener, Ramiro. He would often come into the kitchen through the side door that led to the courtyard. He chatted with Juana while she gave him a glass of cold water, but they would stop talking immediately whenever anyone else walked into the kitchen.

Consuelo was always at odds with Juana. One afternoon I was helping our *tata* prepare our *merienda* while the cook washed dishes.

"You think you're something special, eh, Consuelo?" Juana sneered, staring at the bracelet my parents had given our nanny for her birthday. "Just because you wear a fancy gold bangle and get to travel to America doesn't make you any better than the rest of us."

"*Oye,* Juana, *déjame tranquila, me oístes?*" snapped Consuelo, handing me a plate of crackers with guava paste and cream cheese. Her green eyes had narrowed into slits and her face was hard set.

As I walked away, I could not make out what Consuelo quietly said to the cook. But Juana's belligerent reply was loud and clear.

"*¿Ah, sí?* Well, wake up, *mi hermana;* pretty soon we, too, will get a piece of that pie you're enjoying."

In late summer 1957, my family and I were spending a weekend at Rancho Perea with my grandparents. The servants had the weekend off. On Sunday afternoon, a neighbor called Bibi at the *finca*. He and his wife had gone for a walk and were surprised to see that the porch shades in my grandparents' home were down. They were always rolled up except when it rained hard. As they walked past the house, they noticed that the massive mahogany door was ajar.

My uncle Wilfredo, who was Havana's police commander, was at Rancho Perea that Sunday and immediately called for backup to meet him at my grandparents' home. By the time the rest of the family arrived, three police cars had lined the street in front of *la casa de Belén* and a swarm of officers were milling in and out of the house.

I was supposed to stay on the front porch with Consuelo and my younger siblings, but I was determined to go inside.

"Come here, *niña*, you can't go in there now." I walked quickly down the long hallway until Consuelo's voice was drowned out by the commotion and loud voices of the many people inside Mama and Bibi's home.

I was walking through a war zone.

A dainty Louis XV chair in the formal living room had been knocked over. The glass in Mama's locked *vitrina*, her antique curio, had been smashed, and gone were all her precious porcelain figurines. The walls were stripped of Bibi's valuable oil paintings and the built-in shelves, once adorned with Sevres vases and bowls, were bare.

In the master bedroom, the carved and gilded wooden doors of the locked armoire had been pried open and its drawers tossed on the bed, the contents strewn all over the room. The little drawers in Mama's jewelry box gaped at me, empty of many family heirlooms.

La Virgencita had not been touched. That was the first thing my grandmother checked when she walked into her ransacked home. Seeing the statue of the Blessed Mother safe and intact, she cried.

I meandered through the house, unnoticed in the chaos. My grandfather was in his office with two policemen. Bibi's face was livid. In their search for cash, the burglars hacked open his mahogany secretaire desk, which had once belonged to his father. Scattered throughout the floors were socks, which the robbers used to avoid leaving fingerprints.

In the kitchen, gone were all the electrical appliances; the food pantry was empty. I tensed up as I headed toward my bedroom at the end of the hallway. *Maybe nothing happened there. Who would want to steal anything from two girls' bedroom?* I stood frozen in the doorway; our twin beds were piled with our dresser drawers and their contents. The large closet doors were flung open, most of our clothes, especially fancy dresses, gone. The police later assumed that they stuffed our missing suitcases, which were in storage in the garage, with the clothes they stole.

"This is an inside job, *comandante*," a young officer told my uncle outside my room. "They knew where those suitcases were."

They. Who were they? I inched closer to my side of the dresser. My gold charm bracelet was taken, its empty velvet-lined box left behind as a cruel reminder. What little they did not take was thrown all over the floor.

"*¡Mis muñecas!*" I cried out, staring at the bare shelf on the wall where my dolls had been. "Oh no, Nancy!" Panic struck me as I jumped on my bed and dug through the mess like a dog looking for a bone, tears streaming down my cheeks. "Not Nancy!" I always sat her on my bed by my pillow. She was gone.

Getting off the bed on the other side, I noticed a rubber arm and hand sticking out from under my pillow on the floor. "Nancy!" I kissed and hugged my American doll, my favorite. Then I sat on the edge of my bed and hid my face in her blonde curls.

My mother's bedroom was the last one, beyond ours, in the back of the house. The police theorized that by the time the robbers got there, they were in a hurry to get out. Her room was the least chaotic, although the perpetrators did empty her dresser drawers on the bed. In their rush, they dumped the contents of her jewelry box on the bedspread and made one final scoop before leaving.

"¡*Mira*, Wilfredo! Oh, thank God!" From my room, I heard my mother talking to my uncle.

Her pearl necklace was dangling off the side of her bed, its clasp hooked on the white coverlet's lace. On the floor, barely covered by the bedspread, was a little black velvet box.

"¡*Mi aguamarina!*" Mami cried out. A spectacular aquamarine stone set in a platinum ring with diamond chips had been accidentally left behind. It had been a gift from my father to my mother the day I was born.

The day after the robbery, Juana and Ramiro did not show up for work. They became immediate suspects. By the time police reached their homes for questioning, they were nowhere to be found. Uncle Wilfredo took my grandmother and Mami to jewelry stores and pawnshops with the hope of tracing the stolen valuables, but there were no leads. The thieves were never caught.

※ ※ ※

Uncle Gustavo and his family were still living in our home. My mother was running out of patience with her brother. For two months he kept stalling her, claiming he could not find a suitable enough home. Mami again pressured him to move.

"It's going to take longer than I thought, Ninina," he kept telling her. "And besides, what do you want with such a big house in the country, anyway?"

"*Pues mira, chico,*" my mother replied firmly. "La Coronela is my home. Rolando built that house for his family, and that is where I plan to live with my children." But my uncle did not budge. Exasperated, Mami talked to her father. She found out her brother had asked Bibi to talk her into selling him La Coronela. My grandfather had refused.

Despite my mother's efforts, Uncle Gus did not respond. The stalling continued, and my mother, emotionally drained and preoccupied with other major problems in her life, let it go.

We never again lived in our beautiful La Coronela.

Chapter Ten

A Child of the Sacred Heart of Jesus

I've always had a penchant for all things French. I believe there are two contributing factors to this. One must be genetic. My maternal great-grandfather, Ignacio Perea Fonte, was born in Mexico City, but in 1878, at the age of sixteen and at the onset of the Mexican Revolution, he was sent to live with a family friend in Paris. He lived there for thirteen years and studied art and lithography during the height of French Impressionism. My grandfather Bibi claimed his father spoke better French than he did Spanish. On his return voyage to Mexico, Ignacio's ship docked in Havana for a few days. During that time, he met and fell in love with my great-grandmother, María Regla Cabrera y Hernández, and the ship sailed on to Mexico without him.

The other factor, I am sure, was my early education in Cuba with the nuns of the Order of the Sacred Heart, a well-known Roman Catholic religious society. The order was founded in 1800 amid the turmoil of the French Revolution, by a French nun named Madeleine Sophie Barat. Her dream to establish Catholic schools and convents in France, and eventually throughout the world, was realized when the first school opened its doors in Amiens, France, in 1802. Sister Madeleine Sophie's intention was to teach children, both rich and poor, to know and love Jesus and his beloved mother, to educate the whole person spiritually and morally, and, most importantly, to develop social awareness. She was canonized a saint by Pope Pius XI on May 24, 1925.

The all-girls academies were formed as a family unit. Schools were called houses, students were children, and nuns were mothers and sisters. *Las madres*, the mothers, were the educators and *las hermanitas*, the sisters, managed the households with servile diligence. Together they ran the schools and religious community with dedication and humility. The school also served as a convent for aspiring postulants of the order. Being a member of the Sacred Heart family was an integral part of my young life in Cuba.

Like a palace on a hilltop, the sand-colored structure gleamed under the tropical sun, surrounded by acres of countryside and bordered by Río Kibú. The vestibule of the three-storied building greeted one with formal Victorian parlors furnished with brocade chairs and settees, religious Renaissance paintings, and portraits of our founding nuns. Polished marble-floored corridors wove through harmonious flower gardens and courtyards. At the end of the long entrance gallery, a white, granite, life-size statue of the Sacred Heart of Jesus welcomed all with outstretched arms. An inscription at his feet read *Venid A Mí Todos*— Come to Me All.

Past the statue, a wide winding staircase, lined with brilliant stained-glass windows, led to the chapel, the core of Sacred Heart school life. Behind the main altar was a great mural of the Sacred Heart of Jesus standing on top of the world; the sweet smell of white lilies and roses, of burning candles and the fading scent of incense saturated the air. The peace. High-backed wooden pews lined the walls where the nuns solemnly prayed, with bowed heads and hands folded in unison. Their angelic voices led us in song to *Tantum Ergo*, as we students knelt on wooden pews with torturous, unpadded kneelers.

The Sacred Heart religious lived their cloistered lives behind the convent school walls. They took vows of education, poverty, obedience, and chastity. It intrigued me how these women could be so content secluded from the world. How did they manage without watching TV, listening to American music, or going to the movies? Did they ever wish for a boyfriend? Did they ever have the urge to peel off their hot black habits and jump into the cool waters of Río Kibú for a swim? Or to go horseback riding in one of the school's open fields, their hair free and blowing in the wind? I wondered about that one a lot. The nuns could never wear their hair loose except at night while sleeping. Cut very short, it was always completely covered by their bonnets and veils. Once in a while, a rebellious tuft of hair would peek out from under their white bonnets, and I would think to myself, *aha! Madre Martinez has light brown hair.* But at twelve years old, I was able to comprehend how strong their calling was and how deep their devotion to God, making them seem perpetually delightful, smiling and charitable.

The nuns walked the corridors noiselessly, as if floating. Most seemed content, except for *Madre* Gómez, whose beady eyes burrowed into the students through her wire-rimmed spectacles. In the heat of Cuban summers, the sisters endured their long, black habits without complaint, their perspiring, flushed faces snugly bound by fluted white bonnets, topped by sheer, black veils. A black rosary hung from their waists; they wore a large silver cross around their necks and a plain gold ring on their right hand. They were the brides of Christ. I can still hear their soft-spoken voices emphasizing, "We are a family here"; their runaway laughter as they hiked up their heavy black skirts to jump rope with us or join in a game of kickball, the school favorite.

Discipline, strict rules of silence, good manners, frequent meditations, and spiritual retreats were the backbone of student life. And the black line and clickers: We walked in ranks, from smallest to tallest, down a 10-inch-wide, single black line on the floor on either side of the corridors. In a perfect single file, we walked to and from our classrooms, chapel, lunch, and *recreo*, recess, in complete silence. Our nun walked alongside, policing the hallway with her reliable wooden clicker held snug in the palm of her hand. If we spoke to one another or stepped out of the black line, the loud, snapping clicker would stop our chatter and command our brown oxfords to regroup.

El refectorio—our monastic dining hall—was an enormous room with broad, wood-shuttered windows that opened onto the sweeping green fields and meadows surrounding the school. Tables for eight covered with white linen cloths were set with white dishes, silverware, and crystal glassware. Each table had a vase with fresh-cut flowers from the gardens. Good manners, such as quietly pulling our chairs from the tables, napkins on laps, no talking with your mouth full, and asking politely for something instead of reaching, were imperative during our family-style lunches.

At one end of the *refectorio* a life-size statue of La Immaculata stood atop a cloud supported by plump, rosy-cheeked cherubs. The Virgin Mary's eyes were raised toward heaven and her hands folded across her chest. In the center of the room, reigning supreme on a raised wooden pedestal, sat the keen-eyed nun in charge with a bell and clicker. After prayer, the *madre* read to us as we ate in impatient silence, waiting for the little bell to jingle, finally allowing us to socialize. We had to eat everything on our plates. If we didn't like a particular dish, the nuns would tell us, "Offer it up as a sacrifice for the poor suffering souls in purgatory."

"I hate green string beans," I whispered to my girlfriend Carmen during lunch one day. "I'm not eating them."

"You have to or you'll miss recess," she gasped, watching me expertly spit out my beans into my lovely linen napkin.

"No, I won't. Watch this." I shook the bean-filled napkin under my chair, dumping its contents in a most unladylike manner. Digging victoriously into a favorite dessert, I felt an ominous presence behind me. I looked up at the girls sitting across from me. They were gaping at something above my head. I prepared to become a martyr.

"Señorita Fernández y Perea." Behind me the nun's voice was resolute, emphasizing each word. "Are these your *habichuelas* I just stepped on?" I cringed at the words as a rush of heat raced up my neck and spread over my face. The dessert lumped in my throat while I slowly nodded.

"*Sí, Madre.*" She immediately removed my dessert.

"*Hermanita,*" she addressed the sister waiting on our

table, "please bring this child a fresh serving of beans." As the girls said their prayers and left for recess, I remained banished in the empty refectory to eat a steaming pile of string beans in agony. The *madre* patiently waited on her throne.

"The souls in purgatory, my child," she reminded me.

"Think of those poor souls in purgatory."

There were no souls left in purgatory that day.

In addition to our academic curriculum, we took daily French lessons, studied music, learned songs in Latin and various other languages, and were taught embroidering. We wrote in Italic script handwriting and learned the proper way to curtsy, even while walking. Every week we received a report card in *la sala de notas*, which also served as our auditorium, in the form of three little cards: the pink *muy bien*, above average; the blue *bien*, average; and the dreaded pale-yellow *regular*, barely satisfactory. Silver medals were awarded to students who excelled in a major subject that week. These were turned in at the end of the following week.

We wore two uniforms. The one for daily use was a pretty cornflower-blue pleated skirt with wide shoulder straps worn with a well-ironed, white long-sleeved linen blouse. On its round collar we snapped on a blue bow tie. We wore beige knee socks and brown oxfords with laces. For chapel we fastened waist-length black veils on our heads with an elastic band. Our gala uniform was identical to the daily uniform except it was entirely white, down to the shoes, bow tie, and veil. We wore our *uniforme de gala* on holidays, holy days, feast days, and awards day.

Día de premios—awards day—took place at the end

of every school year. Dressed in our white gala uniform, we gathered in the s*ala de notas* to receive our final report cards and awards for scholastic accomplishments. Mother Superior called the students forward individually and congratulated them, placing a wreath of silk roses on their heads for each subject in which they excelled. (Subjects were represented by different colors of roses.) The teacher then presented the students with a gift, always a hardcover book. As a girl received more than one wreath and book, she removed the previous wreath from her head, hooked it on her right arm and carried the books on her left arm.

After the awards ceremony, we proceeded to the chapel where our parents eagerly waited to see how well we had done by the wreaths we wore and carried. We processed in single file to the front of the chapel and deposited our wreaths in a basket. Carrying our books, we walked back to our pews for a short ceremony and blessing, then on to the refectory with our families for a reception.

The golden rule of silence was ignored on days of *tómbolas*. These holidays consisted of no classes, with games, competitions, and outdoor activities, celebrated mostly on Catholic feast days. The usually silent corridors and courtyards resonated with happy, laughing voices. The seniors set up game booths, and the *hermanitas* treated us to our favorite lunches and *meriendas*.

Christmas was a magical time as we celebrated the birth of Christ, especially *las pequeñas*, who had a close rapport with the infant Jesus. Several days before December 25 we brought a gift to school to honor the Christ child. After Mass we took our gifts to the impoverished girls who were taught in a small schoolhouse on the property, as Saint Madeleine Sophie had instituted. We shared in their happiness as they opened their gifts, and we played together.

On the last day of school before the holidays, we gathered on the immense main courtyard to sing Christmas carols to the Reverend Mother and all our *madres* and *hermanitas*. We sang in Spanish, French, English, German, and Japanese while the nuns stood around the arcaded galleries above us, smiling and wiping their tears. At the end of the concert, a shower of candies rained upon us as the nuns clapped and waved, wishing us *Feliz Navidad*.

My school in Cuba was my refuge, my spiritual home. When the thick wooden double doors closed behind me every morning, I entered a world that was stable and serene. No matter what went on in my family life, life within my school walls was unchanging. I looked forward to the peaceful familiarity and the nuns' genuine care, concern, and affection. But mostly I welcomed the security it gave me.

Others might regard my school as an example of the exclusivity and wealth of the Church, but for me as a child, the Sacred Heart Academy represented constancy, love, and being taken seriously as a student. More than anything else, it was the *madres* and the *hermanitas* who embodied these qualities.

The Sacred Heart nuns' influence on me during those few privileged childhood years in Cuba has remained one of the true constants in my life. They taught me things beyond outstanding academics and good manners. From them I learned about compassion, endurance, and self-sacrifice. They showed me, through their words and actions, how to know and deeply love our Lord and His Blessed Mother.

A Child of the Sacred Heart of Jesus

The Sacred Heart *madres* inculcated in me a secure spiritual foundation that helped develop my strong Catholic faith, which was to be a protective bastion during difficult times in my life.

The doors of my beloved school were closed by Fidel Castro in 1961. Like a thief in the night, the communist revolution stole my opportunity to complete this unique education. But it failed to rob me of my memories, which evoke indelible images of a time gone forever.

I am a nine-year-old pequeña *walking along the polished corridors. I am by myself, on my way back to class from an errand. No one is looking, so I brazenly step outside the black line, enjoying an impish moment. Around the corner of the wide hallway I spot the Reverend Mother approaching. Quickly jumping back inside the line, I smooth out my cornflower blue uniform and straighten up my bow tie. I stick out my chest, proudly displaying the silver medal for English I earned that week. The Reverend Mother gives me a warm smile.*

"Buenas tardes, mi hija," *she greets me, slowly nodding her head as she walks by. Without breaking my stride, I curtsy.*

"Good afternoon, Reverend Mother." I grin and keep walking on the black line. Someone is singing in the flower garden below. I stop and look around; coast is clear. Peering over the corridor balustrade I spot a young hermanita *gathering flowers while singing a French song praising the Lord. The nun's face is radiant.*

I gaze up at the cloudless cobalt sky and smile. "Je suis un enfant du Sacré Coeur de Jésus—*I am a child of the Sacred Heart of Jesus," I declare in my best French, what the nuns have instilled in me since my first day of school.*

A bell rings nearby and an explosion of loud, cheerful voices and shrieks of joy breaks the afternoon silence. I hear the steady beat of thick jump ropes whipping the pavement in the courtyard. I hop back on the black line and playfully zigzag toward recess, my ponytail tickling my neck as it swings in the air.

Chapter Eleven

The Calm Before the Storm

It was a spring Sunday in 1958, and Rancho Perea's rambling veranda was bursting with lunchtime clatter. The *portal* was a sea of tables and chairs accommodating a large gathering of family and friends. My grandmother's *arroz con pollo* was exceptionally good that day, and while servants cleared plates to bring out a favorite dessert, *pudín diplomático*, I listened to snatches of adult conversations on the porch.

"This *guerrillero* Castro is gaining popularity by the minute," Uncle Wilfredo commented to Bibi. He leaned back in his chair to make way for his plate to be taken. As Havana's police commander and a personal friend of President Batista, he was well informed about the rebel's activities. Opposition to Batista was swelling in the misty sierras, with rumors of a revolution brewing. "The *guajiros* are taking up arms and joining him." My uncle took a long sip of water and placed the glass back on the table with a thud.

"He's becoming a Cuban hero," my grandfather said. "Our people are losing confidence in Batista's government."

"This is getting serious, Gustavo," I heard my uncle reply. "Castro's recent attacks on our army units are hitting us hard." Shaking his head, he plopped his elbows on the table and joined his hands in mid-air, making a fist. "Did you hear about the explosions on all the main bridges and railroad tracks?"

"*Sí, como no.* And the *guajiros* are actually supporting this." My grandfather finished eating and pushed his plate aside. "If this keeps escalating, it's just a matter of time before we'll have a rebellion on our hands."

At nine years old, I didn't understand much about politics. I knew Fulgencio Batista was our President. But I was becoming aware of the growing dissent in my country, of an uneasy tension in the air whenever grownups discussed that *guerrillero*, Fidel Castro, and his *barbudos* in the Sierra Maestra Mountains.

My mother yearned for a place of her own.

Despite my grandparents' insistence that we continue living with them, Mami rented a house next door to Mama and Bibi's. Across the street from the park, the white Spanish colonial home was bright and airy. A small wrought-iron gate opened from the sidewalk onto wide granite steps to a columned *portal* surrounded by colorful flowerbeds. An open flagstone terrace hugged the left side of the house and ended by the French doors off the dining room. Low white cement walls edged the entire *terraza*, and a variety of climbing roses in striking shades of red, pink, coral, yellow, and white bloomed along the wall. High privet hedges bordered by areca palms surrounded the property, providing privacy.

Finally, I told myself, we were going to have a home of our own and some stability in our lives. That summer of 1958 marked the blossoming of my few happy years in Cuba. I thrived in school, made new friends, took ballet classes, and especially enjoyed being with my neighborhood pals. We busied the sidewalks on our *calle* playing hopscotch, jumping rope, and roller-skating to the park with our *tatas* and younger siblings trailing behind.

My older sister's passion for rock and roll was at its peak, and she danced a mean jitterbug. Gradually, I watched the gawky, long-legged tomboy in her give way to snug pedal pushers with tight belts and makeup. She had also discovered a cute guy in our neighborhood. Alberto was thin as a rail and sported thick brown hair slicked back *a la* Elvis.

"Psst, Gloria, listen, I need your help," María Elena called to me in a low voice from the other end of our grandparents' porch while we visited there one afternoon. I was playing jacks on the tile floor and was about ready to go for ten.

"*Chica*, you made me miss," I grumbled, pouncing on my red ball as it bounced onto the driveway.

"Sh-hh...*cállate* and listen to me," she commanded, her dark eyes blazing. She was standing inconspicuously behind the bamboo shades. Our grandparents' *portal* was the perfect lookout post to Alberto's home across the street.

"*¿Qué te pasa?* Why are you acting so weird?" I sauntered back to the porch.

"Now pay attention, this is very important," she said breathlessly. "I want you to go on playing jacks and keep an eye across the street." She pointed through an areca palm. "As soon as you see him come out, tell me exactly what he does."

"When who comes out? What's wrong with you?"

"Alberto, *boba*. But don't let him see you telling me, okay?"

"O-o-oh…it's that guy you have a crush on." I sprinkled my jacks on the floor. "I saw him talking to a blonde girl yesterday," I said provokingly. María Elena's eyes shot green spears.

"It's that *sata* Normita, the big flirt." She peeked from behind the blinds' corner opening. "Look, look, there he is." Alberto came out to the walkway by his front porch. "Well, what's he doing?" Her voice was riddled with anxiety; she was biting her nails down to the quick.

"He's just standing there." I tossed the ball up in the air to retrieve my jacks.

"Is he looking over here? Tell me, is he?"

"No."

"Is anyone with him?"

"No, but he looks like he's waiting for someone." She stomped her foot. Suddenly he glanced in our direction. He spotted me and waved. I waved back.

"*What* are you doing?" she hissed. Her eyebrows splayed wide. "No, don't look at me, keep watching him while you play."

"He's combing his hair and looking around," I reported, flustered. "Uh-oh. That *sata* girl and another guy are coming down the sidewalk toward him." It was quiet in the porch corner. Normita and her brother briefly talked with Alberto, then all three got in his car and drove off.

"You better hurry up and get to know him," I said as she darted inside the house. When María Elena turned fifteen that November and celebrated *Los Quince*, Alberto escorted her to dinner and dancing at the Havana Hilton.

* * *

I missed Papi. We visited him often at the sanatorium, never knowing what to expect. Most times he was heavily sedated, and even on good days he appeared quiet and distant. His dark brown eyes were sad and empty, and he rarely smiled anymore. His hugs were stiff, as if he had forgotten how to give them. My father was becoming a stranger to me. It was at this time in my life that subconsciously I began to substitute Papi with Bibi, whom I spent time with daily. Bibi helped me with my homework and taught me how to ride my first bicycle at Rancho Perea. More and more, it was he I went to when I wanted to talk or when I felt sad. My grandfather filled the painful void my father's absence was creating.

The psychiatrist felt that my father could handle being with his family on weekends but not with all five children at the same time. In order to arrange this, Mami rented a furnished condo in a posh section of Havana called Miramar, and we took turns staying with Papi. One weekend María Elena, Roly, and I stayed with our parents, and the following weekend, Consuelo and the twins went, while we stayed with Mama and Bibi. The condo complex was called the Chateau, and our third-floor balcony overlooked the turquoise Caribbean. At dusk the tide rumbled over the coral reefs at the shore's edge beneath the rose-colored clouds of spectacular sunsets.

During our weekends at the Chateau, my father was restless, constantly demanding my mother's attention. Mami was tense and on the alert to his erratic behavior. María Elena was always busy playing her rock and roll records or chatting on the phone with her boyfriend. Most times I was in charge of watching my seven-year-old brother, and we played together often. He looked up to his ten-year-old sister and was in awe of my imagination. When the tide went out, Roly and I were allowed to play on the coral reefs. We pretended the rock formations were castles and we were neighboring royalty. King Roly bravely rescued me from menacing dragons with a sword of driftwood, and I rewarded him with bags of glistening seashells, which we pretended were gold coins.

Sharks were frequently seen swimming by the Chateau. Papi spotted one from our balcony once and called us out to see it. The shark sighting was my inspiration for a new game. When it was high tide, Roly and I were not allowed to play on the reefs. We headed for the swimming pool after hours and played *tiburón*—shark—while our parents watched us from the balcony. The shark was a large gray rock tied to a long string. A small rubber doll, also tied to a string, was our often-doomed swimmer. The swimmer would be bobbing in the water, swimming and relaxing. Then he or she would spot the shark's fin above water in the near distance. (The rock had to be held up near the surface.) Panicked, the doll would begin swimming toward safety, the stepladder at the other end of the pool. The shark would relentlessly chase and circle the swimmer (often we would tangle our strings and get mad at each other), and if the doll made it to the ladder, it was safe.

"I don't want to be the swimmer," Roly would say with knitted brows. "I want to be *el tiburón*."

"You're always the shark," I'd retort. "Last time you tangled the rock in the stepladder."

"I don't want to be eaten by the shark." He'd pout.

"Oh, okay, *tiburón*." I would almost always give in.

"That's what I'm calling you from now on." He beamed.

*　*　*

My grandparents Tito Pepe and Tita Lala also owned a *finca* not far from Rancho Perea. They named the expansive country estate La Casielle, after a village near Cangas de Onís in Asturias, Spain, where my grandfather was born. A long driveway lined with regal palm trees and colorful flowering shrubs led to a gothic-like white mansion. It was ensconced with framboyán, sapodilla, and willow trees, the latter's branches swooping down over the house, keeping it cool during the hot summer months. An old ceiba tree towered protectively over the home's front entrance.

Unlike the casual comfort of Rancho Perea, La Casielle had an elegant country charm. An open stone fireplace partitioned the living room from the dining room, offering heat to both areas. High beamed ceilings, dark Spanish-style furniture, and Renaissance and Impressionist paintings gave it a European atmosphere.

I enjoyed spending weekends with my grandparents at La Casielle swimming in the Olympic-size pool and horseback riding. During my Christmas break in December 1958, I was returning home from a few days stay at their *finca*.

"How was your visit at La Casielle?" Mami greeted me on our porch.

"It was good," I said, looking around for my dog. "Where's Popsy?" My mother's face turned serious. I instantly knew something was wrong. She explained how the gate latch had been left unhooked and he got out and ran into a motorcycle. My Popsy was dead.

I dropped my drawing pad and books on the floor. "Popsy, here boy, I'm home," I called him, tears streaming down my face. "Popsy... I don't believe you, Mami," I cried. Consuelo opened the front door and a brown dog bounded toward me. It sat by my side, looked up at me, and rapidly wagged its tail. Startled, I wiped my tears and stopped sobbing.

"Whose dog is this?" I asked in a shaky voice.

"She's our new dog," Consuelo said, petting her. "Isn't she pretty? But she needs a name." I blinked back tears.

The standard poodle was six months old, and her curly, chocolate brown hair all but covered her hazel eyes. I hesitated before kneeling down to pet her, and she flopped on her back, paws up, exposing her pink belly. Her tongue hung out the side of her mouth as she playfully extended a paw toward me.

"Are you lazy?" I said to her in English. I fought off a smile.

"Lazy. That's a good name for her," my mother put in enthusiastically. "She loves to flop around and sleep a lot."

"*Hola*, Lazy," I welcomed my new dog. She quickly sat up and licked my face, and the tears I had shed for Popsy.

* * *

In late December 1958, news that Fidel Castro and his growing army of rebels were advancing reverberated throughout Havana. The political tension in the island's capital was high. Castro had captured Palma Soriano, the site of the Moncada attack in 1953 that marked the start of his revolution.

We were spending the New Year's holiday at Rancho Perea with Mama and Bibi, relatives, and family friends. On New Year's Eve, we children were wired about staying up late as Mami and my aunts passed out hats, horns, streamers, and confetti. My grandmother was in the kitchen supervising the final preparations for the evening's feast. The men were out on the veranda smoking cigars.

"Our government is falling apart," Felipe, a friend of my grandfather's, said gravely. His teeth clenched his Corona at the side of this mouth. "El Che captured Santa Clara yesterday."

"*Ahora sí,*" Bibi exclaimed. He rapidly tapped his ashes on the ashtray. "This time bomb is about to explode any minute, Felipe. What's Batista doing?"

"He's planning to leave the island *muy pronto.*"

"What a coward!" My grandfather pinched his lips and shook his head slowly. "*Se acabó lo que se daba.*"

"Yeah, it's all over, all right, and now what?" Alejandro, the *finca's* neighbor, asked, putting out his unfinished *panetela*. "Who will be in charge of our crumbling government?" Beads of perspiration formed on his brow. "What of us?"

"General Cantillo will head the armed forces and fight off the rebels," Felipe said emphatically. "It doesn't look good, *mi gente.*"

Around two o'clock, I was in bed, still awake, as the celebration on the veranda was winding down. The grown-ups were dancing to "*Sabor a Mí,*" a popular *bolero*, when the radio announcer interrupted the music.

"We have breaking news." The man's voice sounded urgent.

"Quiet, everyone, quiet," I heard someone say. All merriment on the porch was abruptly silenced. I got out of bed and peeked out the bedroom door.

"President Fulgencio Batista has left the country," the announcer stated dramatically. "*El Presidente*, along with his family and close friends, has left from Camp Columbia airfield for the Dominican Republic." Loud comments followed.

"¡*Ay, Dios mío!*" Aunt Eugenia gave a small scream and clapped her hands to her mouth.

"It's that *condenado guerrillero* again," I said aloud to myself. I had heard Bibi use that derogatory expression to refer to Castro.

I crawled back into bed, feeling quite grown-up using my newly learned curse word. "*Condenado guerrillero*," I repeated with disgust, trying to imitate my grandfather. *He's at it again.* But this time, I had an inexplicable feeling of dread that Fidel Castro's troublemaking was going to do more than cause talk among the grownups. I feared that our newfound happiness, the calm that filled our lives, was coming to a sudden end. The calm before the storm—a storm that might uproot us once again, this time fiercely, without mercy, and change our lives forever.

Chapter Twelve

THE CUBAN REVOLUTION: *COMUNISTAS Y GUSANOS*

Cuca was singing exuberantly off tune: "*Mamá, son de la loma*—they are from the hills." She pushed the wet mop with gusto across the kitchen floor, swaying her hips while she sang. During Castro's takeover, Radio Rebelde, an illicit station, played the song of the 26th of July movement every night. The tune had been banned from other major radio stations. The reason it was playing was understood; Fidel and his *guerrilleros* would soon be in the capital. Batista had been defeated. Our maid reflected Havana's spirit of supreme celebration.

Fidel Castro's revolt had deposed the Batista dictatorship with a brilliant *coup d'etat*, and the rebels had taken over our Caribbean island. On January 3, 1959, Castro and his *barbudos* started their victorious five-day march to the capital, riding atop captured army trucks and tanks. Throughout the island, the revolutionary parade was televised as it advanced toward Havana. On January 8 the *guerrilleros* entered the rejoicing city, and Castro was hailed as Cuba's greatest national hero since José Martí. Havana was enraptured, bursting with jubilation. Church bells pealed, factory whistles blew, and at the harbor, ships sounded off their sirens.

Our neighborhood reeled with people clapping and

singing, honking their car horns, dancing in the streets and cheering "¡*Viva* Fidel!" and "¡Cuba *Libre*!" *Tatas* twirled their wards in midair, chanting "¡*Venceremos*!—we will conquer!" Children were unaware of the day's significance but were caught up in the excitement of a fiesta.

That afternoon of January 8, my family and I went to the home of our neighbor, whose second-floor terrace faced Calle Columbia, the main street where Castro would soon ride by. I stood on the flag-bedecked balcony with the other children and nannies, waving my little Cuban flag and cheering with the euphoric crowd that lined both sides of the street below. But in the house, the mood was more restrained. The adults stayed inside, cautiously peering from the windows, waiting for Castro's arrival with subdued anticipation.

"Look, here comes *el líder*!" Consuelo screamed behind me. Spotting the tanks approaching, she tapped my shoulders excitedly. "Here comes Cuba's liberator!"

The densely packed flock below us roared, as the sounds of heavy marching and the tanks' rumbling grew louder. A group of revolutionaries, their hard, chiseled faces streaked with sweat, marched toward us in front of monstrous armored vehicles. They carried rifles and wore rosaries around their necks.

I could tell straightaway which one was *el guerrillero*. For so long I had wondered what Fidel Castro looked like. Wearing olive green fatigues, he rode atop a tank, flanked by his rebels walking alongside. I could barely see his face, tufted by a thick black beard, topped with a cap and dark-rimmed glasses. But I could see the rebel's teeth flashing through his hearty smile. I had never seen anyone like Fidel

The Cuban Revolution: Comunistas y Gusanos

Castro and his *barbudos*. They looked wild, their hungry eyes scanning the crowds while they clutched their American M-2 rifles against their chests. I stopped waving my flag. As Castro waved and smiled at the swarming masses, he puffed on a cigar clenched tightly in his teeth. I watched astounded as his tank crawled along, stopping often for him to make a short speech or hug and greet someone he knew. His physical presence emanated power, and his immense charisma radiated among the throngs amassing to follow him like a Pied Piper.

His tank paused near our balcony. Fidel Castro looked up in our direction. He was so close, I could see the large medal of Our Lady of Cobre, Cuba's patroness, hanging from his neck.

Near hysteria, Consuelo and Cuca screamed in unison: "¡*Viva* Fidel!" while waving their little flags. Castro's tank started up again. My fixed gaze followed the rebels until they turned the tumultuous corner and disappeared. The rebel entourage marched on to Camp Columbia headquarters, where thousands of Cubans awaited Castro's arrival.

Later on we gathered around Mama and Bibi's television to hear his triumphant speech. Fidel Castro's revolution promised to end social injustice in Cuba. He made it clear that one of the major issues facing the country was the conflict between the elite governmental ruling class and the impoverished masses of *guajiros*. He passionately vowed that every Cuban would have access to proper health care, to his or her own piece of land, and to an education. The immense audience thundered, but my grandparents' living room was silent. We watched in awe as one of the white doves released as a symbol of peace turned in mid-flight and landed on Castro's shoulder. The multitude was jubilant, calling him "The Chosen One" who would lead the Cuban people's destinies. The dove stayed on Castro's shoulder throughout his entire fiery address.

"The bottom line here," Bibi commented as we watched the speech, "is that the *guajiros* will be exchanging their present bosses for government bosses."

"Where is he going to get all this land to give away, Gustavo?" Mama asked.

"There's only one way." Bibi's tone was grave. "Confiscation and redistribution of wealth." Then in a low, fierce voice he added, "This is communism."

At the onset, my family was cautiously supportive of Fidel Castro. They, like most Cubans, were impressed with the young revolutionary's brazen victory in dethroning a corrupt and heavily armed government against difficult odds. It had been an inspiring act, demanding admiration. Listening to Castro's first speech, they welcomed his promise of reform that would benefit the people, hoping this would evolve within the island's existing democratic framework. But they were also skeptical, waiting to decide how they truly felt about Castro until he acted out these promises for Cuba's future.

The takeover in Havana had been swift and absolute. But strong opposition to the revolution gained momentum in the capital as the threads of communism wove their way throughout the island. Growing numbers of antirevolutionary men and women fought the new regime underground. News of property and business appropriations, arrests, shootings, and disappearances were alarming. Many renowned figures in Havana—politicians, businessmen, and journalists—faced the *paredón*, a wall used for firing-squad executions at La Cabaña Fortress. Horror stories of open gunfire, cold-blooded killings, and brutal massacres were rampant in the capital, bringing to light the realization that no one was safe. Our family struggled to maintain balance within the uncertainty of this political upheaval. But at the same time, emotional waves of turbulence washed over our lives again.

In February 1959, my grandfather Tito Pepe lost his battle with advanced leukemia. My father took it hard. My mother lost her only ally in the Fernández family.

In late spring, María Elena, Roly, and I spent a long weekend at the Chateau with our parents. I had not seen Papi for two months. He was extremely thin again, with a heart-wrenching lost look in his eyes. He hardly spoke to us, only to my mother. He fidgeted constantly, mumbling to himself and scribbling notes on tiny pieces of paper, which he then stuffed in his pants pockets. My mother seemed intensely anxious that weekend.

Our new neighbors in the Chateau were a large group of *barbudos* who occupied three apartments on the floor above us. They were constantly patrolling the grounds armed with rifles and dressed in olive green fatigues. Papi became agitated whenever he saw the rebels and forbade my brother and me to play on the coral reefs as we had before.

One early evening, Mami was preparing dinner by the kitchen window when a sudden movement among the reefs caught her eye. She stared in horror through the dusk of sunset as dark figures carrying rifles approached the apartment complex. Instantly, the hallway above us thundered with racing footsteps and angry voices yelling commands. Papi awoke from a nap and wandered into the kitchen as shots rang out from the rooftop.

"Quick, go in the living room with María Elena," my mother urged Papi, pushing him out of the kitchen. "The rebels are worked up about something." She grabbed my brother and me by the hands and took us into our bedroom, bolting the dead lock on the front door as we passed it. She flung open the closet door and sat us on the floor inside.

"Now listen carefully. I need both of you to be very brave." Roly looked up at me, his large brown eyes unblinking as Mami spoke. "There might be some fighting and shooting going on outside." Her words were clipped and fast. "Don't be afraid. You'll be safe here. Papi, María Elena, and I will be in the living room." She put a hand on each of our shoulders. "Sit very quietly and don't come out until I come and get you." A thick cloak of darkness enveloped us as my mother closed the door and ran to the living room.

"Mami-i-i, don't leave me..." my little brother wailed. His thin shoulders trembled next to me in the blackness. My fear dissolved momentarily.

"*Oye, tiburón*, I'm here with you. It's okay," I whispered urgently, tapping his arm. He stopped crying. In the living room, I later found out, my parents lay face down on the floor, each covering my sister with half their bodies, and placed their hands over their heads as machine guns screamed at each other outside. Bullets ripped through the building walls and shattered the glass of the hallway windows outside our front door.

"Cover your ears!" I yelled to my brother. I curled

The Cuban Revolution: Comunistas y Gusanos

myself into a tight ball, put my face down on my knees, and prayed. After what seemed like an eternity, the *tiroteo* ended and the closet door opened at last. Mami scooped Roly in her arms as I sat motionless, my body rubber-like. My little brother's eyes and mine locked for one long moment, then he buried his face in my mother's shoulder as she reached out her hand to me. Outside, Castro's militia surrounded the Chateau, relentlessly combing the area for anti-revolutionaries.

Mami had given Papi a sedative and he sat calmly, staring blankly at the television. I was drawn to the kitchen window, thinking about my pretend castle on the coral reefs. I opened the venetian blinds. In the pink haze of sunset, my imaginary castle loomed over a dark, motionless body. I watched as the rebels encircled the corpse like a swarm of angry ants. Then, grabbing the arms and legs, they dragged it across the rocks toward the road and out of sight.

The following day no one dared leave the apartments. From our balcony we could see other tenants peeking out their windows and portico doors. The pool was deserted, the parking lot full, and I wanted to go home. But Mami tried to keep things normal so we could spend the rest of the weekend with my father. We played board games and watched TV, but the tension was palpable. My father paced the apartment while Mami watched over him, concerned about what he would do next.

At dinner my father's expression suddenly changed and he gave my mother a dark look.

"You want them to take me away to America again, don't you?" he snarled at her across the table. Mami stopped cutting my brother's meat. The utensils clanked loudly on his plate as she dropped them.

"Rolando, it's all right, calm down." She instinctively held on to the arms of her chair, as if ready to get up. "No one is taking you anywhere." Roly's lips began to quiver. Apprehension flickered through me; my sister's eyes darted nervously in my direction.

"I know you and the doctors are up to something." He sprayed spittle in his fury, veins pulsating at his temples, a face like thunder. Pounding the table with his fist, he sprang to his feet. My mother blinked repeatedly, quickly pushing back her chair.

"No, Rolando," she cried out, but my father grabbed his chair and began to lift it.

"I won't let you this time," he bellowed. "I'll break this chair on your head."

My little brother covered his face with his hands. I sat stunned, gaping at my father. Papi's dark eyes widened, blazing with anger. My heart pounded. I held on so tightly to the seat of my chair that my fingers hurt.

"Papi, no. Stop, Papi!" I screamed. I could hardly see through my tears, but I kept my eyes fixed on him. My father put the chair down slowly while looking at me. His face softened; the darkness left.

"Don't be afraid, Yoyi," he said sweetly. "I won't let them take me from you." His entire body slowly relaxed, as if a possessing spirit was leaving it. My mother rushed to his side, gave him another sedative, and took him into the bedroom.

I tossed and turned at bedtime. Papi had hurt Mami once already and had just threatened to harm her again.

The Cuban Revolution: Comunistas y Gusanos

What would happen next? Despite Mami's reassurance that Papi was sick and did not mean to do and say these things, the monstrous look on his face stayed with me. That night I stayed awake for a long time, my mind haunted by our traumatic weekend.

My father's progressive breakdown continued. He was overcome with delusions of persecution by Castro's *guerrilleros*. The doctors prescribed powerful drugs to ward off the hallucinations that agonized him. These drugs made him sleepy and at times catatonic, and we could no longer spend weekends at the Chateau with him. The recent incidents of Papi's hostility prompted my mother to make a heartbreaking decision. After deep soul-searching and countless meetings with doctors, lawyers, and priests throughout the summer, she sought a legal separation from my father. After seventeen years of marriage, she could no longer handle Papi's devastating illness and raise five children at the same time. She felt she had done all she could for him. For her own safety and that of the children for whom she was responsible, she could not go on living like this.

In early September 1959, I was to spend a weekend with my grandmother Tita Lala at La Casielle. She missed my grandfather desperately. Being at the *finca*, which had been his favorite place, eased her sadness. She spent most weekends there, inviting her children and grandchildren to visit often.

Dropping me off at my grandmother's home gave my mother an opportunity to meet with Tita Lala to discuss her decision. Mami had told her by phone that she had to talk to her about my father's worsening condition. Tita Lala invited her to lunch.

I always enjoyed the drive to my grandmother's home on Quinta Avenida in Miramar. Unlike our bustling neighborhood, with children roller-skating on the sidewalks and street vendors singing their sales, Quinta Avenida's main sound was that of traffic, flowing smoothly along the wide, leafy avenue lined with framboyán and palm trees and flanked on both sides by turn-of-the-century colonial mansions and modern condominiums.

I could smell the ocean nearby when I opened the car window, and I knew we were almost there when we drove by a huge billboard of a man dressed up in fancy pants and a red coat. The sign read: "Enjoy a Johnny Walker Red."

My mother was quiet that day, riding in the backseat with me. Our new chauffeur, Raul, kept staring at us from the rear-view mirror.

"Señora, I dreamt about you last night." He gave my mother a sly smile. "You were standing on the rooftop of Belén, with your bare breasts to the wind."

"*Usted es un atrevido,*" she snapped at him, appalled at his insolence. "How dare you talk to me like that in front of my child!" Raul threw his head back slightly and grinned. My mother quickly fastened the top button of her blouse. "I don't want to hear another word from you, and keep your eyes on the road."

"*Sí,* Señora." His tone was mocking. Mami sat up straight and made small talk with me about my upcoming weekend at La Casielle. I knew she was upset with the chauffeur. Raul started to whistle, tapping the Mercedes' steering wheel. I looked up at the mirror. He was watching me and gave me a wink. I flashed him a dirty look and quickly turned away. My grandfather Bibi fired him that very day.

Ever since the Castro takeover, there had been a social awakening among the underprivileged people, an anticipation of Fidel's promises of a change in Cuba that would finally bring them class equality and a better life. My family began to notice an attitude change in many of their household servants. A certain haughty air took the place of deference, a more laid-back behavior replaced dedication, and some servants made open attempts to establish a brazen familiarity with their employers. *Just wait and see,* their snide expressions seemed to say.

As we arrived at my grandmother's, I sensed my mother's apprehension as we walked up the gray marble steps to the front door. The butler led us into the wide foyer. I liked Andrés, a tall, handsome black man in his early thirties. His smile lit up his face, and he had a mischievous sense of humor. He served my grandmother as butler and chauffeur and enjoyed taking care of her houseplants.

Andrés announced our arrival to Tita Lala, who was in the living room. Again, I detected my mother's uneasiness, yet I had no idea why.

"Yoyi, Pilar is making your favorite dessert for lunch today." My grandmother pushed back the hair off my shoulder. "Why don't you go see how she's coming along?"

"Just in time, *niña.*" Pilar looked up as I walked into the kitchen. Her keen eyes smiled at me behind clear plastic glasses. She was pouring the *arroz con leche* in crystal compote dishes. "I'm saving some for you to sample." Pilar had been my grandparents' housekeeper for many years. She was born in Spain, and I loved listening to her Spanish lisp when she spoke. She was a hard-working *gallega* who took great pride in running an efficient household. Tall and muscular, she had a huge mole on her right temple, and she wore her hair plaited, then knotted into a chignon.

"¡*Delicioso*!" I complimented her, licking the creamy rice pudding clean off the spoon. In the dining room, Andrés was filling crystal goblets with ice water as we gathered for lunch. Pilar walked around the table holding silver platters with dome lids. She paused by each person, lifting the lid, offering the lunch courses.

After lunch I visited with Pilar in the kitchen while my mother and grandmother met on the front porch. I wanted to show Pilar my new coloring book and remembered I had left it in the living room. The French doors to the porch were partially opened.

"…no longer take care of Rolando, Clara," I heard my mother say as I entered the living room. She hesitated, then continued. "I ask you to take care of your son now, so I can take care of our children." I moved slowly toward my things.

"What a lame excuse to get out of your marriage, Ninina," Tita Lala replied bitterly. My mother looked dumbfounded. A heated argument ensued, and my grandmother told Mami that her income from Papi's share in the family's lumber business would now be minimal. "Most of Rolando's inheritance has already been spent on his treatments," she said with authority, "so don't expect much from me now."

"Clara, it's not for me only, it's for your five grandchildren." But Mami's words failed to move my grandmother.

The rest of the weekend I was distant with Tita Lala.

When I got home, I talked to my mother about the conversation I had overheard.

"Why was Tita Lala so mean to you?" I sat on a porch step while she deadheaded her geraniums.

"Because she doesn't want to take care of your father." Mami crushed the rotted leaves in her gloved hand and tossed them into a tin pail.

"Why can't we take care of Papi?"

"Because it's too much for me, *m'ija*."

"What do you mean, Mami?"

"You know Papi has been sick for a long time, and I have always taken care of him."

"Yes, I know."

"Well, he needs constant attention now to help him rest and relax so he can feel better, and I also need to take care of you and your brothers and sisters." She looked at me, squinting her eyes in the bright sun. "I can't do both, and I asked Tita Lala to help me."

"Are you afraid of Papi?" Mami took off her gloves and sat on the porch steps next to me.

"No, I never have been," she replied. "But you know that lately he's been more upset. That's why he needs to be in a quiet place to rest."

"You mean that sanatorium place?"

"*Sí*." Her voice was sad, just above a whisper. I remembered my grandmother's harsh words about our minimal income.

"Are we going to be poor now?"

"No, we're not," she said, determined. "Remember we have Bibi and Mama and all our family who care for us very much. We'll manage." But my mother's explanation did not take away the new light in which I had seen my grandmother.

A few weeks later, the doctors allowed my father to spend a weekend with his mother. Even though her home had two guestrooms, my grandmother made Papi sleep with Andrés in the servants' quarters. When my mother found out, she immediately called Tita Lala.

"How can you treat Rolando that way?" Her hand trembled holding the phone. "For seventeen years I slept with him in the same bed, and you won't let him sleep in your home?" Her voice escalated. "How can you be afraid of your own son, Clara." My grandmother retaliated, telling my mother that Papi was none of her concern since he was now in her care. It was at that moment that my mother fully comprehended the initial diagnosis Dr. Naten had given my father.

At the end of the first seven-month treatment, the psychiatrist told her that Papi had a genetic predisposition to neurosis that could have been successfully treated. But it was his medical opinion that what aggravated my father's unstable mental condition, and pushed him over the edge into schizophrenia, was the emotional neglect he had suffered from his mother since early childhood.

My grandmother had wanted her firstborn child to be a daughter. She gave birth to my father instead. He became aware of that at an early age. His emotional pain was compounded when his mother sent him to boarding school in America for eleven years. Now that he was mentally ill and totally dependent on his mother's care, she shunned him even more.

The Cuban Revolution: Comunistas y Gusanos

After the separation, my mother's life changed dramatically. With her income from my father's part ownership of the family lumber business drastically cut by my grandmother, overnight Mami went from being an affluent society lady married into an aristocratic family to a single parent raising five children.

Our next-door neighbor was the principal of the private school my younger siblings attended. He offered Mami a job helping out in the school office, and to make ends meet, she accepted. With Consuelo's help, the constant moral support of her parents and extended family, and her unfailing determination, my mother maintained a steady course in our lives. We continued to attend our private schools, enjoy our extracurricular activities, and live in the beautiful, comfortable house we were finally able to call home.

By 1960, the Cuban revolution had rid the island of the United States' influence, Fidel Castro's primary goal. His intense hatred for U.S. *imperialistas* stemmed from fear that they would steal his revolution. Castro began to court the Soviet Union, seeking their economic help and military protection.

Strong opposition to Castro's embrace of communism first arose among disillusioned businessmen and foreign property holders. But their complaints were ineffective, and soon they realized they could not flourish in this new atmosphere of domestic repression and censorship.

My grandfather's sense of ill-ease was well founded when Castro signed the Agrarian Reform Law, making it legal for the government to confiscate privately owned land for redistribution.

"¡*Ahora sí!*—there's no doubt anymore," Bibi told my mother at dinner one night. "Our island is becoming communist."

"Why do they have to take people's properties?" Mami asked. "Why can't Castro help the *guajiros* and the island's poor without taking away from others?"

"Because this stripping of land, assets, and power is symbolic of taking away status and place in society. *Socialismo*, then everyone is equal." My family now feared what Bibi had predicted about land distribution. The news described how large-scale land holdings belonging to Americans, Batista, and his supporters were appropriated and redistributed to the poor.

The next target was the island's wealthy, a category that included my family. The seizing of property escalated and the terror of arrest and imprisonment was keen. In growing numbers, the gilded members of the crumbling Cuban aristocracy, consisting mostly of white-skinned professionals, business executives, landowners, high military officers, and politicians, along with their families, left their glittering pre-revolution life and fled the island by plane for the shores of Florida, forming a strong exile population in Miami. The communists who remained in Cuba, mostly blacks and the penniless rural *guajiros*, called these Cubans *los gusanos*—the worms, the opposition. They were labeled the traitors of the triumphant "*Revolución Cubana.*"

As more and more of our close friends and relatives fled the island, my family began to contemplate the very real possibility of leaving Cuba. Among trusted family members, friends, and neighbors, there was an intense feeling of "get out while you can," but there was a dear price to pay. The thought of leaving the fruits of a life's work, possessions, family, and country was harrowing. *Where do we go? How will we survive? Will we ever see our relatives again? Will we ever return to Cuba?* Yet there was no doubt that given the fast-approaching choice between communism and freedom, my family would choose freedom.

While the adults in my family watched their idyllic world shatter around them, I was oblivious to the gathering political storm. I was busy with my blossoming social life, looking forward to my twelfth birthday and my first boy-girl party.

Chapter Thirteen

Childhood Interrupted

A drop of perspiration trickled down my chest. I squirmed, quickly pulling at my cotton blouse and peeking down to make sure it wasn't a bug. I was still rattled after finding a *lagartija*, a small brown lizard, between my bedsheets the week before.

It was an unusually steamy afternoon in the late spring of 1960. The porch's tile floor felt cool under my thighs. I sat doodling on my new Deskette drawing pad, waiting for my girlfriends Gracielita and Isis to go roller-skating in the park. I loved my stylish new pad, a feel-better gift from Mami after I got my braces. I was the first one in our extended family to wear braces, and my tin grin garnered much sympathy.

Following my visit to the orthodontist earlier that day, my mother had taken me to *"el ten cen"*—Woolworth's—on Calle Galiano, Havana's downtown main street, to buy me something special and have a Coca-Cola and *panquecito*—a cupcake—at their soda fountain. She always did that. After a doctor's visit in the city, especially when shots, blood work, or pain of any kind were involved, she would take us shopping for a little treat to cheer us up. But visiting *el ten cen* was a treat in itself. The American store was one of the most popular in the city, especially with the young people.

Besides Galiano Street, another favorite was San Rafael Street, near Parque Central in Centro Habana, where most of the major department stores were. Calle Obispo, the main street of Old Havana, had a special charm of its own. The rich scent of *café Cubano*, strong espresso coffee saturated with sugar, wafted out of busy little *bodegas* along narrow cobblestoned streets flanked by sixteenth-century Spanish colonial homes.

I admired my Deskette's hot-pink vinyl binder and scrutinized the teenaged girl on its front cover. She sat across a tufted chair, wearing snug capris while laughing and talking on the telephone. Her legs swung in midair, and her long ponytail dangled over her shoulder. And she had perfect little breasts. I pulled at the front of my blouse to air out my perspiring chest and peeked down again. I was almost twelve, and the development of my breasts was a major preoccupation. At school, there was a raging competition to wear a training bra. I was nowhere near winning.

I went back to my doodling, making a fancy curly-cue on the letter *s*. "There!" I said, satisfied with my work. Carlos. The entire page was filled with fancy variations of the name, with little hearts and flowers floating throughout the letters. He lived around the corner from my house, and I had recently met him while roller-skating at the *parque*. To me, Carlos seemed quite manly at fifteen. He was tall and good-looking, with a flop of thick sandy hair, sea-green eyes, and a sprinkling of freckles across his nose. When he smiled he flashed a chipped front tooth, which made him even more endearing. Plus, he knew all the latest American songs. I felt my face flush, wondering if he would be at the park this afternoon.

Next to me, Lazy woke from her nap and abruptly sat up, growling at an areca palm in the flower garden. Basking on the feathery palm, a chameleon sized up my dog, displaying its brilliant red gill in defiance. With one giant leap, Lazy bolted off the porch into the garden after the lizard. She chased it through the hibiscus and into the rose bushes until she pricked her nose and yelped. With her head down she returned to my side for comfort. I brushed the rose petals off her back.

It was amazing how much I had grown to love this dog in the short time since we'd adopted her. We had bonded immediately. She was smart, loyal, and happy-go-lucky, always ready for a good romp in the yard and especially in the fields at Rancho Perea. Her caramel-colored eyes peeked out through tufts of curly brown hair. The tips of her long, silky ears were often matted with brambles or bits of dog biscuits.

I could tell Lazy my innermost secrets, rest my head against hers to cry when I was sad, or ruffle her face and kiss it when I shared happy news. Each time I did, she cocked her head as if understanding my moods and words. She would often lay her head on my tummy if I was lying down, or on my lap if I was sitting. Sometimes, when I was upset, she would lift and extend her front paw slowly, almost cautiously, and gently rest it on me. She was my shadow, my absolute best friend. I needed her companionship and the unconditional love she gave me.

Lazy's ears perked up at the sound of roller skates on the pavement. She dashed to our sidewalk gate.

"I'm off to the park with Gracielita and Isis," I yelled,

running into the house to drop off my drawing pad and fetch my skates.

"Be careful crossing the street." My mother's voice floated from her bedroom, where she was running the sewing machine. The girls were leaning over the gate petting Lazy, who whined as she watched me roller-skate away from her. I knew she would lie on the porch's top step to wait until I returned.

The park was a favorite neighborhood hangout. There we were discovering the wonderful world of boys and perfecting the art of flirting, which thirteen-year-old Gracielita had already mastered. Prissy and feminine, she constantly worried that her *gomilla* gel was holding her bangs in place, especially the "come-hither curl" on the side of her forehead. A light brown bob framed her pretty face, and she was quickly losing her baby fat.

At fourteen, Isis had clear blue eyes, long dark brown hair, and a golden tan on her athletic body. She was a fun-loving tomboy and the daredevil of the bunch. Like the girl on my Deskette pad, I wore my long brown hair in a ponytail and had gotten rid of my Betty Davis bangs. I had finally learned how to smile again without snagging my upper lip on my braces.

"So, where is everyone?" Isis said, scanning the park's perimeter for the neighborhood boys. Then, as we neared the corner, I saw him. Carlos whipped around a fat crooked palm tree ahead of his three buddies. His roller skates pounded the cement in a steady gait as he led the race. He spotted me and waved, slowing down and heading toward us.

"Here comes your *novio*," Gracielita mocked, in a singsong voice.

"*Cállate, no chibes,*" I hushed her out of the corner of my mouth. Then I smiled at him, nervous and giddy at the same time. Within minutes a large group of kids had gathered and we skated together, laughing as we zigzagged around oncoming kids riding bicycles and tricycles, other skaters, and gossiping *tatas* pushing their baby carriages. Carlos whistled a tune I had never heard before.

"What's the name of that song?" I turned my head, taking in his tanned profile.

" 'A Summer Place,' you like it?" I nodded, looking straight ahead. A sudden breeze made my dress fly up a bit. Trying to hold it down, I missed a huge crack on the sidewalk and tipped forward. Carlos grabbed my arm and steadied me.

"*Gracias,*" I mumbled, feeling stupid. He lowered his hand to hold mine.

"*Por poquito,*" he grinned. I saw his chipped tooth up close as he teased me about my near fall. My heart began to skitter as we skated holding hands.

Nearing the corner where the park faced Tropicana, we could hear the band warming up for rehearsal in *Bajo Las Estrellas*, the nightclub's outdoor theatre. A lively overture started up, with bongos thumping a mambo beat. A man's velvet voice sang, "*Cachito, cachito, cachito mío, pedazo de cielo que Dios me dió…*"

"*Oye 'pa eso.*" Carlos screeched to a halt, seizing both my hands and twirling me around to face him. "That's Nat King Cole, can you believe it? Listen." I plopped on a nearby bench to catch my breath. Carlos sat next to me, his mouth half-open, looking in the nightclub's direction. Turning to me, he sang along: "*Te miro y te miro y al fin bendigo, bendigo la hora de ser tu amor."* Carlos scooted over closer to me; our shoulders were touching, our hands side by side on the bench seat. With my other hand, I fiddled with my ponytail while sliding my skates back and forth on the pavement.

We sat together until the song ended, then, spotting Consuelo and the kids heading our way, Carlos reached for my hand. "¡*A correr!*" he said, and we skated off at high speed in search of our friends.

While I daydreamed about my first boyfriend, life in Cuba was changing fast, creating dangerous political divisions. No one knew who to trust anymore; neighbors turned into spies, and some people feared even those who lived under the same roof. Just being seen with someone who was suspected could get a person in trouble. Every neighborhood, factory, and company had a *chibato*, a member of the newly formed *Comité de la Defensa*—the Committee for the Defense of the Revolution, or, as most Cubans called them, the gestapo. The *chibato*'s job was to keep the police and government authorities informed of any unusual occurrences, such as strangers in the neighborhood, people who spoke against the revolution, and curfew violations. They patrolled Havana's neighborhoods on foot.

Consuelo listened to Fidel Castro's fiery speeches on her radio every chance she had. It was at this time that my mother began to notice a glimmer of contempt in Consuelo's eyes, a shadow of a perilous change that began to affect my mother's trust in her lifelong friend.

By the end of summer 1960, anti-revolutionary groups were gaining impetus in the capital. At the school where my mother worked, the principal was actively involved with an underground movement that recruited weapons from anti-Castro Cubans to help protesting university students form anti-revolutionary groups. The movement also spread propaganda against Fidel Castro. The principal's secretary joined the cause and, unbeknownst to us, so did my mother.

When Mami chaperoned my sister and her friends, we had no idea that she left anti-Castro flyers in restaurants and movie-theatre restrooms. With her red lipstick she wrote anti-revolutionary slogans like "*Abajo Fidel*" in bold letters across the bathrooms' mirrored walls and on stall doors. The donated firearms were inconspicuously delivered to the school. They were then distributed among the staff and taken to their homes to be hidden until the students picked them up soon after. My mother was trafficking arms for these youths in shopping bags, hiding them behind our stereo. Once she had so many, some had to be stashed in the bottom of my grandparents' freezer, covered up with frozen foods. We never suspected a thing.

One evening after dinner, my two little brothers came bounding into my bedroom, dragging their sleeping bags behind them. My mother followed them in and matter-of-factly announced that we were having overnight guests.

"What's going on, Señora Nini?" Consuelo walked in, surveying the activity.

"Our neighbors' sons, Juan and Rafael, will be staying with us tonight, Consuelo. They will be sleeping in the boys' room."

"Why is that?" Consuelo glowered at Mami. I looked back and forth between their faces. I had never heard

Consuelo use that tone with my mother. The two of them glared at each other for a long moment.

"Because they have relatives staying overnight and don't have enough room," Mami said in an offhand manner.

"Whatever you say, Señora," Consuelo said coolly, and left the room.

Our houseguests that evening were university students and close friends of my sister's. Mami let them in after dark, through the French doors off our back terrace. They quietly followed her down the hall past the living room, where I lay sprawled on the floor with Lazy watching *I Love Lucy*. Lazy ran after them, wagging her tail. Standing with Mami in front of my brothers' bedroom, they spoke inaudibly for a few moments. Rafael pet Lazy, then he and his brother went in the room and closed the door behind them. It all seemed so secretive, and I wondered why they did not stop to say hello to me. They always did whenever they saw me roller-skating, but that night they didn't even notice me. While I giggled at Lucy and Ethel's antics, little did I know that Juan and Rafael were being sought by the government for holding a demonstration against the revolution. Thanks to my mother, they were able to hide in our home that night until they were safely smuggled off the island the following day.

※ ※ ※

Fidel Castro's alliance with the Soviet Union became official when he met with Nikita Krushchev in New York on September 20, 1960. At that time he declared to the world that Cuba and the Soviets were one. Upon his return to the island, Castro nationalized $850 million worth of United

States property, including sugar mills, plantation homes, oil refineries, and cattle ranches. The United States stopped buying Cuban sugar and banned all exports to Cuba. Castro retaliated by taking over all remaining American businesses on the island. Overnight, relations between the two countries ceased to exist.

The realization that we were now living in a communist country was a frightening one. There seemed to be an urgency for families to stay even closer together, which for us meant gathering at Rancho Perea every Sunday without fail. Yet beneath all the normal peaceful activities, there was a presence…a low ominous hum, strangled, whispered conversations in the corners of our homes. The adults constantly discussed politics.

"So now he's ticked off the United States."

"*Sí*, we won't be getting anything from *los norteamericanos* anymore." I could hear them talking from the deep end of the pool, where I was practicing my diving.

"This is horrible, Gustavo," my grandmother sighed. "Can't this man see that America has always been our friend?"

Bibi sipped his espresso. "It's just a matter of time, Beba, before this *cabrón* takes over everything."

"*Ay, Jesus mío, ayúdanos.*" My grandmother prayed for God's help out loud.

"*Sí*, Beba." Aunt Eugenia wiped her forehead with her lacy handkerchief. "We have to pray for peace in Cuba."

"We'll have to pray from *el exilio* somewhere," my grandfather's cousin put in. "I'm not staying in a communist country after someone takes everything that I've worked for all my life."

Exilio. Another new word in my vocabulary. I meant to ask my mother later what it meant, but swimming with my cousins, I forgot about it. All too soon that word would come back to haunt me.

* * *

My father was deeply affected by Cuba's strained alliance with the United States. At times he feared that Castro would come after him because he had studied in America for so many years. A few days before my twelfth birthday, Mami took Roly and me to visit Papi in the sanatorium. He wanted to give me my birthday present and hear all about my upcoming party.

It was a crisp afternoon in late September. My father was waiting for us in the garden, sitting in an adirondack chair near a small pond. Hoping to reach Papi first, I walked briskly ahead of my mother and nine-year-old brother. He smiled when he saw me coming.

"*¿Qué tal*, Papi?" I ran to his outstretched arms. His soft polo shirt smelled of antiseptic with a trace of Guerlain cologne.

"Yoyi! Now, let me look at you." He was flashing his old beautiful smile, the one I remembered seeing when I was a little girl and saw so rarely now. My spirits soared. He seemed relaxed and happy. His face was tanned, and he looked strong and handsome. "I like your hair," he remarked, noticing the "come-hither curl" on my forehead. With Gracielita's help, I had finally gotten the hang of it. "You look very grown-up."

"Well, Papi, I'm almost a *pepilla*." I sat on the wooden

ottoman in front of him.

"That's right, next year you'll be a teenager." He reached for a large bag on the grass next to him. Mami and Roly had stopped by the pond to look at the koi fish. I relished the special time with my father.

"*¡Feliz cumpleaños!*" he said happily, handing me a brightly wrapped box with cascading pink ribbons. "Tita Lala took me shopping." Papi gave me the first two books of the Pollyanna series I had been eager to read and a box of *dulce de leche*, my favorite cream-and-caramel candies. I gave his cheek a kiss and thanked him.

"There's another gift yet," he said, waving at my mother. At the bottom of the box I found a small bundle wrapped in pink tissue paper.

"A shell box!" I exclaimed, admiring the tiny shells adorning the little wooden box. Inside the red velvet–lined box was a gold bracelet with dainty seashells dangling like charms. With both hands I held it up, marveling at the beauty of each shell.

"That's so you always remember Kawama." My father gazed at me with a sweet, faraway look in his eyes. "Remember how you loved going for walks on the beach with me?" I nodded, still fascinated with the bracelet.

"This is the best birthday present I ever got, Papi." I hugged his neck and closed my eyes. Kawama. I recalled our fun-filled vacations at Varadero Beach. I knew in my heart I would never go there again with him. "The best, Papi. You know just what I like," I said, pulling away from him.

"How about the time we saw a shark, *te acuerdas?*" he asked me while browsing through one of my books.

"*Sí,* Papi, I remember." I put the bracelet down, a

quick shiver running through me. "*El tiburón.*"

We talked about my upcoming birthday party until my mother and brother joined us. Toward the end of our visit, my father's demeanor changed. His smile vanished, and he seemed edgy. He kept looking past the garden fence at the quiet tree-lined avenue, insisting that we keep our voices down. We were saying our goodbyes when two military jeeps drove by at high speed and disappeared around the corner, heading away from the sanatorium.

"Oh God! They found me!" Papi yelled, springing to his feet, his face pale and rigid with fear. "Ninina, they're coming back to get me. Castro knows where I am." He had trouble catching his breath, and his eyes were wide open. "Help me, Ninina. You have to hide me." He stood holding onto the back of his chair, anxiously looking around him.

"No, Rolando, no one is coming to get you," my mother said soothingly, placing her hand on his forearm. "Let's go inside now." As she turned away to help Papi, Mami gave me an urgent look.

"Take your brother and go see the fish. I'll be right back." I knew that look well; I had seen it so many times before. *Go away from here quick. You're not supposed to see this.* My little brother moved closer to me, staring at our father, who seemed oblivious to our presence. I reached for Roly's hand, and, holding my gift box under my other arm, we walked away from our parents as two orderlies rushed to my father's side. He was screaming now: "Please, don't let the *milicianos* take me away!" He gasped for air. "I'm a good Cuban, I love my country, please!" My brother and I walked toward the pond without saying a word and sat on a bench by the water's edge. Roly's face brightened as a large mottled koi swam by. A fat gray one swam off by itself.

"Look, that one looks like a *tiburón*." He pointed excitedly and jumped up to get a closer glimpse.

"*Sí*, just like a shark." I said the words slowly, absent-mindedly. Taking the bracelet out of its box I put it on my wrist. "Kawama," I whispered to myself, holding onto one of the charms and watching the orderlies and my mother take my father into the sanatorium.

After that episode, the doctors increased Papi's sedatives, and we children were not permitted to visit him often. Mami went to see him every week. When she returned she would go to her room and close the door. I often heard my mother sobbing, gently at first, then louder. I never asked her what was wrong. I knew.

* * *

I twirled around in front of the tall oval mirror that had once been my mother's.

"What do you think, Lazy?" My dog cocked her head at me from my bed, where she lay chewing her rubber bone. I loved the swishing sound my new dress made when I moved around. It was white with small blue flowers throughout, sleeveless with a scoop neckline and a fitted cobalt-blue cummerbund. I wore the bracelet Papi had given me with my new pearl ring, a *tú y yo*, a gift from Mami. I preened in my finery and looked at myself in the mirror. *I'm going to dance with Carlos tonight*, I mused, holding my full skirt out with both hands.

In the dining room, Cuca and Consuelo were hanging up the last of the colorful balloons, and Mami was putting candles on the cake she'd baked for me. Pink and white streamers decorating the open French doors waved in the balmy evening breeze. Outside, the *terraza* had been set up with folding chairs and small side tables. In the living room, my favorite records, plus a few I had borrowed from my friends, were stacked next to the high fidelity. The doorbell rang, announcing the beginning of my party.

Carlos was the first to arrive and offered to be in charge of the music. My school and neighborhood friends soon followed, along with several chaperoning moms. Following the awkward boy-girl introductions, the rock-and-roll dancing began. Then, a slow song came on. Frankie Avalon crooned his hit song "Why," and Carlos asked me to dance. Our living room was crammed with dancing couples, and the mothers craned their necks to supervise. I had no idea how to slow dance, but I didn't care as I swayed around in Carlos's arms, feeling his hand on my back and giggling as I stepped on his toes.

Suddenly, Lazy began barking furiously at someone approaching our porch. My mother wove her way through the kids to the open front door, while Consuelo took hold of Lazy's collar and led her to the kitchen, trying to calm her down. Carlos and I were dancing near the open living-room window. Over the music, I could hear Mami talking to someone. The record ended, and Carlos left me to play the next one. I inched toward the front door while everyone started to wonder what was happening outside. I could see a *miliciano's* cap and his heavy gun belt as he faced our porch light. I stood near the door listening to him tell my mother that we were violating the ten o'clock curfew.

"*Esta fiesta se acabó.*" With a hate-filled voice, he heralded the end of my party.

"*Me cago en la mierda*—shit!" Manolo, Gracielita's boyfriend, whispered through his clenched teeth. Carlos walked over and stood next to me while Elvis sang "Jail House Rock." I felt his arm next to mine as our hands clutched in the folds of my skirt.

"I hate Fidel Castro," Carlos snarled under his breath.

"I do too," I said, just above a whisper.

"*Compañeros*, we must obey the rules of the revolution. ¡*Viva* Fidel!" the rebel hollered, opening our garden gate and disappearing into the night.

I remember the day my childhood ended.

I woke up in high spirits the morning after my party, despite the *miliciano* cutting it short. My twelfth birthday celebration had culminated with an evening of many firsts: my first boy-girl party, where I danced my first *danzón* with my first boyfriend, Carlos, whose hand fumbled nervously up and down my back while his other clammy one squeezed mine in midair. Yet I floated in his arms as if on gossamer wings, lost in my dreamy moment.

As we did every Sunday, Bibi and Mama's children and grandchildren were gathering at Rancho Perea for a day of relaxation. I looked forward to Sundays at *la finca*. In this peaceful setting I spent a carefree day swimming and enjoying the playground with my cousins. But what I anticipated doing most on this Sunday was riding my new bike, a birthday gift from my grandparents. Being the second oldest daughter, I often got hand-me-downs from María Elena. Having my own brand-new bike was a big deal. Sky blue with white-walled tires and thin spokes, my 24-inch *bicicleta* gleamed in the Cuban sunshine. I had the *finca's* long, winding driveway all to myself that afternoon. There was no battling my siblings, cousins, or nannies to get out of the way. Infused with a burst of energy, I stood on my bike's pedals and pumped as fast as I could, testing its speed, the handlebars' multicolored plastic streamers whipping the backs of my hands. I let go of the handlebars, extended my arms out to either side, and allowed the bike to steer itself. I relished my newfound freedom and the sun on my face while breathing the sweet air fragrant with gardenias, jasmine, and citrus. The thick areca palms and colorful hibiscus lining the driveway seemed to whiz by. Towering throughout the property, sleek royal palms rustled their fronds in the warm trade winds.

On my bike, I was alone with my thoughts, free to daydream about Carlos and my party. I stopped to pluck a coral hibiscus and put it in my hair, over my right ear. Humming the tune of one of the songs we'd danced to, I pedaled to the end of the driveway and reached the locked gates. As I turned my bike to head back, I heard the distant rumbling of a vehicle, crunching its tires on the dirt road leading to our *finca*. I stopped and straddled my bike. Through an areca palm I saw a military jeep with four soldiers fast approaching. They wore olive green fatigues and brandished machine guns. The driver hollered "*Aquí es*" and stopped the jeep in front of our gates. In an instant, I was face to face with Fidel Castro's *milicianos*.

"Open the gates, *chiquilla!*" the dark-bearded soldier ordered, scowling at me. My eyes were cemented on the machine gun resting beside him. A voice unknown to me came from my open mouth. "I can't. They're locked."

"Then go get someone to open them, *pronto*!" he barked and laid on his horn. I raced to the front porch, grateful for my fast new bike.

"Bibi, Bibi!" I yelled for my grandfather. Hearing the persistent honking, Uncle Gus was already on the driveway.

"*¿Qué pasa, niña?*" he asked me. My grandfather was standing on the porch steps, following his son to the driveway. Looking at Bibi, I told them both:

"*Milicianos*. They're here in a jeep with guns and they want to come in, now!"

My uncle turned to my grandfather. "Papá, I'll take care of this. You stay here." Taking his keys from his pants pocket, Uncle Gus rushed past me toward the front gates. His clenched jaw twitched on his tanned face. Someone dropped a glass on the porch tile floor. My aunts and nannies raced around, gathering the children.

"*¡Ay, Dios mío, milicianos!*" screamed the cook, abandoning her serving tray on the porch table and running into the house. I kicked the stand on my bike and stood by my grandfather. Bibi put his arm around my shoulder, pulling me close to him. My grandmother stood on his other side, her fingers tightening around Bibi's forearm. I looked for my mother, remembering she was by the pool on the other side of the house, with the rest of the family.

The jeep roared past my uncle onto the plantation grounds, screeching to a halt in front of the rambling veranda. A bearded, scruffy militiaman jumped out of the passenger seat and stood on the driveway facing my grandparents and me. He threw his cigar stub on the pavement, stomped on it, and spat.

"Where is the owner of this property?" he demanded.

There was a piercing silence.

"I own this *finca*," Bibi replied bluntly, his hand tightening on my shoulder. My grandfather's voice was serene, without a trace of the inward seething and panic I felt sure were rising inside him. "What do you want?"

"You have fifteen days to evacuate these grounds," the *miliciano* announced. "After that, you cannot take so much as a nail from this place, *¿me oye?*" Mama heaved a sigh. The men in the jeep burst out laughing. The rebel handed my grandfather the official government papers. "This land has been appropriated by the revolution for use as an army training center." He took his time saying the words, all the while scanning the petrified faces of my relatives gathered on the porch. He spun around and jumped into the jeep without opening the door. "*Dale, arranca,*" he ordered the driver.

My grandmother lamented, almost inaudibly, "*Ay,* Gustavo," as the jeep revved up to go.

"*¡Viva* Fidel!" the rebels shouted, raising *el puño,* the revolution fist. "*¡Viva la revolución!*"

"*¡Cabrones!*" my grandfather cursed under his breath, his eyes brimming. His beloved Rancho Perea had been confiscated. Of all their possessions, none would be more painful to lose than this one. As the jeep turned around to leave, its back bumper rammed my new bike, hurling it into the air. I watched, horrified, as it crashed onto the pavement.

"*¡Cabrones!*" I swore to myself, running toward my bike. I lifted the bent handlebars, my cheeks burning with rage. The front fender was crunched into the tire. I stood on the driveway, holding my battered birthday present. The coral hibiscus fell from behind my ear as I watched the jeep disappear among the palm trees.

Pictures

Newlyweds Ninina and Rolando
—Marianao, Habana, Cuba, March 1943

Gloria María's grandparents Tito Pepe and Tita Lala
—Kawama Beach, Cuba, April 1943

*Three generations: Abuelita Sofía, Mercedes, and Ninina
—La Víbora, Habana, Cuba, 1946*

María Elena and Gloria María with Nancy
—Lumberville, Pennsylvania, 1954

*Ninina and her five children the day they left Cuba
for Doylestown, Pennsylvania
—August 1956*

Entrance to Rancho Perea—"La Finca"

Rancho Perea—"La Finca"

Bibi in his office at Rancho Perea

La Virgen de las Mercedes—*Our Lady of Mercy,*
beloved by our family for four generations and still with us

Mama and Bibi, happy days at Rancho Perea
—1957

*Gloria María (center) with friend, siblings, and cousins
at Rancho Perea
—1957*

*"A small joy among the sadness" someone wrote
on the back of this picture of Gloria María in Jamaica
on her way to "Neverland"
—February 1961*

Ninina and her children reunited in exile
—Miami, Florida, June 1961

*The Howard family's home on Maple Avenue
—Doylestown, Pennsylvania*

Bibi enjoying his first snowfall in "la casa de Maple"
—*Doylestown, Pennsylvania, 1963*
"*Like a Palm Tree in the Snow*"

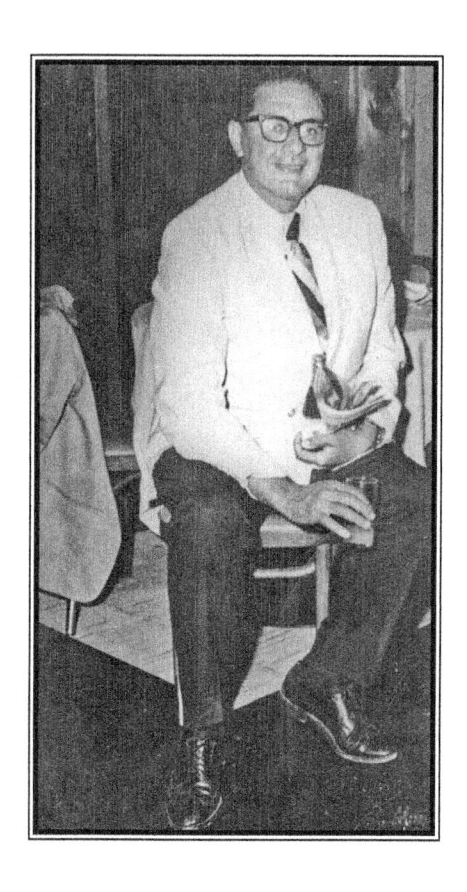

Gloria María's Papi, Rolando, shortly before his death
—April 1972

*Ed Howard and Gloria María recalling
the day he found out she could speak English
—Howard home, early 1990s*

Gloria María's grandparents Mama and Bibi
—Miami, Florida, 1966

Gloria María and her Mami, Ninina
—Michigan, 1995

Chapter Fourteen

FLYING TO NEVERLAND

After the seizing of my grandparents' *finca*, I became more aware of the political situation in our country. I paid close attention when adults talked about Castro and his revolution. *Who are these people? What's happening to Cuba?* But when I asked my mother questions, she would always say, "Pray for peace in Cuba, *m'ija*," and nothing more, just like the nuns at school. I decided to scavenge for up-to-date news from my girlfriends at school, some of whose fathers were well-known communist political figures.

"My father says Fidel Castro is going to send kids to Russia to become communists," a pesky girl named Bernadette told a group of us at recess one day. *Madre* Pérez overheard her and immediately called her aside. Bernadette's face turned red as she followed the nun inside the classroom.

"She's a show-off commie, trying to scare us," Miriam said, starting the jump rope with Beatriz. "*Andale*, Gloria, it's your turn." I leaned my body forward a couple of times, trying to gain momentum to jump into the whipping rope. But Bernadette's words stayed with me, casting a shadow of fear as I joined in the game.

Bernadette had been right after all. One evening in

October 1960, a radio station made an announcement that the government would soon take schoolchildren away from their families, sending them to Russia to be indoctrinated in communism. The news spread like a terrifying wildfire among upper-class parents. Soon the growing fear led parents to send their children off the island to avoid communist indoctrination. In January 1961, an exodus of Cuban children began by way of a visa-waiver program.

My mother, my relatives, and the nuns at school did an exceptional job of sheltering us children from the tidal wave of panic that was washing over the island. I never had a clue. When I asked Mami about the rumors I had heard from Bernadette, she dismissed them as nonsense and quickly changed the subject. But as Christmas drew near, we heard of more and more neighborhood children and girls at school who were suddenly going on vacation alone to spend time with relatives or family friends in America—a Neverland from which they would never return.

* * *

Navidad. I had been looking forward to Christmas. Since I was now twelve, I would be allowed to stay up with the adults to celebrate *Nochebuena*, our traditional Christmas Eve festivity. Afterward, we would attend Midnight Mass, *la Misa de Gallo*, which was the focal point of our Christmas celebration. *Nochebuena*, literally meaning "the good night," was primarily a grown-up holiday. The children participated in the late dinner feast but then went to bed, while the adults stayed up celebrating, attended Midnight Mass, and then continued partying until dawn.

During the latter part of the Advent season, from December 15 to 20, many families prepared a *nacimiento*, or nativity scene, in their homes to commemorate the birth of Jesus. It was always displayed in the formal living room, next to *el arbolito*, the Christmas tree, for everyone to see as they entered the home. My grandmother Mama was famous in our neighborhood for her *nacimiento*. She transformed the corner of her living room into the rugged hillside of Bethlehem, which she made out of paper mache, then painted. Mirrors laid flat became lakes surrounded by palm and olive trees. The crèche was displayed until January 6, the feast of the Epiphany, commemorating the coming of the three kings Melchior, Caspar, and Balthasar. That day was the children's true celebration of Christmas. Gifts for them and all family members were set out around the crèche and exchanged as a symbol of the holy season.

Our Christmas family gatherings had always taken place at Rancho Perea, but not this year. Fidel Castro had put an end to that. But he could not ruin our love of the blessed holiday or the joy of being together as a family. On that Christmas of 1960, we gathered at Mama and Bibi's home for *Nochebuena*. The packed house held a more subdued celebration that year. Occasionally, someone would reminisce about our past Christmases at *la finca*, and my grandfather's eyes would well up. I missed Rancho Perea, too. Knowing that we could never go there again was excruciating. But the thought of soldiers running around and practicing target shooting on my grandparents' beloved plantation made me furious. What right did this *guerrillero* Castro have to do this? *That's what happens in a communist country*, I heard grownups say. I sensed a fearful tension around me—and within me. *What else were they going to take away?* There was a feeling of intense family union on that *Nochebuena*. Despite our great loss, we celebrated the birth of Christ in the same tradition we always had.

Our Christmas Eve feast included the customary roast pork, white rice and *frijoles negros*, and *turrones*, Spanish nougat and marzipan cakes for dessert. Spanish hard cider, Bacardi Cuban rum, and Champagne were passed around to adults throughout the night. "¡*Feliz Navidad*!" everyone wished one another with lackluster spirit. My last Christmas in Cuba was void of the merriment I had always known before.

* * *

On January 3, 1961, the United States broke all diplomatic relations with Cuba. Soon after, Castro announced to the world that his revolution was socialist and that he was a Marxist-Leninist. As the island's prime minister, he controlled all policies, and there was only one political party: the Cuban communist party. The Cuban people's dream of a democratic system died that day.

Watching the televised speech, I didn't understand most of what Castro was saying, but I knew it wasn't good.

"¡*Ay, qué horror*!" my mother said. She shook her head and covered her mouth. Watching with us, Consuelo whispered animatedly to Cuca while looking at Mami.

"¿*Qué pasa*, Consuelo?" My mother startled her.

"*Nada*, Señora." Consuelo's mouth pursed in displeasure. "I was commenting to Cuca that *el líder* gave a great speech."

"¿*Ah, sí*? Do you think what Fidel is doing is right?" My mother's eyes blazed across the room at our nanny.

"¡*Sí* Señora, *y bien que sí*!" A dark look veiled Consuelo's face. "It's about time the government took away from the rich to give to the poor." Cuca gasped, giving her cousin a look of disbelief, and quickly left the room. Mami's mouth dropped open.

"¡*Ay*, Consuelo!" She sighed, slowly shaking her head. "How can you say that after being a part of our family for so many years? You've had a good home with us. I've always paid you well, cared for all your needs: your food, clothes, uniforms, medical bills. We've taken you with us on our trips to America, on all our vacations, and you..." Her voice grew hushed..."you are my friend, Consuelo. We have been through so much together. How can you say that to me?" Consuelo's face remained stony, her normally luminous eyes a steely green. She stared at Mami without saying a word, then left the room.

Fidel Castro proclaimed 1961 the year of education. When he took over the island, forty percent of the six million Cubans were illiterate. Once in power, one of his main objectives was to make the entire country literate and educated in communism. The revolution needed more teachers in rural areas and immediately began recruiting university students and high school graduates to teach the uneducated throughout the remote Cuban countryside.

At school, the nuns were happy to have us back after Christmas break. On our way to class one morning, my best friend, Carmen, and I quietly chattered about our Christmas gifts. She and I could often get away with talking without being caught. Being among the tallest girls, we walked our hallways' black line toward the back of the file. The *madres* were usually more concerned with the front of the line and where they were headed.

As we approached the school's main entrance, the closing of the wooden double doors resonated throughout the silent hallways. The heavy clicking of boots on marble floors echoed in the gallery, and gruff, male voices invaded the cloistered female environment.

Our single line had to pass by the vestibule, where two *milicianos* were talking to an *hermanita*, who was nodding vigorously. They were demanding to see Mother Superior. Two *madres* walking opposite us hurried down the hallway toward the commotion. The *hermanita*, her cheeks flushed, hastily left the vestibule, wringing her hands. As we walked by, I noticed one militiaman holding a large brown folder, but my eyes focused on the revolvers holstered on their belts. The pungent smell of sweat, citrus *gomilla*, and stale cigarettes permeating the air made me recoil.

"*Cochinos.* They are such pigs." Carmen's low voice was contemptuous. "They think they're still in the mountains and don't have to bathe." One of the *milicianos* looked our way as we filed by. His eyes were registering Carmen, who was quite developed for her age. His lips formed a wolfish smile as he stared at her breasts. *Madre* Gómez motioned to us to move along more quickly, and seeing me looking at the *milicianos*, she slowed down to walk next to me. Her usually beady eyes were wide open, filled with a softness I had never seen before.

"Straight ahead, my child. Look straight ahead and walk quickly." She gently patted Carmen's shoulder, the last girl on the line, and as she did so, glanced back momentarily at the *milicianos*. She walked the rest of the way behind us, which she never did.

A few minutes into our mathematics lesson, a senior girl walked into our classroom and spoke inaudibly to *Madre* Gómez. The nun told us to work on our homework while she was gone and immediately left, leaving *la mayor* in charge. Sitting next to the open window facing the corridors, I noticed the *madres* leaving their classrooms one by one. Like busy ants, they scurried down the hallway leading to Mother Superior's office.

"Psst...something's up," Beatriz whispered next to me. I nodded.

"Maybe the *milicianos* are taking over the school," I said, thinking of Rancho Perea. I felt anger welling up inside me. *They took away my grandparents' finca. Now they're here, at my school.*

"*Ay, Dios,* do you think they are?" Carmen sounded panicky behind me.

"*Silencio, niñas,*" the senior girl reprimanded, but the murmuring continued, and no one was working on their homework. When *Madre* Gómez returned, her face was pale as she spoke to us.

"Girls, school will be dismissed early today." Instant gasps and chattering broke the silence in the room, but our outbursts were subdued with the *madre's* clicker. "Shhh...shhh...before you go home, we will go to chapel for a special blessing and to pray for your safety outside our convent walls." She paused for an instant, taking her time to look at us. "From now on, we will be doing this at the end of every school day." A sea of hands went up in the air.

"*Madre,* what's wrong?" Carmelina asked in a wispy voice.

"*Sí, Madre,* why are we going home so early today?" Miriam sounded jittery.

"Did the soldiers come to take us away, *Madre?*" Teresita was near tears.

"*Niñas, por favor,*" Madre Gómez pleaded. Her hands circled nervously in the air as she paced from one end of the classroom to the other.

"*Madre,* is Fidel Castro taking over our school?" I asked, feeling my voice catch. There were muffled cries as all eyes turned on me. The nun's eyes seemed huge behind her spectacles. She pinched the edge of her fluted bonnet, pulling it away from her flushing face.

"*Niñas,* everything will be all right," she told us, trying to gather her fast-crumbling composure.

"I want to go home now," Yolanda whimpered quietly in front of me as we filed to chapel. *Me too,* I thought, as my shaky hand rubbed my friend's shoulder.

Fidel Castro's year of education had begun. The *milicianos* had come to our school that day in early January to obtain a list of the 1961 graduating seniors. These were the students the revolution was rounding up to send to the rugged, isolated Cuban provinces, to the wild mountain sugarcane fields to teach illiterate *guajiro* children to read and write. My sister's name was on that list.

Relations between the Catholic Church and the communist government had been far from amicable and were worsening by the day. Castro had begun closing down Catholic churches and parochial and private schools, banishing its clergy and religious from the island. La Catedral de la Habana was boarded up and abandoned. The revolution made pariahs out of Cuba's Catholic faithful. The nuns of the Sacred Heart, fearing their days in Cuba were numbered, embarked on a risky undercover program of their own to save "their daughters." Mother Superior promptly notified the parents of the girls whose names she was forced to provide to the government.

Because of her connection with the underground Catholic youth movement, my mother was able to quickly obtain a student visa waiver for my seventeen-year-old sister. María Elena was set to leave Cuba in mid-January, one week after Mother Superior's phone call. I was not told the truth about my sister's leaving. Mami casually said she was going on vacation to Miami with her boyfriend, Alberto, and his parents, but first they would stay in Montego Bay, Jamaica, for a few days.

"How come she gets to go in the middle of school?" I balked. "And where is Jamaica, anyway?"

"Alberto's parents have invited her to go with them," my mother said convincingly. "She'll be back in two weeks." But the truth was my sister had been given an early final examination in order to graduate and was fleeing to the United States via Jamaica. She had to stay there until her residency paperwork was finalized for her to go on to Miami. If the Cuban government found out that someone was leaving the country permanently, especially to the United States, that person would be detained. The only way out was to call the trip a vacation. The revolution allowed each departing person one suitcase only and $5 American dollars. If adults did not return to Cuba in two weeks, the government confiscated everything they owned, classifying them as *gusanos,* traitors to the revolution.

Life felt as if it was on fast-forward. My immediate family was rapidly dispersing. Aunts, uncles, and cousins were leaving Cuba to visit relatives in Spain or friends in Mexico, or to vacation in Costa Rica, Columbia, or Venezuela. But most headed for Miami, where the majority of Cubans were fleeing. Even Carlos and his family were off to visit friends in Chicago. He came to say goodbye two days before he left.

"Don't worry, we'll be back in two weeks. I'm going to miss you." His eyes watered a bit as he left our porch. My first boyfriend was off to Neverland.

In the park, there were fewer kids skating each week. Instead, groups of angry-looking militia youths—children I had never seen before—marched on the wide sidewalks, loudly chanting "¡Cuba sí, Yankee no!" and "¡*Viva* Fidel!" as they pushed us out of their way. I bombarded my mother with questions regarding so many of my friends and family leaving.

"It's a good time to vacation right now, *m'ija*," she told me nonchalantly. "The airlines are offering good prices, so people are taking trips." That same day Carmen called to tell me she was leaving on vacation the following day.

"*Oye*, Gloria, you won't believe this," she said confidentially. "I just found out today. I'm going to fly to Miami by…my…self tomorrow," she enunciated the words, "to visit my godmother. Isn't that incredible?" Carmen was always in a big rush to grow up. "I can't believe Mami and Papi are letting me go alone. ¡*Estupéndo*!" I couldn't get a word in. In the background, her mother was calling her. "I have to get off now and finish packing, but I promise I'll send you a postcard as soon as I get there. I'll see you in ten days, *adiós*."

"Carmen, wait, I…" But she hung up the phone. I never heard from her or saw her again.

A few days before María Elena left, Tita Lala came to stay with us. She was accompanying my sister on vacation to Jamaica. Knowing my grandmother's passion for traveling, I did not think this was odd. I figured she, too, was taking advantage of the great airline prices. I was not aware that my grandmother had sold her home in Miramar and her *finca*, La Casielle, and was leaving Cuba for good.

One night Cuca had just served our family dinner. Suddenly we heard what sounded like fireworks nearby.

"¡*Es un tiroteo*!" Consuelo shouted from the kitchen. The rapid popping sound got closer, almost outside our terrace. My mother yelled for us to get down on the floor under the dining table and to help my grandmother, who struggled to go down on her knees. Lazy huddled beside me as we all crouched under the table. While the shooting grew louder, my mother was running from room to room, fastening the wooden shutters and locking the doors.

"¡Señora Nini, *por Dios*, hurry up and come!" Consuelo yelled. Roly sat beside me. He looked at me as if saying, *I know what to do. We did this before, you and I*. Mami turned the lights out and crawled under the table with us. Realizing Cuca was missing, she called for her.

"It's all right, Señora." The maid's voice sounded distant. "I'm safe under my bed, *está bien*."

The next day we found out Castro's *milicianos* had been chasing a man in the park across the street from our home. They hunted him down until they found him cowering behind the fountain wall and shot him dead. After that incident, we were forbidden to go to the park, roller-skate on our neighborhood sidewalks, or play in our yard. We could only be outside on our front porch and terrace. We yearned for the old routine, the normalcy of our daily lives. Gone were the cheerful sounds of children playing. Even the street vendors stopped coming. Our neighborhood seemed like a ghost town. The apprehension inside every home spilled out into the deserted streets.

The day my sister left Cuba, I had a presentiment of *el desparramo*, a feeling that things were falling apart. We gathered on the porch to see María Elena off. Consuelo and Cuca stood by the doorway while Mami smoothed out the lapels on my sister's jacket.

"Call me as soon as you get to Jamaica." María Elena nodded, then turned and looked at me. I threw my arms around her. She stood stiffly, not one for ever showing affection, and I felt a soft pat on my shoulder. I looked up as she turned her misty eyes on me.

"*Oye*, so now you'll be *la mayor*, the oldest here while I'm gone." She smirked. "I'll see you soon." Picking up her train case, she hurried down the front steps to the waiting car. She turned to wave one last time, then wiped her cheek with the back of her hand. Why was she so sad if she was going on vacation?

The next day my mother told me that Papi had also gone with María Elena and Tita Lala. At first I was glad for my father, that he was able to leave the sanatorium for awhile. But something didn't feel right about all these vacations. They were getting longer and longer, and none of my friends and relatives were coming back when expected.

At my grandparents' home, our remaining family members started visiting more often, not just on Sundays as was customary. As they prepared to leave the island, relatives brought their most valuable and meaningful boxed possessions and left them in the care of family or friends staying behind, with the hopes of recuperating them when the revolution was over and they returned to Cuba. They knew that once they left "on vacation," two weeks later *milicianos* in government trucks would come and ransack their home of all their belongings, leaving it empty. All their assets and real estate would go into the hands of the government.

In mid-February 1961, Mother Superior called my mother again, requesting she come the following day for a parent/teacher conference regarding me. Nothing was ever discussed over the phone. In Havana, phones were bugged, mail was searched, and we lived under constant surveillance in our neighborhoods. No one could disagree openly with Castro or the revolution. If caught, one would end up in prison or dead. Anything important or confidential had to be dealt with face to face, behind closed doors.

The next day, Saturday morning, Mother Superior met my mother and me in the parlor. She suggested I walk around the school while she talked to my mother. I worried what this was all about. I was struggling with math, but was it that bad? As I strolled toward the corner of the corridor, the sweet scent of stargazer lilies lured me into a chapel-like alcove. Sunlight streamed through the wide windows, illuminating Mater, a life-size statue of the Blessed Mother as a young woman. As I often did, I knelt on the pew and said a prayer—this time, that I didn't fail math. *Mater Admirabilis, ora pro nobis,* Mother most admirable, pray for us.

I loved hearing our nuns tell the miraculous story of Mater. In 1844, a young Frenchwoman named Pauline Perdreau, who later became a Sacred Heart nun, had a yearning to paint a picture of Our Lady on a convent wall in the Trinita dei Monti house in Rome, Italy, where she was a student.

"We need to have Our Lady in our midst," she pleaded with the nuns, until they gave her permission. The nuns were aghast when they saw the completed work. It was not a becoming representation of the Blessed Mother. Her face was disproportionate to her body, her hands too large, and the colors in the painting clashed. They covered the mural with a tarp until it could be painted over.

On October 20, 1846, Pope Pius IX visited the Trinita house and insisted on viewing the fresco. Reluctantly, the nuns unveiled it.

"She is truly Mater Admirabilis!" the Pope exclaimed. An exquisite painting of the young Virgin had replaced the original artwork.

"It is a miracle," the nuns proclaimed reverently. One by one, they genuflected and crossed themselves.

"Someday, I'm going to Rome to see you, Mater," I said, rising to leave, my eyes fixed on her peaceful gaze. As I wandered the silent halls I glanced at the parlor. What were they so urgently discussing?

The *milicianos* had been at school the day before, demanding another student list. The revolution had begun enforcing phase two of the Year of Education program. The government needed the names of all Cuban children ages eight to twelve to begin the process of their communist indoctrination in Russia. They did not say when these children would be taken, but Mother Superior feared it would be soon. My name was on that list.

I was talking with my English teacher, *Madre* Smith, in the courtyard when I noticed Mami motioning across the open gallery for me to come. As I walked back to the parlor, I purposely did so on the center of the floor, far from the black line on either side of me. *No black line today*, I gloated.

On our ride home from school, Mami seemed uneasy, fidgeting with paperwork the nun had given her. "Mother Superior says you have to work harder on your math," she said. That afternoon, as I reveled in my relief at not failing math, my mother immediately began to arrange my departure from Cuba.

The following day Mami told me that I, too, was going on vacation for two weeks. I would be leaving in three days, flying to Montego Bay, Jamaica, staying overnight with María Elena, Papi, and Tita Lala, then flying on to Miami the following day, where I would stay with Aunt Emma, my father's sister. I was not particularly close to my aunt. We did not see my father's family as often as we saw my mother's. Recently divorced, she had always impressed me as a bit on the strict side. But this would be a short holiday, an adventure. I felt I could easily make the best of staying with Aunt Emma for two weeks.

"All by myself?" I asked Mami and stopped sketching.

"*Sí*, but it's a short flight. In Jamaica, María Elena, Papi, and Tita Lala will be waiting for you at the airport." She was talking unusually fast. "You'll get to visit with them overnight before you go to Miami." *Just like Carmen*, I thought, feeling the excitement I was sure my best friend must have felt. *All by myself,* my mind repeated the words she had used when she called to tell me. I felt extremely grown-up, important. The thought of traveling in an airplane again, to visit Jamaica and another part of America, buoyed me. Getting out of school for two weeks wasn't hard to handle, either.

My mother explained that Aunt Emma, Aunt Blanca, and Uncle Luis would be living in America for a while because they weren't happy with the way things were in Cuba. Aunt Blanca and Uncle Luis would be waiting for me at the airport in Miami and would then take me to Aunt Emma's. I picked at a hangnail.

"I can't wait to tell Carmen when we both return from our vacations," I told my mother, not noticing how quiet she had become.

The night before my trip I sized up the one small suitcase the government allowed me to take. After Mami packed my few clothes, I squeezed in my Deskette pad and pencils, two of my favorite books, my Catholic missal, and my *abanico*. The Spanish hand-painted fan had been a birthday gift from my godmother, Milly, and was the first one I ever owned. I had finally mastered its tricky maneuvering; a quick forward flick of the wrist spread out the delicate, pleated panels to display an array of pastel flowers. I showed off at mass, taking my cue when the ladies around me started fanning themselves. It was a most grown-up feeling, and my *abanico* was coming with me. I put my autograph book and my silver rosary in the purse I would be carrying, and Hildi, a small doll that Tita Lala and Tito Pepe had brought me from Austria and who had replaced Nancy as my favorite, was also coming along. There was no room for anything else.

February 26, 1961, was a brilliant winter morning in Havana. I woke up to luminous sunshine streaming through the gaps between the *persianas* on my window. The sweet scent from my mother's rose garden wafted into my bedroom. As I finished dressing, Mami rushed in carrying a black velvet box. She helped me put on my pearl necklace and checked to make sure I was wearing my pearl ring. Then she began to adorn me with some of her best jewelry. I was wearing a suit: a skirt, blouse, and jacket. Under my blouse I wore her pearl necklace, with mine on top of the blouse. Four gold brooches with diamonds and other gemstones were pinned on my blouse, concealed by the jacket. Two additional less showy pins went on my jacket lapel. Several bracelets worn on each arm were hidden by my jacket's long sleeves, and I wore a ring on each hand.

I looked at my arms, feeling like a gypsy woman I had seen in a movie. "Why can't you put them in a bag or something inside my suitcase?" I asked my mother. Her face turned serious and her eyes fixed on mine. She placed her hands firmly on my shoulders.

"Listen carefully, *m'ija*, this is very important." I felt her fingers gripping me. "Do not take your jacket off until you get to Jamaica, not even if you're hot."

"Why not?" A nervous apprehension raced through me.

"Because if the *milicianos* see the jewelry, they will take it away from you," she explained. "As soon as you get to Jamaica, María Elena will take it and keep it safe." Thoughts of a bearded rebel pawing me, ripping off the gems, gave me resolve.

"Don't worry, Mami, they won't steal our *prendas*," I told her with bravado. I didn't know that my mother had smuggled valuables also with my sister. Partially hidden in our clothes, sewn inside skirt hems, and tucked inside suitcase linings was the only way to smuggle jewelry, money, and important documents. The challenge was not to arouse suspicion.

Lazy was restless that morning, following me everywhere and occasionally prancing excitedly, eager to play with me. At breakfast she put her head on my lap. I stroked her curly top while I finished my *café con leche* and toast.

"I won't be gone long," I murmured to her, smoothing out a tangle of hair in one of her long ears. I missed her already. I bent down and kissed her wet nose. My mother called for me. I gave Lazy her daily tidbit, my last bite of toast. She ignored it and followed on my heels as I went into my room to get my things. Lazy jumped on my bed, wagging her tail as if saying *drop everything, don't go, just grab a book and lie here by me, like you always do*. I sat at the edge of my bed next to her and draped my arm around her in a hug. I reached for Hildi, leaning against my pillow, and lifted her slowly, admiring her pretty face and long blond braids. As I pressed her close to my chest, I had an impulse to look carefully at everything in my room as if to take it all into my memory. Mami called again. I placed Hildi inside the train case, and gathering my things, I reluctantly left my bedroom.

I sat on the porch steps while our chauffeur packed my suitcase and train case. Lazy straddled across me and plopped on my lap, as if to prevent me from moving. My dog's anxious behavior seemed odd. She had never acted like that when I'd gone somewhere before. It was as if she knew I would always come back.

"Be good, Lazy," I said falteringly. I hated leaving my dog, even for two weeks. "I love you, girl. I'll be back soon." She licked my face. I felt like crying. As I walked toward the car, Lazy ran after me and gave a high, frantic yelp. Consuelo held her back as she closed the sidewalk gate behind me. To this day, I can still hear my dog's long, heart-wrenching howl as our car drove around the corner and was out of her sight.

My flight was scheduled to leave at 10:30 a.m. At Rancho Boyeros airport, parents rushed around with their children in tow, anxiously looking for their flight information. Walking the crowded hallways toward my KLM gate, I passed several younger children wearing nametags. I strained to read them as they passed by. Underneath their names were the names and phone numbers of the people meeting them when they arrived at their destinations. A little boy lagged behind his father, holding on tight to his hand. On his tag, under his name and age, it simply stated, "Please take good care of me." Some children were crying; others did not say a word. No one seemed too happy to be leaving. The air was notably tense, and the word *"vacación"* was heard constantly.

At the KLM check-in counter, we were told my flight had been delayed. The time of departure would be announced when available. Two hours later, there was still no word. My mother asked my grandparents to go home since we did not know how long it would take.

"We will stay with you until she leaves," Bibi told her, sitting next to me at the gate. *Milicianos* patrolled the airport hallways and escorted people to interrogation rooms.

We soon found out that was the reason for the delays. It was the government's relentless attempts to find any reason to prevent Cubans from evacuating the island. They periodically stopped by our gate, calling someone's name off a list to come with them. Each time they did, my mother's face tensed up, Bibi's jaw clenched, and Mama prayed under her breath. At that moment, I began to have second thoughts about my trip.

We spent hours waiting and worrying, but we did not leave our gate for fear my flight would be announced and leave without me. We dared not complain. We took turns walking the nearby halls and going for something to eat, always leaving one of us behind to listen for the announcement. At times I felt warm and tempted to take off my jacket, but the sight of a *miliciano* reinforced my determination to outwit them. After a grueling twelve-hour delay, my flight was finally ready to board. It was almost 10:30 at night.

Despite the long, tense wait, my family had remained upbeat throughout the day, cheering me up about the trip. When it was time for me to go into *la pecera*—the fish-bowl—as Cubans called it, where the soldiers did final passenger checks before boarding, Mami held my hand tight, so tight the rings on my fingers hurt. She and my grandparents walked with me to the doorway of the glass-enclosed room. Bibi clasped me to his chest. I could feel him drawing a deep breath. He held my face with both his hands. I searched for the usual twinkle in his eyes, but instead they were brimming with tears.

"'*Pa lante, como el elefante,* Yoyi." Forward like the elephant. He smiled, quoting a favorite *refrán*, and kissed my forehead.

Mama hugged me and gave my cheek a kiss. "*Que Dios te bendiga,*" she sniffled. Then I said goodbye to my mother. She hugged me to her, tight, and kept me in her embrace while people going into the room bumped into us. Looking me in the eyes, she said, "Everything will be all right, *mi amor.* Have a fun vacation and I'll see you in two weeks."

A formidable woman with an impeccably made-up face walked by and spoke to my mother. "Don't worry. I'll keep an eye on her." Mami's jaw dropped. It was Olga Guillot, a well-known Cuban entertainer. My mother and aunts had many of her records. One night, from our grandparents' courtyard, we had heard her sing at the Tropicana.

"*Un millón de gracias,*" Mami thanked her. Olga acknowledged my mother's gratitude with a nod, gave me a quick wink, and trotted off with the boarding passengers. I sat in a chair next to the glass wall where my family could see me until I left. By then, my excitement had fizzled out, replaced by a stomach-tightening sensation. The room was filling up fast as *milicianos* yelled at teary-eyed parents to leave the room if they were not on the flight. I clung to the box of cookies Mama had given me as soldiers milled around. I looked down at my jacket, making sure it was buttoned, and pulled my long sleeves as far down as they could reach. The *milicianos* paced the aisles back and forth, their expressions glaring defiance. I did not look at their faces as they passed me, so close I could see the worn releases on their holstered guns. The *miliciano* standing in the front of the room spotted my tin box. He walked slowly toward me, his eyes fixed on the container.

"*¿Qué llevas ahí, chiquita?*" He snatched my tin with a swift, hungry movement. My heart was beating in my neck. I watched his black-rimmed nails all over the lid as he forced it open. *Get your grimy paws off my cookies*, asqueroso! I wanted to yell at him. I stared at the man, despising every inch of him. I glanced at my family just as Mama crossed herself and Bibi's eyes tore into the *miliciano*. But Mami's eyes, calm and unblinking, were on me. *Be brave*, they were telling me.

"Who gave you these?" he growled.

"*Mi abuela.*" I looked up at his face. He seemed so young underneath the bushy beard. Another *miliciano* called him from across the room. The young militiaman grabbed a guava turnover and stuffed it in his mouth, half of it hanging out. Slamming the lid back on, he thrust the box at me. I finished closing it and set it back on my lap, placing both my hands over it.

Two girls close to my age hurried into the room and sat next to me. They were sisters going on vacation, of course, to visit relatives in Miami. I envied them having each other. I wondered if Carmen had still felt excited about her solo trip as she sat in the same room to board her plane. Had she changed her mind and felt like I did? I wanted out—no vacation. I wanted to go home to my dog. I turned to look at my mother. Her eyes were unusually brilliant. Was she fighting off tears? How could I be happy about going on vacation when parents and relatives were so visibly upset? What was going on? How could I know of the agony that plagued my mother that day, not knowing if she would ever see me again. A *miliciano* slammed the door shut and yelled at us to get up and prepare to board the plane. *Why do they have to be so rude?* I reluctantly picked up my train case. Another door opened at the far end of the room and people rushed toward it. My head spun sharply to look at my family. Bibi stood between Mami and Mama, his arms around both their shoulders, drawing them close to him. He smiled at me while Mama gave little waves. I nervously smiled back, waving goodbye, but my eyes were riveted to my mother's as I got up to leave. *Be strong*, they were telling me this time. A man hurried by me, banging my train case hard into my knee. Strangely, I felt no pain. I summoned what remained of my courage and moved slowly toward the door to give the agent my boarding pass. I turned to look at Mami one last time but couldn't see her through the people piling behind me. I stood on my toes, craning my head while everyone wove around me. Over someone's shoulder I spotted her face for a split second, then I was pushed sideways and it was gone.

Someone pulled me by the sleeve. *"Vamos, ven conmigo."* Olga Guillot was urging me to walk with her. *"¿Qué te parece?"* She asked what I thought as we walked out onto the runway. "You and I are going to fly together." I did my best to raise a smile, and felt glad that I had brought along my autograph book.

The plane was packed with children of all ages, many traveling alone like me. They walked down the aisle as if in slow motion, their eyes widened with curiosity. *Is that what I look like?* I wondered. The stewardesses were shepherding them toward their assigned seats while adults spoke loudly to each other in confusion, shoving their way to their rows. I inched my way down the cramped aisle, letting everyone pass me. I had memorized my seat number but could not find it with so many people around me. Finally, a stewardess helped me to my seat. It was 11:30 at night. I was sleepy, but sitting by a window perked me up. I pressed my forehead to the pane in hopes of seeing my family, but my window faced the runway and the menacing darkness of the night.

The engines started up. Slowly, the aircraft cruised down the runway. I stared out my window again. Nothing. Looking across the aisle out the other windows, all I could see was a blur of lights. The louder the engines rumbled, the more I wanted to scream: *Stop the plane! I don't want to go on this vacation.* The vibrations in the cabin caused my train case to shimmy too close to my feet. As I bent down to push it further underneath the seat in front of me, one of the two pearls on my *tú y yo* ring popped off and bounced on the floor. In one suspended moment, it seemed to gleam in midair in the moonlit cabin. I watched helplessly as it disappeared. My fingers felt the empty spot on my ring where the pearl had been. I could not know then that I was losing another pearl that night—Cuba, the pearl of the Antilles.

The propellers revved up, and as the plane turned one last time to head down the final runway, I could barely see the airport through my tear-filled eyes. In a flash, the airport lights were far behind me as the plane sped into the humid night. A tall royal palm, la Palma Real de Cuba, was silhouetted in the moonlight as I watched my homeland disappear amid the sleeping clouds.

Chapter Fifteen

Las Playas Del Destierro

As the plane gained altitude, sporadic shouts of joy broke out in the crowded cabin. Across the aisle a mother with two young children thanked God out loud: *"¡Ay, gracias, Dios mío!"* The elderly woman sitting next to me was silently praying her rosary, nervously rubbing each bead. But soon the mood turned somber, with an occasional burst of anguished sobs. Passengers seated near me dozed off, but with the propellers' loud rumbling and the aircraft's vibrations I could not fall asleep.

"¿Estás bien?" Olga had stopped by to check on me. I was okay, I told her, and eager to see my family in Jamaica, and oh, would she please sign my autograph book?

"We'll be there before you know it." Her voice was cheery as she scribbled on the pale pink page. Shortly after she walked away, the soft strumming of a guitar floated from the back of the cabin. A man sang a melancholic ballad about leaving Cuba. *"Cuando salí de Cuba, dejé mi vida, dejé mi amor."* His strong voice echoed a soulful lamentation. With each verse, others joined him, their voices sad and yearning. By the end of the song, a full chorus sang the last stanza:

"Cuando salí de Cuba, dejé enterrado mi corazón." The lady next to me cried softly. Her sadness was contagious.

In my quietness, I felt sure there was something going on besides vacation trips.

After a smooth landing in Montego Bay, I was met by my family at the gate. The first face I saw was my father's. He looked tired but happy to see me. Behind him, my grandmother waved rapidly, and next to her, my sister looked concerned. At customs, an official interrupted our chatter when my turn in line was up.

"*Señorita, su pasaporte, por favor.*" I looked at María Elena, then at the stern-looking man.

"This is all I have." I handed him my flight information folder with my tickets, student visa pass, and boarding pass. He scrutinized them, then me, and demanded my passport again.

"Give him your passport now, it's okay," my sister said, nodding. She waited for me to produce the document, looking hard at me. I shook my head.

"I don't have one," I blurted. People behind us were becoming impatient as the official continued with his interrogation. He told my sister that without a passport I could not go on to America. My father became agitated, telling the man to stop bullying me.

"We'll wait for you at baggage claim," Tita Lala told María Elena and quickly took Papi out of the room.

"My sister is tired, sir, and doesn't remember where she put it," María Elena spoke calmly to the man. "I will look for it and you will have it first thing tomorrow morning before she goes on to Miami." The official raised a skeptical eyebrow at me.

"If you do not have her passport by noon tomorrow

she will be sent back to Cuba on the first available flight," he said, addressing María Elena. My sister did not flinch. I stared at him, startled. He stamped something in my folder and gruffly handed it to María Elena. "Next," he barked out. Relief bathed my sister's face. I practically had to run to keep up with her as we hurried to baggage claim.

"We can't go to sleep tonight until we find that passport," she fumed. "Think, where did Mami put it?" Her eyes were blazing black ebony. "You're in big trouble if we don't find it."

"I don't know what you're talking about, I told you. I don't know." People were staring at us. "And stop yelling at me." My sister took my train case from me so I could walk faster.

"Fine. We'll talk about it when we get to the boardinghouse. C'mon, hurry up, and don't talk about this in front of Papi, okay?"

"*Está bien.*" Maybe it was just as well if I did get sent back to Cuba. The trip was turning out to be a pain. I knew nothing of the whereabouts of my passport. I didn't even know what it was or what it looked like, or that my mother had concealed it from the *milicianos*. She knew that if discovered, my passport would have been a dead giveaway that I was leaving the country permanently, and I would have been detained. She could not risk telling me and instead took a chance that María Elena would find it. Mami had explained the student visa waiver to me and told me it was all I needed for my vacation. My sister knew that Mami had stashed my passport somewhere in my things, but she didn't expect that I wouldn't know where. When she realized that I didn't have a clue, her frustration turned to fear for my safety.

When we arrived at the boardinghouse where they were staying, María Elena called my mother to let her know I had arrived safely in Jamaica. *"Ya llegó el paquete. Todo está bien."* Knowing the phones in Cuba were tapped, they had to use code words. *El paquete*, the package, was me. *"¿Todo está en la caja?"* Is everything in the box? my sister asked. The box was my luggage.

"Sí, sí, todo va…" my mother's words were cut off and the line went dead, but María Elena had received the confirmation she needed. It was sometime after one in the morning when she tucked me into a cot next to her twin bed in the small room she shared with our grandmother.

"Don't you want me to help you look for my passport?" I asked her, half-asleep.

"No, Tita Lala will help me." She held the sheet up while I hopped in bed. "You get to sleep now. You have to get up in a few hours," she said, impatient and miserable. She looked at me before turning out the overhead light. "Are you *sure* you don't remember Mami showing you where she hid your passport?"

"De veras, I don't know anything about it." I turned on my side to face her. "Does this mean I'm not going on vacation to Miami?"

"Don't worry, you're going. If I have to stay up all night, I'll find that *condenado pasaporte."* Tita Lala came in to say goodnight and help my sister with the search. My father had already gone to bed. I watched drowsily as my sister and grandmother rummaged through my suitcase, removing every single item and going over it carefully. María Elena took the jewelry off my clothes, piece by piece, and placed it in a small box. She felt around the hem of my suit skirt and, to my surprise, ripped open one spot and slipped out some documents.

"¡*Perfecto*!" she said. "Here's your birth certificate." She folded the papers and put them in the box with the jewelry.

"Did you find it?" I asked sleepily.

"Not yet, but I will. Go to sleep." She handed my skirt to my grandmother and asked her to sew up the hem where she had ripped it open. The last thing I saw before drifting off to sleep was my sister, frantically searching through my train case while Tita Lala stitched my skirt hem. As my eyes grew heavier I heard a far-away voice exclaim, "Tita, I found it!" just as I gave in to the beckoning slumber.

When I awoke, María Elena gave me the good news while victoriously holding up the little book. Mami had hidden my passport behind the mirror on my train-case lid. My sister smiled for the first time since I arrived.

I hardly touched my breakfast. Who could stomach cold fish so early in the morning? While waiting for the taxi, I sat with Papi on a swing in a shady corner of the porch. He was not coming to the airport with me; the medication made him feel tired, he told me, but I knew he was upset to see me go.

The morning's cool, newborn light would soon be brilliant and hot. I was glad to be wearing a short-sleeved cotton dress instead of my three-piece suit weighed down with hidden jewelry and documents. The fragrance from gardenia plants and pots of flowering jasmine scented the soft breeze. A gardenia plant limb laden with blossoms cascaded over the railing near me. I plucked a flower, held it to my nose momentarily, and tucked it in my hair behind my right ear. My father planted both feet on the floor, causing our seat to stop swinging. He looked at me, cocked his head, and smiled.

"You look just like your mami." His fingers lightly touched the gardenia petals; his gaze went beyond me, lost in a memory that was his alone. I waited for him to reminisce. But the cab pulled up and gave a quick honk. I did not want to leave him. My father hugged me and kissed me on the cheek.

"I'll see you soon." His beautiful brown eyes were vacant.

"I'll write you, Papi, I promise." I took the gardenia from my hair and gave it to him. The porch's screen door flung open as Tita Lala came out to say goodbye, followed by my sister and the Alvarez family, who would be accompanying me to the airport. From the taxi's window I looked out at Papi to wave goodbye, but he sat gazing at the gardenia in his hands as the swing slowly rocked back and forth.

At the airport María Elena gave me final instructions: "Aunt Blanca and Uncle Luis will be waiting for you at Miami airport. It's a short flight, so don't worry, okay?"

"Okay. Well, I'll see you back in Cuba after vacation." I looked up at her as we walked to the runway door. "Yeah, right," she answered, looking straight ahead. She handed my boarding pass to the agent and pointed to me. Flipping open my purse, she tucked the flight folder in it and checked me over quickly.

"You ready?" I nodded. Her hands were on my shoulders.

"You gotta go, now." We looked at each other for a moment; my sister's eyes softened.

"*Adiós*, Meffy," I addressed her by the nickname I had given her and turned to walk out onto the sunny runway. As I followed other passengers to the airplane staircase, her voice rang out behind me: "Go, go, go!"

The Cuban passengers on board rejoiced when we landed in Miami. Large groups of people streamed out of the airport onto the runway to greet the arriving exiles. I stayed in my window seat while people hustled to get out. *I'll get trampled for sure*, I thought, deciding to wait a few more minutes before getting up. I looked out my window, searching for my aunt and uncle. A wave of panic assailed me when I did not see them. The cabin was almost empty when I spotted a stewardess approaching me.

"Are you all right, honey?" Concern marked her voice. I nodded, picking up my train case. "C'mon, I'll walk you out to meet your family." When we reached the bottom of the long staircase, the crowds had thinned out, and my relatives were nowhere to be found.

"They're not here," I told the young woman. She scanned the area carefully.

"Oh, they will be. You just stand here and wait for them. Right here." She pointed to a spot next to the railing, then turned and sprinted back up the stairs to the airplane. I watched as airline employees unloaded our suitcases and drove them in an open cart toward the building. Two huge jets took off, three more landed, and I was still standing there when the flight crew came down the stairs to leave.

"You're still waiting?" The stewardess seemed startled

to see me. I nodded again. "Wait here, okay?" She left the group and rushed toward a man standing near our Pan American airplane. She pointed at me while talking to him. The kind-looking older man looked my way. Together, they hurried toward me. He wore a uniform, a cap, and a Pan American Airlines nametag. Something about him reminded me of Bibi.

"This man will help you find your relatives, okay? Don't worry, everything will be all right, honey." She dashed off to catch up with the crew before I could thank her.

"So, little lady, do you speak English?" he said with a cheery smile.

"Yes."

"Well, that's good news. Now, who are you waiting for?"

"My aunt and uncle."

"All righty, you come along with me. We'll go inside and find them." My legs felt like lead as I followed him to the information desk where my aunt and uncle were quickly paged. Minutes later, they hurried down the hall toward me, all smiles and happy to see me.

"*Hola, gorda,*" Aunt Blanca greeted me. I cringed. She had called me chubby since I was a baby, but at twelve, I no longer thought it was endearing, especially since I had long ago shed my baby fat. Uncle Luis told me they'd been in the cafeteria lounge waiting for my plane to arrive.

"*Oye,* Blanca, I can't believe we lost track of time, *vieja,*" he joked with his wife. I felt like a forgotten piece of luggage that was finally claimed. Walking with them down the crowded, noisy airport halls, surrounded by strangers bumping into me, I was lost in the shuffle, a foreigner in my own skin.

On our way to Aunt Emma's, my aunt and uncle made small talk about my trip. I wasn't in the mood to chitchat. Picking up on that, they soon left me alone and continued talking with each other. Looking out the car window, I was amazed at how different Miami was from Pennsylvania. The palm trees and tropical landscape reminded me of Cuba, but the pace seemed faster.

The car turned onto SW 24th Street, a tree-lined residential area of modest homes built close to each other. We pulled into a short driveway next to a small, mint-green house. Aunt Emma and her two young boys came out to greet us.

My aunt's rented, furnished cottage was nothing like her luxurious Miramar home. The living room was dark and cluttered, its furniture shabby and dingy. Toys, coloring books, and crayons were sprawled on the floor. I sat on a mud-colored couch, still holding on to my cookie tin. There were no porcelain figurines, crystal ashtrays, or silver-framed family photos on the chipped wooden endtables. Only my cousin's teddy bear with a missing eye.

Aunt Emma's home was not what I had expected. I did not want to stay there. What kind of a fun vacation was this going to be? Next to me, Aunt Blanca was fidgeting. She and Aunt Emma exchanged nervous glances. Uncle Luis lit up a cigarette. Aunt Emma tucked her heels underneath the rocker she was sitting on to abruptly stop its motion. Her eyes darted from her sister to her brother-in-law then back to me.

"This is not a vacation, honey." I stiffened at her words and glimpsed at Aunt Blanca and Uncle Luis. They shook their heads simultaneously, their faces drawn. My uncle momentarily looked away. Silence.

"What do you mean, *Tía?*" I clutched my cookie tin.

"Well, honey, you and many other children had to be sent out of Cuba in a hurry." She paused and looked at Blanca and Luis.

"*Sí, ese desgenerado* Fidel was going to take you away from your family and ship you off to Russia for a long time to turn you into a commie," said Uncle Luis, ill-concealed disgust in his voice. He took a drag from his cigarette.

"You're lucky, *gorda*. At least you have family here in Miami to come to." Aunt Blanca put in. "Many of these kids had no one to go live with and are now in orphanages, waiting for a relative to arrive from Cuba." The room suddenly seemed smaller, the air thicker.

"You mean, I can't go back to Cuba?" I heard myself ask, looking at all three of them. I could feel my heart pumping inside my chest.

"No, honey, you're in exile now with the rest of us. You'll be living with me and the boys until your mami comes," Aunt Emma replied. Now I understood what *el exilio* meant. I felt frightened and betrayed. I kept my mouth closed, though I could feel my lips quiver. I sucked in quiet, jagged breaths, but no tears came. I suddenly wished I had wings so I could fly out the opening screen door as my little cousin came in from the porch. Fly away, hard, fast, never stopping until I reached Cuba. But a shiver ran through me as I recalled the day the *milicianos* came to my school. *No, I don't want to go to Russia and become a communist.* Whatever that meant, I knew it was bad. *I have to stay here where I'm safe—alone and afraid in America.*

My thoughts whirled out of control as I tried to understand what was happening to me—communism, exile, escaping from Cuba, leaving my loved ones behind. My way of life, as I had once known it, had ended.

"María Elena will be coming soon." Aunt Emma's attempt at cheeriness reeled me back to reality. "And she'll be living here with us, too."

"But I thought she went on vacation to Jamaica with Papi and Tita Lala." I knew the answer before my aunt responded that my sister, father, and grandmother were also leaving Cuba for good. Despite my confusion, a twinge of comfort spread through me. *My big sister is coming.*

"When will Mami come?" I heard my voice cracking, fading out.

"We don't know when, but soon, we hope," Aunt Blanca chimed in. It all made sense now, the cover story of my vacation in Florida, the sadness and tears of the passengers on the plane. All the people leaving Cuba "on vacation" had been fleeing the island to escape communism. Just like me. I thought of my dog and tears pricked the back of my eyes. I silently raged at Fidel Castro and his *milicianos*, feeling the anger rise to my face, but not a sound came out of my mouth.

Aunt Blanca cleared her throat and looked at her husband. Uncle Luis uncrossed his legs and inched forward in his seat. Then they rose to go.

"We'll see you soon." Aunt Blanca's hug was brief. I nodded.

"*Hasta pronto,*" Uncle Luis said, and they were gone.

El paquete—that was the code name my mother and sister had used for me when I arrived in Jamaica. That's what I felt like, a dumped package.

"Can I call Mami?" I asked Aunt Emma as she closed

the door behind my aunt and uncle. She coached me on how to talk to my mother before making the call. Not a word about what I had just heard. Only talk about my trip and pretend vacation. I had to be careful and quick so my mother would not get in trouble, since the government had the phones tapped. My aunt picked up the telephone and started dialing.

"Just tell her you arrived safely and are having a nice vacation, honey." *I don't ever want to hear that word again*, I wanted to scream at her. She picked at her lower lip with her long, polished fingernails while waiting for the operator. It took a long time to get through to Havana. My eyes remained fixed on my aunt's lips, waiting for her to say my mother's name.

"Ninina? *Sí, sí, es* Emma. *Todo está bien. Un momento.* Here's your daughter." My aunt handed me the phone. "*Coje, coje;* here, quick, talk to your mom."

"Mami…?" I stammered into the mouthpiece. When I heard my mother's voice all the tears I had been holding back since the moment I left Cuba welled up in my eyes. Wiping away a runaway tear, I asked, "When are you coming? When will you come on vacation to Aunt Emma's?" I looked up at my aunt, who nodded in approval. My mother spoke quickly, reassuring me that we would be together soon.

"Be good, listen to your aunt, and say your prayers." I heard her sharp intake of breath, followed by a soft silence.

"I will, Mami."

"I love you, *mi'jita*, and I…" A click. Then nothing.

"Mami, Mami, are you there? Mami?" I pressed the phone harder against my ear, listening to the dial tone, waiting to hear my mother's voice again. My aunt took the phone away from me, listened for a moment, and placed it back on the receiver.

"She'll be here soon honey, you'll see." Aunt Emma draped her arm around me and hugged me to her. "Now let's get you settled in; you must be tired." I nodded with weary resignation and followed her to a small room, cozy with sunlight. Painted light yellow, it had two twin beds, barely enough room for a dresser, and a narrow little box of a closet. The only window faced the tiny backyard, which had an orange tree in its center. The neighbor's house was so close, I could see a big apricot-colored tabby preening itself on a sunshiny kitchen windowsill, while a woman standing behind him sang "Blue Moon" as she washed dishes.

Sitting on one of the beds, I stared at the other one. It comforted me to know I was looking at the bed that would be my sister's. But when would María Elena be here? My mind was bombarded with questions that I could not answer. What's going to happen to me now? Will I ever see my parents and siblings again?

An intense longing for home enveloped me. To see the late afternoon sun filtering through the areca palms, scattering tiny slits of amber light across our porch floor. The wooden shuttered window over my bed, gaping wide open, welcoming me into my cheerful bedroom; to smell the musky, indefinable scent of my dog, laying on my bed, waiting for me.

All the small, comforting details of my life in Cuba seemed so very far away in this bare, unfamiliar room. A peripheral movement caught my attention. The cat next door was stretching on the windowsill. He looked totally content, basking in the sun. He sat and looked my way.

Noticing me, he meowed softly. It was then that I cried.

My sense of security was bolstered three weeks later when my sister arrived from Jamaica. My father and grandmother had to stay longer because of a delay in their paperwork to enter the United States.

María Elena did not waste any time resuming her role as *la mayor*. My vacation of sorts was over. The following Monday, she and Aunt Emma enrolled me in a public elementary school two blocks away. It was hard enough being in a foreign country and going to a new school in the middle of the term, but not knowing anyone was the worst. Armed with happy memories of the welcoming first-grade children in Lumberville, I felt confident enough the following morning as I walked into the noisy sixth-grade classroom. But I was not a novelty this time, the little girl from an island in the Caribbean. The heavy influx of Cuban exiles to Miami had put our *islita* on the map.

I dreaded going to school. In the crowded classrooms I missed my friends in Cuba and the Sacred Heart Academy. I wished I could wear a uniform to school. Seeing the majority of girls in my class wearing the latest fads made me conscious of my limited wardrobe. All I owned were a couple of skirts, a few blouses, and my blue cotton dress. What to wear to school seemed so unimportant to me, yet I quickly learned that it was a key popularity factor. I felt totally isolated.

At first I ate lunch by myself every day. But eventually I met other Cuban children. Most lived with their parents, except for Raulito, who along with his older brother was also living with relatives until their parents arrived from

Cuba. We formed a little group and gave it a name: *"los Cubanitos del exilio."*

* * *

"You're so lucky you don't have to go to school anymore," I grumbled one night while reading my American history book in bed. My sister sat cross-legged on her bed poring over the newspaper spread out in front of her.

"*Oye*, it's not easy trying to find a job either, you know? Sometimes I wish I was still in school." María Elena had been tirelessly looking for a job. Every day she took the bus to downtown Miami to apply for secretarial jobs.

María Elena hopped off her bed and conspicuously took a brown paper bag out of her dresser drawer.

"*Mira*, I got a treat for us today on my way home. This will cheer you up." She pulled out a bag of cookies from the bag. They were dark chocolate with a white filling. "These are great with milk. Here, enjoy your first Oreo." She popped one in her mouth and handed me several.

"But what about your pimples?" I cried out. "You're not supposed to have chocolate stuff." María Elena had had a bout with acne in Cuba, and even though her skin had cleared up nicely, she was supposed to watch her chocolate.

"Oh, don't worry." She slowly pulled the cookie apart and ate the half with the white cream. "See how dark this chocolate is?" she said, showing me the other half. "That's because they burned off the ingredients that give you pimples when they baked them."

"O-oh…" I stared at my cookies, fully convinced.

"Let's go ask Aunt Emma if we can have a glass of milk

and we'll bring it back to our room," she conspired. "But don't say a word about our cookies. This is our stash."

Our aunt strictly rationed our food, and we were not allowed to eat anything without her permission. "I don't have much money, and we have to make these groceries last the whole week." We heard that litany every Friday when we got home from the supermarket and helped her unpack the bags. Whenever María Elena got a car ride downtown from my aunt, she used her allotted bus money for that day to buy a treat for the two of us. Even though I fell for my sister's chocolate fib, those Oreos became our comfort food.

Life at Aunt Emma's was an unendurable waiting game. Every day I asked myself, *Is this the day I'll know when I'll see my mother again?* On my way to school each morning, I would see moms walking their young children to the corner, watching them until they reached school safely. In the afternoon, they would be waiting for them at the same corner. It was a painful reminder of my constant fear that I would never see my mother again. I had never imagined the loneliness of being without my family.

I missed my dog. At night I would lie in bed and instinctively reach out for Lazy. Closing my eyes, I imagined her thick furry body lying next to me. I recalled Consuelo's harping not to let her on my bed because she might be dirty or have *bichitos*, little bugs. But Lazy always slept with me. Who was caring for her now and loving her the way I did? Was she sleeping in someone's comfy bed at nights or in a grimy kennel cage? Once I woke up crying after dreaming she had been abandoned, hungry and dirty. I could hear her sad howling as she wandered my neighborhood's empty streets and the park searching for me.

It was at bedtime that my thoughts inevitably turned to my family and Cuba. I thought about my home, my bedroom, and the favorite things I had left behind. My eyes burned with tears remembering my school and Rancho Perea. I longed for the smell of Cuba's rich, humid red soil; the fragrance of my mother's roses blooming in the garden outside my bedroom window; the thick, salty sea air. Instead, I was smacked into reality by the pungent smell of sauerkraut and fried fish that often drifted into our bedroom from our neighbor's kitchen.

I looked forward to Fridays. As Catholics, we could not eat meat on that day. Tired of fish sticks and tuna fish, my aunt often treated us to waffles and vanilla ice cream for dinner at the nearby Waffle House. Afterward, we would go food shopping at the Food Fair, and recalling how sparse Havana's supermarkets had become after Cuba's breakup with the U.S., I was amazed at Miami's bountiful stores and the variety of foods to choose from. I remember standing in awe in front of a perfectly formed pyramid of apples in the produce section. I loved apples, and since they were not a common fruit in Cuba, I had not eaten one since we lived in Pennsylvania, four years before. My aunt handed me a small brown bag. She smiled.

"Go ahead and fill this." Her voice was flushed with affection. She wasn't so bad after all, my Aunt Emma. That night I wrote my mother a letter while crunching on a sweet red Delicious.

At times in Miami I thought I was in Cuba. Not only because of the similarities in the environment, landscape, and weather, but also because of the many Cubans arriving daily. Hearing the familiar speeding, clicking Spanish almost everywhere I went made me feel at home. One day, as we walked toward my aunt's car in the grocery-store parking lot, a man getting into his station wagon nearby overheard us speaking in Spanish.

"This is America, you know?" he hollered across the roof of his car. "We speak English here." My aunt ignored him, but he railed on: "If you don't like it, then get the hell back to where you came from!" An older man, with thinning gray hair and dark-rimmed glasses, he glared at us while Aunt Emma hurried the boys into the car. I stood gawking at his angry face. He scowled at me, shaking his head. "Stinkin' spics!" he growled.

"Why is that man so angry with us?" I asked my aunt, still looking at him.

"*Andale*, get in the car, honey, hurry." Her face was livid. I could not make out what the man was shouting to Aunt Emma, but his face was beet red. She opened the driver's side door and, just before getting into the car, turned and yelled back at him, "Get rid of Fidel and we gladly will!" Once inside the car she muttered, "*¡Prejuiciado!*" Still mumbling, the man scrambled into his car, slammed the door, and peeled out of the parking lot. Aunt Emma's jaw was set like stone, and her teeth clenched as she turned on the ignition.

"*¿Porqué, Tía?*" I asked. "What did we do?"

"*Nada*. It's nothing we did, honey." Her voice sounded shaky. She drove faster than she usually did.

"He doesn't like us because we're Cuban?" I held on tight to the armrest as we whipped around the corner.

"No, because we're different," she declared, stopping at a red light. "*Los Americanos* are good people, but not all Miami folks are thrilled to have us here."

"Is that why he called us stinkin' spics?" My aunt's eyes blazed like two hot coals as she turned to address me. I thought she was about to cry and curse at the same time.

"*Sí*, because people like that are narrow-minded, ignorant, and insecure." She grimaced, as if tasting something bitter. The light turned green. It was a quiet ride home to my aunt's bungalow as I wrangled with the meaning of a new word in my English vocabulary.

Prejudice.

* * *

While I struggled to cope with the difficult adjustments of life in exile, I was unaware of how dangerous circumstances had become for my mother in Havana.

Where Mami worked, there were rumors that the school was under surveillance. Random searches by *milicianos* took place with increasing frequency. There was no doubt that the government suspected the school administration's involvement with the Catholic Youth Underground movement. Under perilous secrecy, the principal held a final meeting with his staff. "We have to leave Cuba immediately; they are on to us. It's just a matter of time before we are all arrested," he told them. "The movement has dissolved and recommends that we take refuge in the Venezuelan Embassy." But my mother did not want to leave the island via Venezuela; she had to go to America.

Soon after, the school principal and the monsignor who headed the organization in Havana left Cuba, but the school secretary was arrested. I cannot imagine the terror my mother must have felt when she heard the news. That very day she met with a family friend employed as an agent for an American airline.

"I can get you and your three children out of Cuba, but don't smuggle any money, jewelry, or documents. Nothing they can nail you for, Ninina," he instructed her. "Just bring five American dollars and one suitcase for each of you." He handed her the visas and necessary paperwork for departure on March 27. Once she made the decision, Mami had three days to settle her accounts and dispose of personal items and possessions without arousing suspicion, especially from Consuelo.

My mother entrusted her father to close our home after she left and to distribute household items among the servants and relatives. She left Consuelo $500 cash in Cuban money and gave Lazy to our laundress, Felicidad.

My mother was anguished at leaving her parents behind. Booking flights to leave the island was becoming more difficult with each passing day. Since my grandfather held a government position, Mami was afraid it would not be easy for him to leave Cuba.

"*No te preocupes, mi'jita,*" Bibi reassured her. "Your mother and I will soon follow. You have to go now, while you can." Family members could not risk losing their reservations while waiting to leave with loved ones, especially in my mother's case.

"Why are you leaving for Jamaica so suddenly?" Consuelo asked my mother. She was helping her pack my brothers' suitcases. "Will I be going along to help you with the children?"

"No, Consuelo, not this time." Mami continued packing. "I'll be gone for a few days only, just to see how *el caballero* is doing."

"Then why are you taking the children with you?" She closed a suitcase and gave my mother a cold stare. "Why not leave them here with me?"

"Because it would be good for them to see their father. He misses them." Mami pushed the dresser drawer harder than she meant to. "I need you to stay and take care of our home while I'm gone, Consuelo."

"Bueno, qué más da," Consuelo rolled my brother's socks into a tight ball. "It's just as well that Cubans who don't want to be here leave our island."

"It's just for a few days, Consuelo."

"Sí, Señora, for a few days." The nanny finished folding my brother's shirt while looking at my mother.

* * *

The night before her trip, Mami sewed some jewelry and the deed to her property, La Coronela, inside the lining of my sister's coat. Aware of rumors that adults were being searched at the airport, she did not hide anything in her own clothes. She stashed her and the children's birth certificates and passports inside the lining of her train case.

My mother did not have sufficient time to exchange Cuban money for American dollars to take with her. Doing that in itself was risky, and she was already in enough danger. All she took was the $20 allowed for the four of them. She felt confident that once reunited with Tita Lala and Papi in Jamaica, my grandmother would help her and the children financially. During their years of extensive travel abroad, my paternal grandparents had invested money in America. Prior to Castro's takeover, Tito Pepe began transferring large sums of money out of Cuba to the United States. Knowing this, my mother counted on her mother-in-law's help during her exodus. After all, hadn't she taken Tita Lala into her home and helped her prior to her leaving the island?

On March 27, 1961, one month after I left Cuba, my mother, nine-year-old brother, and the eight-year-old twins, along with Mama and Bibi, arrived at Rancho Boyeros airport in Havana at 8 a.m. Their flight was scheduled to leave at 10 a.m. The anxiety at the airport was heartfelt; the long flight delays and thorough interrogations created chaos, but what Mami feared the most was an arrest for her involvement with *la contra revolución*.

By 1 p.m. they were finally called into the "fish-bowl room" to await boarding. As when I left, the soldiers patrolled the room, up and down each aisle, intimidating the nervous passengers with their guns and suspicious stares. The incessant passenger questioning continued for more than an hour. Suddenly, like a death call, a *miliciano* yelled out my mother's name. Terrified, she gathered the children and followed a rough-looking *miliciana* with a black beret to another room. The children waited in the hallway with my grandparents. My mother had been randomly selected for a body search. She was ordered to empty out her pocketbook, take off her clothes and shoes, and jump up and down several times. The children were not searched.

They were finally ready to board the plane at 3 p.m. Mama openly wept as she watched her daughter and grandchildren leave the room. Bibi comforted his wife while watching a piece of his heart rip away from him, the pain almost unbearable, as his daughter waved goodbye one last time. Inside the airplane, *milicianos* meandered up and down the aisles, further delaying departure with their last-minute questioning. It was not until the plane was in the air that my mother accepted the fact that she had left Cuba safely.

Many times throughout my life I have tried to imagine how my mother felt the day she left Cuba. I visualize her standing by the front door of our home in Marianao. Her one hand rests on the brass handle of the mahogany front door; the other holds the one suitcase the government allows her to take. She sets it down on the tiled porch floor for the chauffeur to carry to the waiting Mercedes. How did she fit a lifetime of memories in one small suitcase? How did she decide what to bring and what to leave behind, knowing she might never be able to return?

My mother turns around slowly, a revolving movie camera taking in every detail surrounding her. She scans her home's interior as if preparing to take one final shot, one that includes everything so that she can remember it always. The teardrop crystals in the chandelier above her clink softly in a sudden breeze; they sparkle in the morning sunshine streaming into the foyer. In the living room, a coloring book and box of crayons are strewn on the seat of a Louis XVI chair. The tip of a crimson red has marked the delicate cream-colored fabric, but what does that matter now? Her bedroom door is ajar; she can barely see the brocaded trim of her bedspread, a wedding gift from her grandmother. In full view is the dining-room hutch, filled with family heirlooms she hoped one day to pass on to her daughters. How did my mother feel at that moment, fearing she was leaving it all behind forever, abandoning her wealth, her past, her way of life?

The long hallway, usually bustling with the noise and activity of children, dogs, nannies, and housemaids, is now desolate. The only sound is the faint clanking of plates from the kitchen as the cook washes the breakfast dishes. Did my mother wonder how the servants would react when they realized she was not returning? Would they understand her betrayal in leaving them?

It had taken my mother so long to finally find a home of our own after many years of an uprooted life. She had loved this house on sight. It became the respite she needed after her painful separation from my father. At last, a place to provide stability for her children. Now, she faces an unknown destination.

My mother grips the door handle a little tighter. Did she shudder at the thought of *barbudos*, with greasy hair and unkempt beards, rummaging through her home and throwing her belongings into an army truck parked in front of the house? She knew this is what would happen if she didn't return in two weeks from her "vacation." Her home and its contents would automatically become government property.

My mother knows the *barbudos* will be angry; to them she is a *gusano*, a fleeing traitor of the Cuban revolution. In their eagerness to pillage her home, surely they will trample

Las Playas Del Destierro

through the rose bushes lining the brick walkway. They will empty the dining-room hutch of all its precious contents, thrash about the rooms tossing everything into large cartons, yank her delicate bedspread from the bed to wrap the things they will haul off to the waiting truck.

The heavy wooden door settles into its waiting frame as it closes behind her. The familiar catching sound seems to resonate louder than usual. She is reluctant for a moment, then slowly lets go of the handle. My mother descends the wide marble portal steps onto the brick walkway. Her roses have never looked lovelier. She glances over her shoulder for a final look. A pair of gardening gloves lay on a glass-topped table next to a white wicker rocker she will never sit in again.

How did my mother withstand the fear that burdened her? The terror that she might be arrested for her anti-revolutionary activities just minutes before boarding the plane that will take her to freedom. The anxiety of going alone to a foreign country with three small children in tow, without money and with limited use of the language. The gut-wrenching dread of never again seeing her two oldest daughters, whom she had already sent off the island to save from communist training. How intense must be the panic that drives a parent to take such a desperate measure, never doubting it was the right decision. Apprehension must have gripped her heart at the thought that her parents and remaining relatives might not be able to leave Cuba.

The chauffeur unlatches the black wrought-iron gate that opens onto the sidewalk. "*¿Está lista,* Señora?" he sneers, holding it open for my mother. His insolent gaze must sicken her.

"*Sí, desgraciado comunista,* I'm ready to go," I'm sure she wished she could reply, but she suspects he's a *chibato,* an informant who's been surveying her every move. She walks past him, avoiding eye contact. "¡*Sí, vámonos!*" Does he notice the uneasiness in her voice? The gate slams hard behind her, but she doesn't flinch. My mother steps into the car and doesn't look back again.

Arriving safely in Montego Bay, my mother was met at the gate by her contact, an elderly priest who provided her with boarding passes for their connecting flight to Kingston, Jamaica. Before parting, he blessed her and the children. When their short flight landed in the early evening, Tita Lala gave them an icy reception and questioned my mother about her plans. While the children chattered with Papi, Mami was finally able to disclose her situation to her mother-in-law. She had no money except for $20, no place to go, and she was counting on her help.

"Well, I don't have any money, either," Tita Lala said curtly. Mami knew that was a lie.

"*Pues de una a otra,* Clara—one way or the other I guess we will all suffer together. Wherever you and Rolando are, that's where we will be." My grandmother agreed to let them stay with her and my father that night, but the following morning she made arrangements with her landlord to find another boardinghouse for Mami and the children. Tita Lala made Mami spend her $20 for the first two days. By the end of the second day, my mother and the children walked several blocks to see my grandmother. Trying to understand why her mother-in-law was shunning her and the children when they desperately needed her help,

Mami figured it must be resentment toward her for having separated from her son. But her children didn't deserve to be punished. Tita Lala opened the screen door just as Mami was about to ring the bell.

"Clara, I have spent the money I had, and as of tomorrow, the children and I will be literally out on the street if you don't help us." She swallowed her pride, knowing she was at the mercy of a woman who did not like her. "*Por Dios*, Clara, these are your grandchildren." My grandmother gave in on one condition: Mami could move in with her and Papi, but Tita Lala would not give her a cent.

One large room accommodated all six of them. A partition in the center divided a section where Tita Lala slept in a single bed and Mami and my sister shared another. On the other side, Papi had a single bed and my brothers slept on small cots next to him. The room did not have a private bathroom. Boarders had to use an outside bathroom in the backyard with an adjacent shower stall. There was no hot water.

Exile in Jamaica was a harsh awakening for my mother. In addition to the financial and emotional hardships, the heat and humidity were intolerable, especially at bedtime. Mealtimes were family style with the landlords and other guests. Breakfast was minimal; sometimes they had fish, but mostly it was juice, milk, and toast. Lunch was usually lemonade with bread and butter. Dinner was most times chicken, vegetables, and bread. The food passed around on platters was scarce; by the time my mother got them she was lucky to snatch the chicken wings for the children, who often complained of being hungry. They grew thinner by the day. Mami asked Tita Lala to buy some condensed milk and Ovaltine for them.

"No, we have to save our money," my grandmother replied each time. It took the children themselves asking her for the sweet milk and chocolate before she gave in and bought it for them.

Living together in such confined quarters, my father's bad days were hard on everyone, especially my mother. While he was in Jamaica, Papi was not under psychiatric care. My grandmother kept him calm with sedatives whenever necessary.

The children passed their days in the tiny backyard, playing with small lizards, chickens, and a caged parrot that often bit my father as he persistently poked his fingers through the bars to pet it. The children treated the chickens as pets, giving them names, and cried inconsolably when the landlady killed them for their dinner. They refused to eat it. My mother had to stop them from playing in the backyard. Instead, she and my father, when he was having a good day, walked with my siblings to a nearby beach where they could play. Expecting they would not be in Jamaica for long, Mami did not enroll the children in school.

My mother wanted to enter the United States as a resident instead of a refugee. She was afraid that as a refugee, she might be sent anywhere in the States to live. As a resident, she knew she had the right to live wherever she chose, and she wanted to go to Miami. Twice a week she walked downtown in the scorching heat to the American Embassy to fill out forms, have pictures taken, receive vaccinations, and follow up on the necessary paperwork to obtain U.S. residency for herself and the children as soon as possible. Tita Lala was encumbered with embassy delays concerning Papi's residency papers. Because of his mental illness, the embassy required intricate legal proof verifying who would be responsible for my father in America. Her resentment toward her daughter-in-law intensified. My mother resigned herself to endure whatever injustices came her way, counting the days until she could leave Jamaica to reunite with my sister and me and start a new life in America.

* * *

By April 1961, thousands of Cubans were struggling to start a new life in exile. A short, temporary one, they hoped, until they could return to Cuba. Most settled in Miami, only ninety miles from the island. They felt hope being so close to their homeland. Perhaps they thought the breezes that carried the scent of frying green plantains to them were born on the beaches of Varadero. There was comfort in knowing they were breathing the same tropical air that swept over their enslaved island. "It will soon be over, this bad dream. Soon we will go home again." They lived each day with that belief, which helped them endure the heartbreak and hardships of exile.

The deep yearning for their lost *patria* and loved ones left behind drove a brave group of Cubans to plan an invasion to liberate Cuba. Backed by the CIA, approximately 1,500 exiled Cuban men began training in Guatemala. These men were mostly ex-Batista officers, soldiers, and sons of wealthy Cuban families. The invasion was named Brigade #2506, in honor of the first volunteer who died while training in Guatemala and whose serial number was 2506.

On April 11, 1961, the first boat carrying the well-trained and equipped exiles sailed for Cuba in an attempt to reclaim their oppressed homeland. The plan was to invade the southern coast of the island at the Bahía de Cochinos—the Bay of Pigs. On April 15, the expatriates made an air raid on Cuba with two B-26 light bombers. They struck Castro's three principal military bases: Cuidad Libertad, less than half a mile from Castro's command headquarters, and the air force bases at Santiago de Oriente and at San Antonio de los Baños, near Havana. These air strikes were meant to demolish Castro's air power, thus assuring total air control for the invading Cubans, who would land two days later.

The air attack destroyed five planes in Castro's small air force, but with four British-made Sea Fury light attack bombers, one B-26, and three T-33s, Castro made a strategic comeback. He commanded the rocket-equipped Sea Furies to attack and destroy the advancing ships, which had no anti-aircraft weapons. The T-33s were set to take care of any further air attacks. Castro's planes sank three of the invasion's main vessels: The Houston, transporting the Brigade's 5th battalion; The Barbara J, the CIA's command vessel; and the freighter Rio Escondido, carrying ammunition and vital communications gear. Castro's strategy was to isolate the invasion on the beachheads. With no air or vessel aid, the exiles would be crushed.

The invasion arrived first on Playa Larga, then at its eastern entrance on Playa Girón. Early in the morning on Monday, April 17, the exiles reached Cuban soil on crafts from the ships that had left Puerto Cabezas, Nicaragua.

Castro's militia patrols saw the advance approaching and started the first fire exchange. Fired up with the expectation of U.S. military backing arriving at any moment, the valiant exiles fought hard for two days. But President Kennedy chose not to send aid, and consequently, the Cubans were annihilated and captured by Castro's forces.

On the first day of the invasion, Miami was aflame with Cuban patriotism—the exhilarating hope, despite the fear for the invaders' safety, that this was going to be the liberation of our country. That we would soon return to Cuba, to our homes, schools, friends, pets. To life as we knew it. The TV and newspapers constantly blared information about the futile battle, but it was at school where I got the details from our *Cubanitos* group. During the siege, we brought our rosaries to school and prayed for our brave compatriots every day at recess. I was worried about Raulito. His nineteen-year-old brother, Enrique, was fighting in the invasion. Most times, Raulito was so visibly upset he could not say the rosary aloud. His eyes filled with tears, and he would mouth the words, unable to speak.

After the invasion failed, Raulito did not come to school for a week. Our teacher told the class that Raulito's brother had been killed during the attack. I later found out it had happened during the first volley exchange as his craft reached the beachhead. On his first day back to school, Raulito cried at recess; he heaved and sobbed, his thin shoulders shaking. I put my arms around him, trying my best to comfort my friend as his tears fell on my blue cotton dress.

As a result of the invasion, Castro lost 161 men to the Brigade's 107 and took 1,189 prisoners. It was not until

December 23, 1962, after many had already died in captivity, that most of these prisoners were released in exchange for $53 million worth of food and medicine from the U.S.

The Bay of Pigs affair was the main cause of the Cuban missile crisis, in October 1962. After the invasion, Fidel Castro and other Cuban leaders feared a more powerful attack, this time from the United States, to take over the island. I prayed, along with thousands of exiled Cubans, for this to happen. We were so sure that it would. Castro asked the Soviet Union for military support. In return, the Russians sent forty-two nuclear missiles to the island, where three launch pads, strategically aimed to hit several major U.S. cities, including Washington, D.C., had been built.

U.S. reconnaissance planes quickly discovered what Castro had done. F8U Crusader planes flew over the missile sites and provided President Kennedy with detailed, blown-up pictures of the military installations. The Cabinet, Chiefs of Staff, and Presidential Council held meetings on what to do. The U.S. had a massive air attack planned that would wipe Cuba off the face of the earth. President Kennedy had to choose between establishing a naval blockade to prevent further shipment of arms to Cuba or bombing and invading the island. Realizing thousands of lives would be lost with an invasion, the president opted for the blockade.

President Kennedy contacted Soviet leader Nikita Khrushchev and demanded that he remove the threat to the hemisphere, but nothing was resolved. Russia remained prepared to launch the missiles, and Fidel Castro was ready with his army. President Kennedy ordered the naval blockade and gave a televised talk to a stunned nation. He explained the grave situation to the American people, promising continued surveillance of Cuba and warning that America would retaliate against any nuclear attack from the island.

The United States sent twenty-five blockade ships to Cuba, prepared for military action. If the Russian ships did not stop, the U.S. would fire a first warning. If the Russians pressed on, then the U.S. would hit the advancing ship's rudder, preventing it from advancing. At this point, the United States feared the worst. The Soviet ships, escorted by Russian submarines, continued on their way to Cuba. They paused at the blockade line. At that moment the world stood still at the brink of nuclear war. The Russian ships opted to turn back.

The United States and Russia made a final pact. The Soviets would remove the missiles and not bring them back to the island. The U.S. vowed not to invade Cuba as long as the Soviets did not install offensive weaponry again. Fidel Castro was furious with the two superpowers for reaching this agreement without his knowledge. The failed *invasión* squelched the hopes that buoyed Cuban exiles with dreams of returning soon to their *tierra libre*, their free homeland.

A few days after the invasion, Aunt Blanca and Uncle Luis invited us to their home in Coral Gables for dinner. Going to visit them was like being in Havana. They lived in a quiet neighborhood of elegant homes with manicured lawns. The nannies in their starched white uniforms pushed fancy strollers along the tree-canopied sidewalks. It was obvious to me that my relatives were not facing the hardships of exile that my sister and I were.

En route to Coral Gables that day, Aunt Emma's car cruised through Calle Ocho, 8th Street, my favorite Cuban neighborhood. Every day more Cuban stores opened up in Calle Ocho with the same names as the ones in Havana. It wasn't long before that section of Miami was labeled "Little Havana."

I rolled down the window, took in a deep breath. Cuba. My heart danced as I listened to Cuban music blasting from busy little kiosks that sold *café Cubano*, *media noche* sandwiches, and *cangrejitos de carne*, tasty pastries filled with meat. The rich aroma of sugary *pastelitos de guayaba* and *dulcecitos* floating from the *pastelería* made my mouth water. The street was normally always bursting with sounds and activity. Garrulous Cuban *recholateo* interlaced with traffic noise, people milling in and out of shops and men sitting on storefront benches, smoking cigars and grinning as they gave *piropos*, flirty compliments, to the vivacious women walking by.

But on this day, *los Cubanos* walking the streets of Calle Ocho appeared subdued, despite the upbeat music. A feeling of mourning veiled the usually animated community. The domino park was empty except for a few old men slouching on wooden chairs, wearing loose cotton shirts and faded Panama hats to shade their tanned, wrinkled faces. They communed with their friends over the smooth, small ivory rectangles while drinking *un cafecito* and puffing on cigars. As we drove by Coral Gables Park, two men were taking down a banner hung next to a huge picture of José Martí. Our car stopped at a red light, allowing me to read the idolized Cuban hero's quote imprinted on the cloth: *"No son bellas las playas del destierro, hasta que se les dice adiós"*—

"The shores of exile do not seem beautiful, until you bid them farewell."

I watched the two men fold the banner carefully, almost reverently, their faces drawn with sadness. A little boy stood nearby, waving a tiny Cuban flag at passersby. He spotted me and gave me the most remarkable smile, as if he knew me. I smiled back. We held our gaze until the car turned the corner. *These are my broken people*, I thought. At that moment, I felt an intense connection, a feeling that I was part of something so profound that I was unable to grasp its true meaning. But I understood José Martí's words. I dreaded that the shores of America would not seem beautiful to us exiled Cubans for a long, long time.

Chapter Sixteen

LA NOCHE QUEDÓ ATRÁS

The two and a half months of waiting were over.
The U.S. embassy finalized authorization for my mother's entry to the United States as a resident on May 5, 1961. When we were reunited at the Miami airport, my mother's face appeared etched by the strain of living. She was rail thin.

"*Gracias, Dios mío, al fin. Gracias.*" Her voice was tight, emotional. The twins stood quietly alongside, shifting nervously on their feet. My brother Roly draped his skeletally thin arms around my waist in an embrace.

"*Oye tiburón,* you finally got here," I said to him. He smiled, his large brown eyes dominating his drawn face. We all looked thin and anxious to one another, but we were together again. In that we found our sustenance.

Our new home in exile was a street-side apartment in a complex on South Miami Avenue, near downtown Miami. The connecting one-storied units formed several sections divided by walkways. Ours was a corner dwelling facing an ample front lawn alongside a busy main street. A side path flanked by small trees and hibiscus bushes provided privacy. This apartment maze was like nothing I'd seen before, a far cry from our gleaming white Spanish colonial house across the street from the park in Havana. In my twelve years of life I had moved so often. I had become weary of wondering if we'd ever find a permanent place to live and call our own. I studied my mother's face as she surveyed what was to be our next home. She reminded me of an embattled warrior in a *Flash Gordon* episode I had seen in Cuba. Exhausted from battle but undefeated, with a look of determination to make a difficult situation work. I could see it in her eyes; her strength had been reinforced by her children. Somehow I knew we were going to make it.

Then we walked inside. The heat in the tiny living room almost gagged me. A dank smell with a trace of stale cigarettes permeated the apartment. There was no air conditioning, not even a fan. After opening the windows it still felt like a hot oven. Our home was a minute efficiency apartment with sparse, dreary furniture and paint peeling off the walls. The front room served as both living space and kitchen area. To the left of the living room there was a closet-sized bathroom and one very small bedroom. My mother joined together the two twin beds to accommodate herself, Madeleine, and me. The boys would share the small sofa bed in the living room, and María Elena would sleep on a foldable cot next to them.

In the kitchen area, a chrome and Formica dinette set, its vinyl chair pads stained and worn, was crammed in the corner. An old refrigerator rattled on and off next to a grease-splattered gas stove. The heavily scratched countertop had a few burn marks. A sudden movement in the far corner, where a chunk of Formica was missing, caught my eye.

"¡Mami, *una cucaracha!*" my little sister screeched. I had never seen such a huge cockroach. As the insect scurried across the countertop, my mother smashed it with her shoe, white goo exploding from its shiny, dark brown body. She calmly cleaned it up and flushed it down the toilet.

"I don't want to live here," Madeleine moaned, leaning against my mother. Her soulful brown eyes were glued to the spot where the bug had been. The rest of us looked at Mami, waiting for her response.

"This is where we have to live for now," she addressed all of us. "The most important thing is that we are together again, *gracias a Dios*." She glanced at María Elena and me. "You'll see, once we get it all cleaned up it will be fine." My sister and I exchanged rueful glances. But our mother was right. After being apart for so long, dealing with the stifling heat and giant bugs was a small price to pay to be together again.

My mother's cousin Yoya, herself barely getting by in Miami, had paid for our first month's rent and bought us food and basic necessities to tide us over until we could go downtown to El Refugio, the Cuban Refugee Center. María Elena and I helped Mami spread peanut butter on slices of white bread for our snack. I took one slice, folded it in half, and handed it to Roly, who was sitting on the edge of the lumpy couch, quietly looking around, while the rest of us settled in.

"Welcome to America, *tiburón*," I said, sitting next to him. He liked it when I called him shark, a reminder of our swimming pool games at the Chateau apartment in Miramar. He struggled to form a half-smile that quickly disappeared.

"I miss Cuba," Roly said quietly. "And Consuelo, too," he added. He had a picture cradled in his hands and was looking at it intently. The small black and white photo was faded and crinkled at the edges. In it, Consuelo stood ankle-deep in the Caribbean at Kawama Beach, her thick black hair tied back, with runaway strands floating in the breeze. She was holding three-year-old Roly in her arms. They were gazing at each other with huge smiles on their faces as small waves lapped about them.

"Oh, I remember that day." I inched over to get a closer look. "That was a fun vacation even though you wrecked my sand castle." A single marble-like tear rolled down his cheek and splashed on his hand inches away from the photo. I silently cursed Fidel for my brother's sadness. Somewhere outside children laughed. A boy chasing a ball whizzed by our window. Pulling up the venetian blinds, I recognized a neighbor from Cuba.

"It's Joshi! Look, Roly, it's your friend Joshi, and there's Pedrito, too. *Mira*, come and see!"

Roly stood next to me grinning, his mouth framed with peanut butter. Hearing me, everyone came over to the window. We huddled together, staring at the group of children playing on the huge front lawn. Within minutes, we were outside with them. It felt liberating to run and play outside again, to fling open the windows and leave the front door open, with only a screen protecting us from the outside world. It took us awhile to realize we no longer had to live in fear.

Fidel Castro's revolution and subsequent alliance with the Soviet Union forced thousands of Cubans to emigrate in search of freedom, primarily to America. The U.S. considered us to be refugees fleeing from a dictatorial regime and the oppression of communism. Between the years of

La Noche Quedó Atrás

1959 and 1960, close to two thousand Cubans arrived in Miami each week. By 1961, approximately 135,000 Cubans had fled to southern Florida. Even though many of these refugees were among the wealthiest and most educated in Cuba, the majority traded their wealth for liberty in America, arriving with nothing but their will to survive. Enterprising, industrious, and grateful for America's welcoming open arms, these Cubans now earned a living washing cars, pumping gas, and working in convenience stores, fueled by the hope that soon Castro's government would be overthrown and they could return to Cuba. Cuba's upper and middle-class citizens were thankful for any work that the tolerant city of Miami had to offer them.

In February 1961, the U.S. government opened the Cuban Refugee Center in Miami, offering food and medical and financial aid to Cuban exiles. The morning after she arrived, my mother, who a month before had been driven to Havana's airport in a chauffeured Mercedes, officially registered herself and her five children for aid in America. Once a month, the government provided us with $100 cash and one large box containing dried foods and necessities such as flour, sugar, powdered eggs and milk, rice, canned beans, canned beef, soap, detergent, and toilet paper. They also included a carton of cigarettes for smokers. Our rent was $85 a month, utilities $15.

Mami joined María Elena in her quest to find a job. Every day they walked the long blocks to downtown Miami. There was no money for bus fare. In the wretched heat, they went into every store and business they passed. One miserably hot and humid afternoon in late May 1961, they came home exhausted. María Elena hurried into the bath-

Palm Trees in the Snow

room and closed the door. Despite the sound of running water in the sink, I heard her sobbing. I was worried. My big sister never cried.

My mother enrolled me in the nearby elementary school for the last month of classes. Sixth grade had been a grueling year for me to complete. This was the third school I would be attending in one term. It was a chaotic experience. There were more Cuban children than American in the steaming, overcrowded classroom. I felt invisible, as if I wasn't part of the environment surrounding me. As in the school I attended while living with Aunt Emma, at recess the Cuban children grouped together. Unlike the American students, who played games, we mostly talked, and Cuba was the usual topic. There was a stunned, disassociated feeling in our group. We seemed to be on guard, as if at any moment, our lives would change again.

The frazzled teacher, a no-nonsense older woman with myopic eyes and heavy makeup, yelled at us constantly. I felt sorry for the students who spoke no English. They were in a state of limbo and totally ignored. A few of us Cuban children who did speak English were assigned to translate for them. I often found myself daydreaming during the noisy classes. My thoughts traveled to my school in Cuba. I wondered if I would ever see the Sacred Heart *madres* and *hermanitas* or my friends again, walk the marble-floored halls in silence, or wade barefooted in the cool waters of the school's Río Kibú while picnicking on a saint's day holiday.

The teacher's shrill voice, ordering us to open our books to page whatever, would startle me back into reality. A reality I wanted no part of. I did what I had to do to get by and counted the days until mid-June.

My father and grandmother arrived in Miami shortly after my mother and siblings. They moved in with Aunt Blanca and Uncle Luis in Coral Gables. At Papi's insistence, Tita Lala brought him to see us a week later. They took a bus to Miami and stopped at a convenience store near our apartment, where Papi bought us cookies and candy. Sitting under a palm tree in the front yard, I waited anxiously for their arrival. When he was still a long block away, I recognized my father's tall frame and casual saunter. I sprung to my feet, waved, and dashed down the sidewalk to meet them. I knew from his broad smile and trademark wave, an arm raised high with an open hand held momentarily, that Papi was himself. There was no doubt in my mind as his arms wrapped around me in a secure embrace.

My father was talkative and affectionate toward us children and Mami. As he handed out the sweets, we acted as if they were bags of gold. We had not eaten many treats since we left Cuba. My grandmother and mother hardly spoke to one another. Tita Lala sat stiffly on our old couch, her legs crossed daintily at the ankles. She placed her leather purse on her lap, then folded her hands on top of it as if afraid to touch the sofa. She took in her surroundings with repugnance. I brought her the glass of cold water she asked for and sat next to her. My grandmother was appalled to see me barefooted.

"But it's so hot, Tita," I said, stretching my toes out in front of me.

"They're filthy. You're going to get a scratch and then an infection, *por tu vida*," she castigated me. "Put your sandals back on," she added reproachfully, with ill-disguised annoyance in her voice. While I reluctantly slipped into my flip-flops I recalled my grandmother's promise to take me to Paris on my thirteenth birthday. It seemed foreign to me now, like the woman sitting next to me with flushed cheeks, pinched lips, and fiery eyes. My grandmother had washed her hands of us financially and emotionally.

When it was time for them to leave, my father paced our tiny apartment, checking out the bedroom and bathroom. He picked up the empty carton from the Refugee Center and slammed it down on the kitchen counter.

"Ninina, you can't live like this," he told my mother. "This is not right. I need to help you and the children." My grandmother and mother exchanged anxious looks. It was as if they knew what was coming and what they had to do.

"*Cálmate*, Rolando," Mami said, controlled. "*Todo está bien*—we'll be all right."

"No. Let me stay and help you. I'm your husband, for God's sake." His voice was escalating. Madeleine whimpered. The boys stopped eating their *merienda* and stared from the kitchen table.

"*Vamos*, Rolando," my grandmother said forcefully. She reached for his arm. He swung it away.

"No, Mamá, leave me alone. I'm not leaving my family like this." The agony in my father's voice made my stomach tighten.

"Here, Rolando, it's time for your medicine." My grandmother gave him a sedative with a glass of water to wash it down. Hesitantly, his strong, tanned hand reached out to get it. I knew he would soon be quiet, zombie-like. Five minutes later, like two strangers, my father and grandmother walked past me and were gone.

After they left, my mother explained to us that we would not be seeing my father as often as we had in Cuba, when we could frequently visit him in the sanatorium. He was under Tita Lala's care now and would live with her and our relatives. He depended on my grandmother to bring him to visit us, and I could see that was not something she enjoyed.

I felt exiled from my father and his family, as if we were living in two separate worlds. *Why did our relatives live in comfort while we had to struggle? Weren't we supposed to help one another?* It was difficult to comprehend how only three months before, we had lived in a beautiful house with maids, nannies, and a chauffeur who drove us to ballet lessons, Rancho Perea, and our private schools. Now we had nothing. Lying in bed that night, my cotton nightgown stuck to my body with perspiration. The pillowcase beneath my head was sodden with my sweat. I thought of our relatives in Coral Gables, sleeping peacefully in their air-conditioned rooms. I pulled up the venetian blinds as far as they could go, but no breeze came through the window, only the fading sounds of car motors, night birds chirping, the faint smell of gardenias from a garden nearby. Gardenias. Cuba. Tears pricked my eyes. I resented my grandmother for casting us aside. Mostly I detested *el destino*, that merciless thief, destiny, who stole my Papi—this time, I feared, for good.

One afternoon in June 1961, our screen door flung open and closed with a loud bang.

"Hey everybody, I've got good news!" María Elena

announced cheerily. She flew into the kitchen, where my mother was preparing an omelette for lunch with fresh eggs our neighbors had given us.

"*¿Qué pasó, m'ija?*" Mami set the spatula on the stove and wiped her hands on a dishtowel. She watched my sister pour herself a glass of water from a plastic pitcher in the refrigerator.

"*¡Encontré trabajo!* I got a job!" María Elena snitched one of Roly's crackers as he bickered with Jorge over the butter.

"*¡Ay, qué bueno!*" my mother sighed, relieved. "Where? Doing what?"

"I'm going to be a secretary. Remember the law firm across the street from that new Cuban restaurant you liked?"

"Ah, *sí.*" Mami nodded.

"When do you start?" I asked, setting the table.

"Next week—*and*, guess how much I'll be making?" Her eyes were glowing with excitement. "$35 a week. *¿No es fantástico?* Now we can afford to take the bus downtown, Mami; no more walking *en este calor asqueroso.*"

The following Friday, when my sister received her first paycheck, my mother put aside $5. "If we save a little each week, we'll have enough to buy some extras," she said, serving us our dinner of red-bean *potaje* and white rice. "I think today we should celebrate María Elena's new job." She smiled at us, the proverbial Cheshire cat. Our eyes flicked from one to the other. "*Sí,* after dinner we'll go to White Castle and treat ourselves to a milkshake, *¿qué les parece?*" Our little apartment was inundated with shrieks of joy.

"*¡Un batido, sí,* Mami, *sí!*" we cheered simultaneously. That steamy evening, our happy caravan walked to the corner White Castle. We sat at a picnic table under a shady palm tree and savored our cold milkshakes.

Soon after my sister's employment, my mother found two jobs: one selling Avon products and the other peddling bidets and bathroom supplies. Every day in the sweltering summer heat, she walked door to door for hours. Since our exodus from Cuba, I had begun to observe my mother in a totally new light. An unfamiliar side to her personality was emerging, as if it had been restrained and now was set loose.

I had always been aware of her love for me, but in Cuba, I didn't often experience it directly. When we were young children, the *tatas* were our primary caregivers. The nannies were the ones responsible for our schoolwork, our playtime, and our park and beach excursions. They tucked us in bed each night and read us our bedtime stories; tended our skinned knees, bumps, and bruises; and settled our fights. In my mother's case, it was even more so because of my father's illness. As it progressed, his care demanded most of her time, with constant visits to the sanatorium and trips abroad during his long treatments. Her concern for him consumed her both physically and emotionally. Now in exile and legally separated from my father, she was solely in charge of her five young children. It was as if we were reborn to her in that wretched apartment in Miami, and for the first time ever she gave us each her all.

I was also getting to know the twins for the first time. In Havana, because my father was unable to handle being with all five children at the same time, we were often separated from the twins. At home, it seemed Consuelo was often whisking Madeleine and Jorge here and there, enforcing the Cuban custom that very young children had a place of their own at certain times, often apart from their older siblings and parents. For example, at mealtimes, young children would eat at a small table in the hallway adjacent to the dining room so as not to disrupt the adults' meal with their inevitable childish behavior.

When our golden years of wealth and privilege in Cuba were shattered by the communist revolution, we were thrown together in exile as a penniless, fatherless family with an intensity we had never experienced before. We did everything together now, and it was a new and comforting experience for me.

My mother continued saving money whenever possible. We looked forward to Fridays, when she would take us to the nearby grocery store. Here we took turns buying one special treat we wanted. I almost always asked for Oreos. Mami bought extra items like bread, eggs, cereal, crackers, milk, and fresh vegetables to supplement our refugee rations. She tried to stock up on several cans of Spam to make her famous *carne fría*, a concoction she invented to camouflage the bland taste of the dreaded *carne del refugio*, the Refugee Center's rank-tasting canned beef. Mixing the beef with Spam, eggs, milk, onions, and seasonings, my mother then shaped the mixture into a long roll, dipped it in beaten eggs, and rolled it in breadcrumbs. She then wrapped the meat in foil and baked it. My mother's *carne fría* was eaten warm the first time, then, after refrigerating the remaining roll, we would eat it cold, hence its name.

My mother's spirit of survival, her inner strength, and her fierce determination to provide a better life for us shone before my eyes during those grueling, hot summer months in Miami. She made the worst time of our young lives memorable, not because of the hardships we had to endure, but because of the joy we felt being blessed with health and being together in a free country.

On my last day of school in June 1961, my mother was sitting at the kitchen table reading a letter when I walked in the front door, happy to be done with sixth grade forever. Holding the letter with one hand, Mami rubbed her forehead with the other. Then, with one long, slow motion, she ran her fingers from the temple all the way back to the nape of her neck. My mother had received news from her parents in Cuba, telling her that in two days, they, too, would be leaving "on vacation" to Costa Rica.

After the fiasco of the Bay of Pigs invasion, exiled Cubans were overwrought with anxiety for their loved ones still in Cuba, where the political situation was worsening with a brutal repression. Communication by phone was nearly impossible. My father's family had been able to leave Cuba, but some of my mother's still remained. My grandparents, Mama and Bibi, were our biggest concern.

When his children and grandchildren began to leave Cuba, my grandfather knew no peace. He vowed he would not leave the island until they had all left safely. In May of 1961, after all his children had left, Bibi began to plan his and my grandmother's escape from communism. My grandfather knew that soon the government would appropriate everything he owned, just like it had with Rancho Perea. Because of his government position as the vice-treasurer of the ICEA, the Cuban Institute for the Stabilization of Sugar, Bibi was aware that he was *fichado*—the government had his number and would not easily let him go.

By late spring of 1961, the Castro regime had imposed stiffer regulations on citizens leaving the island. All flights to America had ended in January 1961 as a result of broken relations between Cuba and the United States. In Havana, there were rumors that soon airlines would no longer be permitted to make reservations for any departure from Cuba. Using whatever connections he had, my grandfather was able to book a flight for him and my grandmother to leave Havana on June 8, 1961.

My grandparents' odyssey to freedom was preserved in letters that he wrote to my mother before he left Cuba and then from exile. Using a combination of narrative and his own words, I have attempted to translate the painstakingly detailed information my grandfather penned.

The only available way out of the island for my grandparents was through Mexico City, then on to Costa Rica, to which their daughter Milly and son Gustavo and their families had fled. Bibi knew he could not leave the country without authorization from the ICEA. The conditions there were worsening by day. *Milicianos* had taken over the Institute, performing daily body searches on all workers entering and leaving the building.

The savage repression by what the employees called the Cuban Gestapo, groups formed by the new "Spanish Volunteers" within all business offices, led to the arrest and abuse of *gusanos*, the suspected anticommunist Cubans. Workers denounced coworkers, resulting in twenty arrests in my grandfather's department alone. Bibi's assistant, a man who was imprisoned and later released, told my grandfather of his experience.

Those arrested were held from fifteen days to a month

in improvised prisons at Hotel Blanquita, Palacio Deportes, Hotel Príncipe, and La Cabaña. Men and women were imprisoned together. They were not fed for the first three days and had no change of clothes or access to bathroom facilities. The communists took the prisoners' personal belongings—money, jewelry, papers—and had their homes searched. In a letter, Bibi wrote: "This tragedy weighed heavy on my spirit, like a nightmare that relentlessly tormented every hour of my days."

Though suspected of being a *gusano*, my grandfather was spared from arrest because he was greatly needed at work. The government was in the process of dissolving the ICEA, and Bibi was an integral part of the procedure. He knew he was under constant surveillance.

Bibi met with the Institute's administrator and requested vacation time in June. He was turned down on the spot because of ICEA's dissolution. "That is precisely why I do not wish to be here." My grandfather presented his argument. "I helped found the ICEA, and it is too painful for me to see it end." The administrator was adamant. He told Bibi the final decision would have to be made by the Federal Administrator of the Sugar Refinery, who was a well-known communist. My grandfather met with him the next day.

Bibi was told how indispensable he was, highly admired and respected. They were extremely grateful to him for his dedication to his work, the man said. He suggested Bibi postpone his trip. The administrator concluded by offering my grandfather the even higher government position of General Administrator of the Sugar Refinery, along with a considerable raise. With this new position, Bibi would not be subjected to the daily searches or have to deal with the militia in any way.

The following morning, after a sleepless night, my grandfather met with his superior again. It took two hours for him to convince the administrator to authorize his June vacation. In order to accomplish this, Bibi accepted the new position beginning upon his return, knowing in his heart that this trip would have no return. My grandfather had one month to prepare for the first and only trip he would take out of Cuba. He wrote:

> *It is a sad and difficult thing to have to undo and tear apart your home. To sell and give away all your possessions in order to start a new life with one hand in front and the other behind you. I have to leave things behind that had been collected and acquired with love and devotion. My precious books, stamp collection, my paintings. Our antique Spanish colonial bedroom set and all our furniture; all my priceless porcelain figurines, my writing, the family heirlooms. How do I leave behind my father's mementos? The infinity of irreplaceable things that were a part of my life, the fruit of fifty years of intense labor in my life. In addition to all this, my beloved finca, Rancho Perea, robbed from me, with everything in it. Our home in Belén, our car, our real-estate properties.*

The black market was thriving in Havana, as wealthy Cubans quickly sold their possessions in order to flee the island before their homes and valuables were appropriated. My grandfather sold all the belongings he could in return for U.S. money. He arranged to leave that which he could not sell, liquidate, or give away with my grandmother's cousin, Eugenia. Having been close to my grandmother during their childhood, Eugenia, a quiet, mild-mannered woman in her early seventies, was deeply devoted to Mama. She had never married and had become anxious living alone in her mansion in Vedado after Castro took over the island. My grandparents invited her to live with them, and she had done so for the past two years. But Eugenia was terrified of exile and chose to remain in Cuba. My grandparents left their home in Belén, along with all their remaining belongings and those of their children, in her care. But Tía Eugenia was not left alone. Consuelo, who had asked to stay on with my grandparents after my mother left Cuba, also remained in *la casa de Belén* to help the elderly woman.

In her forties now, Consuelo had never married. Her grandmother, with whom she spent every weekend, had recently died. Her older sister, Carmen, and her family had moved to Santiago, and her cousin, Cuca, had married a communist and was working in the sugar cane fields of Matanzas.

Meanwhile, Consuelo had begun to have a change of heart concerning the revolution. A few days before Mama and Bibi fled Cuba, Consuelo asked to speak to them. My mother's lifelong friend and our nanny then told my grandparents how much she missed my mother and us children. She was realizing that Castro's revolution was not what she had hoped for. A devout Catholic, Consuelo was both furious and terrified at Castro's interference with the Catholic Church, restricting its religious celebrations and processions. Soon after, he closed the doors of all

Catholic churches, forcing hundreds of nuns and priests to leave the island. The practice of Catholicism became prohibited in Cuba.

Consuelo's green eyes were tearful. "I am going to write to Señora Nini and ask her to send for me, *caballero*," she told my grandfather. An air of optimism softened her face. Bibi let out a weary sigh.

"Señora Nini and the children are struggling in America, Consuelo." He said the words slowly, as if to himself. "They have no money. Our family has lost everything. I'm sorry, Consuelo. I don't think that will be possible."

"*Pero caballero*, I know she needs my help, and I miss the children so..." She sobbed in desperation. "I should have never turned against Señora Nini, *nunca*." She wiped her tears with her white linen apron. "Señora, *perdóneme*," Consuelo cried out, looking at my grandmother.

"There is nothing to forgive, Consuelo," my grandmother comforted her. "This revolution has been a disgrace for all of us."

"But I have to try, Señora." Consuelo composed herself. "I don't want to stay in Cuba. I belong with Señora Nini and the children." As she thanked my grandparents and left the room, Mama looked at Bibi imploringly. Before she could utter a word, my grandfather answered her plea.

"No, Bebita. There is nothing we can do."

Three weeks later my mother received a letter from Consuelo. I sat alongside Mami at the kitchen table while she read the contents of the onionskin paper. Our nanny wrote that our home in Marianao had been partitioned into four apartments; that it was hard to find aspirin in Havana and that she missed us terribly. Then Consuelo asked Mami to bring her to America to live with us.

"¡*Ay*, Consuelo!" Mami sighed aloud to herself. "I have no money, no way to get you out of Cuba now."

That night I wrote Consuelo a letter. I carefully taped four aspirin pills on the paper, along with two sticks of Juicy Fruit gum, which had always been our *tata's* favorite. When Consuelo wrote back, she asked me not to bother sending her any more aspirin or gum. She never received either.

"I will see you and your family again someday," Consuelo ended her letter. "I will find a way." Her words haunted me. Each time the news televised a rescue of Cuban *balseros* who had drifted into American waters on their flimsy canvas and inner-tube rafts, I searched the emaciated, sun-blistered faces for Consuelo's. Not seeing her, I feared she had been part of that journey and had died of thirst along the way, or worse, had been attacked by a shark as she attempted to reach us in America.

I always thought Consuelo would come. But she stayed in Cuba, living with our family's only remaining relative in Havana. Our *tata* helped her raise her three daughters and faithfully served the family until she died at the age of 88.

My grandfather's letters to my mother helped me reconstruct the day he and my grandmother left Cuba:

June 8, 1961. A famous day in the story of my life. I leave behind a whole lifetime. I go in search of peace, my children and grandchildren and freedom. In Cuba remain invaluable memories, joys and sorrows, past glories, happy moments and painful deeds; the tombs of my parents, brothers and friends. I leave behind my homeland. Only God knows when I will see her again. Only God knows with how much pain I have left her behind and only God knows the agony one feels in this absence. But if this is my destiny, I give thanks to God because He is allowing me to be reunited with my children and grandchildren and has given me the hope of a better future for all of you. We have nothing, but we are full of optimism because we have our faith, our lives and our health intact to battle on with. Our trip began at the airport search office. We were fortunate that we were not forced to take our clothes off. Much of our jewelry was confiscated, but we managed to smuggle the most valuable ones.

My grandparents' worst moment during this search was when Mama almost lost her beloved Virgencita, the statue of Our Lady of Mercy. Knowing that the *milicianos* would seize all religious articles, my grandmother had dressed the statue as a doll and warned my grandfather that she would not leave Cuba without her. When the soldiers questioned her about the "doll," she calmly told them it was a gift for her granddaughter. The *miliciano* in charge, who had just confiscated my grandmother's pearl necklace, ripped the doll from her hands and began tearing off the clothes to inspect it. My horrified grandmother wept, begging him to stop while my grandfather looked on, helpless, trying to comfort his wife. Another *miliciano*, a young man in his twenties, intervened and convinced his superior to let it go. "*¡Qué carajo!*" the older militiaman cursed, thrusting the half-dressed statue at him. Gently, the young *miliciano* handed it to my grandmother. "*Que Dios te bendiga, hijo,*" Mama said above a whisper, tears streaming down her face.

"*De nada,* Señora," he replied, visibly moved by my

grandmother's gratitude. Painstakingly dressing the statue again, Mama reverently held it close to her chest, so protectively that she never once set it down during the remainder of the trip.

Bibi's letter continued:

Our flight was greatly delayed. We were scheduled to depart at 4 p.m. but were not allowed to leave until 7:30 p.m. Until the last minute, there were interrogations, searches, and delays. We landed in Merida, Mexico, at 10 p.m. and left at midnight en route to Mexico City. We arrived at 2:30 a.m. Exhausted, we thought we would be able to go to a hotel to rest and visit the city later on that day until our flight left, but instead we were detained in the airport waiting room. We were kept there without sleep or rest and were escorted by police to the airport restaurant for a meal. I was heartbroken. I was looking forward to visiting the Basílica of Our Lady of Guadalupe, a dream of both your mother's and mine, and experiencing the beauty of the capital of the country where my father was born. Finally, we were let go at 1:30 p.m. on June 9. We boarded a jet plane to Guatemala, where we connected one final time en route to our destination, Costa Rica, and freedom.

All in all, my daughter, it was a good trip for being such a long one. After arriving in Costa Rica, I wanted to forget everything. It was like a bad nightmare. When I recall our trip, it is as if it was someone else's story, not mine.

I am hopeful for a better future and that soon we will know peace and good times again. While we await that happiness, we trust in God and the Blessed Mother, who have always taken care of us and solved all our problems.

Kisses to all from all with the blessings of your father,
Gustavo

My grandparents began their lives in exile living with their daughter Milly and her family in San José, Costa Rica. Bibi wrote my mother:

It is so difficult, after a life filled with hard work and sacrifices striving toward a peaceful old age, to have to start all over again, when my strength and energy are no longer what they were when I started fifty years ago. I know I am not the only Cuban going through this hardship, and I am one of the lucky ones that was able to get away from the maulings of the communist beast, the bloody titan who is destroying our Cuba.

I give thanks to God every day for the good and noble children He has blessed me with and for the invaluable treasure that is my beloved grandchildren, so beautiful and intelligent, who are my pride and joy and hope for the future. My family has always been the greatest blessing of my life. Even though God has crowned my life with all these blessings, on a bad day I cannot help but feel discouraged, as I realize the rewards of my life's material work, obtained through sacrifice for my old age in order to never be a burden to my children, and be able to help them, has been destroyed and lost forever due to the devil who tortures Cuba. In the end, all we can do is totally accept the will of God and never lose faith in Him.

La noche quedó atrás, mi hija. *The night, being the inferno that is Cuba today, was left behind. We have to hope that the dawn of our future, especially our children's and grandchildren's, will be realized in these free lands of America, where there still exists democracy and a decent form of living and thinking.*

Exactly two weeks after my grandparents left Cuba, members of the Office of the Recuperation of Goods, the official title of Cuba's legalized government thieves, went to my grandparents' house and took a complete inventory. They gave cousin Eugenia four days to move out. She was permitted to take her personal belongings and the contents of her bedroom. Eugenia immediately made plans with Consuelo to move in with my grandparents' niece, the only other remaining relative in Cuba, who was married to a doctor known to be a staunch communist. Terrified of getting in trouble with the government, Eugenia followed orders and took with her only her personal things. She left behind all the family members' belongings, including my mother's, that had been entrusted to her care. All of my grandfather's real-estate properties, and our home, La Coronela, were also confiscated.

The day after Eugenia and Consuelo moved out, an army truck came and *milicianos* emptied my grandparents' beautiful home. After they left, a next-door neighbor, a woman who had been friends with my grandmother, retrieved some photos that had fallen out of albums as the soldiers tossed them into the truck. She took these pictures with her when she left Cuba for Miami, hoping to someday give them to a member of our family. Many years later, a few of these photos reached my mother's hands. One of them is an 8 x 10 black-and-white portrait of Mami on her wedding day. The bride's expression is pensive; her eyes are downcast, gazing at her gown's elaborate lace train. They seem fixed on the exact spot where a *miliciano's* boot print irreparably damaged the picture.

As I pore through my grandfather's letters, I am in awe of his philosophic resignation and acceptance of the difficulties in his life. I cannot imagine the anguish he and my grandmother felt as they left their homeland for the first time in their lives, fully aware that they might never return. Their once close-knit family had been unraveled by the revolution, scattering their children and grandchildren throughout Costa Rica, Mexico, and the United States. My loss was insignificant compared to theirs. I had a child's resilience. But in their mid-sixties, how did my grandparents endure the pain of such great losses? How did they deal with the uncertainty of their future in a foreign country? My answer came in one of Bibi's letters from exile: "I have faith that someday we will get all our things back. For now, we cannot dwell on our losses. We have to forget <u>everything</u> that we had before so we can think about what we have now. We must be thankful to have our most valuable belongings still with us: our lives, our faith, and our freedom."

In spite of the sadness that weighed down his spirit in exile, my grandfather always searched for the silver lining in the many dark clouds that filled his days. His unselfish, fathomless love for his family deeply inspire me. Bibi will always be the glowing candle in my darkness. He never gave up hope, and his indomitable spirit was victorious as it left the night behind.

Chapter Seventeen

TÚ SÍ PUEDES

It had been a scorcher of a day in Miami in August 1961. The blistering midday heat kept us from playing outdoors for long. To pass the lethargic hours we stayed inside reading, exchanging books and comics with our neighboring friends. We did not have a TV or radio. I wrote letters to my father and sketched pictures of Cuba: of Rancho Perea, our home, my school, the park, Kawama Beach, and my dog, Lazy. I needed to create a scrapbook of my memories of Cuba.

I was glad that summer was almost over. Our confining apartment, with the stifling heat and humidity, had become close to intolerable. On some days, a rusty thermometer hooked outside our kitchen window registered as high as 102 degrees. The thick air felt like warm hands pressing my face. As the heat relented by late afternoon, we kids bolted outside as if released from captivity. I sat on our front steps sketching, the dry, brownish grass prickly under my bare feet. At sunset, neighbors trickled out of their apartments to welcome the respite of the evening breeze.

Our communal front lawn resembled a neighborhood park. Animated *recholateos* and *dime-y-diretes*, conversations and gossiping, filled the air with fast, clicking Spanish. It was there that our life in exile was played out. A comfortable camaraderie existed among the apartment complex's tenants, many of whom were friends and neighbors from Havana. Parents sat on folding chairs under shady palm trees, visiting with friends while their children played *chucho escondido*, tag and hide and seek.

The main topic of daily conversation among the adults was always the same.

"Maybe next week, or next month, we will all return to Cuba," Pedrito's mother said, a deep longing in her voice.

"Remember walking along the *malecón*?" Joshi's father relived in detail the pleasure of strolling along the famous seaside boulevard in Havana, salty mist spraying the tropical air as the Caribbean waves crashed against the low sea wall. Others reminisced about the life in Havana they once knew. They yearned for the sugary sands of Varadero Beach. They clung to the ever-shrinking hope of recuperating all that was left behind.

The exiled Cuban community was steadfast in their belief that Castro's revolution would not survive much longer. How could a young *guerrillero* with an army of rebels convince the island's democracy-hopeful people to accept his communist dictatorship and menacing alliance with Russia? The exiles were convinced that any day the people in Cuba would revolt and put an end to this terrible nightmare. And then, with the help of the United States, Cuba would be a free, democratic republic.

But while the Miami refugees pined away for their lost homeland, the well-educated, enormously self-confident, charismatic Fidel Castro was weaving a spell over the Cuban people that increased their loyalty to *el líder*. Spanish colonialism on the island was all but ended. Castro understood his people. He constantly mingled with them, inspiring them to work hard for a better life that only *la revolución Cubana* would bring.

Cuban music always drifted out from a neighbor's window. On that day, the radio blared an unfamiliar song: "C'mon baby, let's do-o-o the twist." The man's voice sang on: "And it goes like this." Several teenagers were dancing the new rave on the lawn. Imitating them, I gyrated my hips from side to side, my jet-black ponytail swinging to the beat of the music. It reminded me of doing the hula-hoop in Cuba.

But the heat soon got to me and I headed to the opposite corner of the yard for some cold lemonade, where my mother sat talking with Lilí and Vicente, the parents of Alberto, María Elena's boyfriend. I liked them. Lilí was a soft-spoken woman with dark wavy hair framing her fine-boned face. Everyone loved Vicente. Easygoing and laid-back, he was always *choteando* with his effervescent sense of humor.

"*Sí,* Ninina, you've got two big advantages for making the move," Vicente said as I approached them. "You know English, and you have friends in Pennsylvania."

The Cubans in our complex were anxious to find higher-paying jobs to provide a better home for their families. The heavy influx of refugees in Miami was making the job search difficult. Factories were full, and stores were not hiring.

"I think your idea is excellent, Ninina," Lilí put in, smiling at me as I joined them. "*¿Quieres limonada?*" she asked me, starting to pour lemonade in a plastic tumbler.

"*Sí, gracias.*" I plopped on the grass next to my mother and reached for the icy drink. I leaned my back on the side of Mami's folding chair, sensing the importance of their discussion.

"Doylestown sounds like a good place to live," Lilí continued. I stopped guzzling my lemonade and looked up at my mother.

"We're going to live in Doylestown?"

"We're going to try our best," my mother answered. The determination in her voice made it sound like a done deal. Thinking of my girlfriend Kathy in Doylestown, with whom I had corresponded from Cuba, I sprung to my feet.

"I'm going to write Kathy and tell her we're coming back to Doylestown," I announced happily. The thought of snow made me forget the heat as I sprinted off to our apartment.

As I observed my mother's resolve, my grandfather's words resounded in my mind: *Tú sí puedes*—yes you can. Mami had often told us that Bibi used those words to encourage her during difficult times in her life. As a child, when she was terrified of night-time thunderstorms and had to stay in her bed. When my father's illness spiraled dangerously and she had to make the devastating decision to separate. When she had to send me out of Cuba alone, not knowing if she would ever see me again.

I had first heard those words in Lumberville when I told my mother that I could not go to school because I didn't know English. *Tú sí puedes…*

My mother wrote to three Doylestown friends that she'd made when we lived there in 1956-57. Mami asked for their help in relocating to Pennsylvania. Within ten days, their response was unanimous: "Come up right away, and we will help you."

With their combined savings, Lilí, Vicente, Alberto, and my mother came up with $60 to buy a used car. Vicente and Alberto found a 1955 Chevy; it had no heat but was in fair condition. Once they arrived in Doylestown, Lilí and Vicente planned to take a bus to New York to visit relatives, then return to Miami. Mami and Alberto, who was also moving north with us, would give themselves one week's time to find work in Doylestown. If things did not pan out, they would return to Miami.

Alberto had proposed to María Elena in Cuba, shortly before the mayhem of leaving the island broke out. Assuming that their wedding would take place soon after we were settled in America, he had made the commitment of staying with us in Doylestown instead of returning to Miami with his parents. Exile had forced my mother to toss some of our culture's courtship rules out the window. In Cuba it would be unheard of to have your daughter's *novio* living under the same roof. But due to our circumstances, Alberto was now undeniably a part of our family.

My mother left María Elena in charge of us four children. Using some of the little money she had scrounged for the trip, Mami ordered an inexpensive *cantina* service to deliver daily meals for us while she was gone. As happy as I was about returning to Doylestown and not having to endure a hot, overcrowded seventh-grade classroom in Miami, I was not looking forward to another separation from my mother. Aware of my growing anxiety, she reassured me: one week. By the end of that time we would be together again, either in Doylestown or in Miami. If she remained in Doylestown, the Refugee Center would provide airfare for us to relocate.

My mother seemed upbeat on Thursday, September 6, 1961, the day we saw them off on their journey.

"I'm going to find a better life for us," she said decisively when she kissed us all goodbye. The car was packed with minimum luggage, several thermoses of coffee, and a cooler filled with sandwiches, fruit, cookies, water, juice, and sweet guava paste for energy. Memories of the day I left Cuba pelted my thoughts with anxiety as I watched the old Chevy sputter out from the curb and into the stream of traffic.

The trip went smoothly with the exception of a flat tire and the unexpected expense of a ferry ride to cross over to Norfolk, Virginia. The $70 that they had barely stretched to cover for their stay at the Doylestown Inn on Saturday night.

On Sunday morning, Don and Erma Sands offered the weary, hungry group a hearty welcome breakfast at the inn. My mother had befriended Erma through our school in 1957. The Sandses owned a shoe store in town, where we had been customers. With four children of their own, they opened their hearts and home to my mother and her friends, offering to share all meals with them. Don and Erma accommodated Lilí and Vicente in their guest room and rented two rooms in a neighbor's home across the street for Mami and Alberto.

The other friend my mother had contacted was now the public school system's superintendent. Marion Franco-Ferreira was an assertive woman, well respected in the small community. She and the Sandses had been researching jobs for Mami and Alberto. Being an educator, Marion's influence was limited to that field. She needed help from someone with business authority and a big heart. Marion knew what she was doing when she phoned Ed Howard.

Marion and Ed had worked together on the school board. Married with five children, he was president of the PTA at his children's elementary school. Ed was also president of the National Fiberstock Company in Philadelphia. Hoping he might know of available jobs, Marion asked Ed to meet with her. She told him how she and Mami had become friends in 1957. She reminisced about her visit to Havana, where she met our extended family at Rancho Perea. After explaining my mother's struggle in Miami, she concluded, "These people need jobs, Ed, and a place to stay when the children arrive. I want to help settle them in Doylestown. Can you help?"

The Howards were active members of their church. They were also involved in various community activities and were already committed to several projects. Afraid of biting off more than he could chew, Ed told Marion he was interested in helping but had to discuss the matter with his wife first.

"Hey honey, how would you like to be part of a cultural experience?" Ed Howard waltzed into his kitchen and planted a kiss on his wife's cheek. Barbara Howard was draining hot noodles for dinner.

"What did you volunteer us for now, Edward?" While feeding their dog, Ed told his wife about his meeting with Marion.

"Geez, Ed, I don't know," Barbara said halfway through the story. "Who are these people?"

"Marion knows them well. She even met the entire family when she vacationed in Cuba." Barbara stopped slicing the meatloaf.

"Cuba? You mean, from Fidel Castro's revolutionary mess?"

"Yeah, honey. This is one gutsy lady, this Ninina." Ed spread out the dishes on the counter for his wife to serve. "She's lost everything. Her country, her wealth, she's separated from her mentally ill husband, and she's got five young kids to raise, just like us."

"Wow... and she came to Doylestown by herself?"

"On a wing and a prayer," he nodded.

"She's come this far, Ed. There must be something we can do," she said with a sudden resolve. "We've got plenty of room here. We'll make it work."

"Are you sure, Barb?"

"Positive. Let's tell the kids at dinner."

The next morning Ed Howard met with my mother and Alberto at his office in Philadelphia. Mami thought the tall, outgoing American had an easy smile and a ready wit. She liked him from the start. With Alberto's background in business administration and ability to speak English, Ed hired him on the spot to work in his accounting department. He then invited Mami and Alberto to his home that afternoon to meet his family.

When my mother stepped into the foyer of the Howards' home on Maple Avenue, she felt instantly welcome. An easy rapport between her and Barbara sparked a unique friendship—one that would last a lifetime.

"You were not at all what I had imagined," Barbara revealed to my mother. "I expected a shy, dark-haired woman who couldn't speak English. Instead, you are this feisty strawberry blonde, with your own version of English."

Mami and Alberto sat with Ed and Barbara in their warm living room, where my mother shared her plight with them. As Mami spoke, Barbara instinctively got up off the couch across from her and sat on the floor next to my mother, listening intently. She abruptly placed her hand on my mother's arm. Barbara looked at her husband.

"Ed, we have to help them." He nodded. Barbara turned to my mother. "Ninina, you and your children are welcome to live with us. We will help you make that good life here in Doylestown." She held my mother's hand firmly, as Mami sat speechless.

"That's settled then." Ed sprung to his feet, heading for the telephone. "We've got work to do, honey." It was late afternoon by then, but Ed Howard felt there was still enough time to tackle the top-priority issues: a job for María Elena and bringing us children to Doylestown as soon as possible. He phoned my sister in Miami, interviewed her, and offered her a secretarial position in his company.

Next he called the Refugee Center. Due to the growing problem of overcrowding in Miami, the Center was glad to assist Cuban families in leaving the area, but in order to do so, they required proof of employment. Ed verified Alberto and María Elena's jobs. The Refugee Center then provided airplane tickets for us children to reunite with our mother.

With two phone calls, a man my mother barely knew

had helped realize her hopes for a brighter future. "Don't worry, Ninina," Ed told her, flashing his huge grin. "We'll find that job for you, too." During the following week, while we prepared to leave Miami, my mother found work in a hosiery factory in town.

It didn't take long to prepare for our trip to Pennsylvania. We each had only one small suitcase, packed with basically the same belongings we had brought from Cuba: our clothes. We left Miami on September 17, 1961.

I had no regrets leaving our cramped, hot apartment with its occasional fat *cucarachas*. But en route to the airport, a part of me already missed Miami and the way it reminded me of Cuba. My spirits livened up thinking of Doylestown, snow, and my American school friends, though I was skeptical about meeting the family with whom we would live for a while. Would we ever put down roots of our own?

Chapter Eighteen

Doylestown de Mis Amores

As our plane prepared for landing, happy memories of my father and our previous trip to Pennsylvania ganged up in my mind. This time Papi would not be waiting for us at the Philadelphia airport. His radiant smile floated in my thoughts, the joy on his face as he watched us hurry down the airplane's open staircase and into his outstretched arms.

My father was now totally out of our lives. Tita Lala had discouraged our phone calls, claiming they upset him. All I could do was write to him. He answered me periodically, but most times his short letters made little sense. A few lines or a couple of sentences, often signed Rolando. *Did he realize he was writing to me, his daughter?* After awhile I stopped writing him so often. I had decided that the personal disconnection I felt from my father after reading his notes was too painful.

"Welcome to Philadelphia, folks," the pilot announced cheerily. "We've got a beautiful 73 degrees out there and plenty of sunshine." I absentmindedly smoothed out the skirt of my suit, the one I wore when I left Cuba and was now fast outgrowing. I picked up my old train case. *Here we go again.*

The American man, Mr. Howard, was the tallest man

I had ever seen. At well over six feet, long legged and lanky, he sported a sharp crew cut and dark-rimmed eyeglasses. His wide smile showcased a mouthful of gleaming white teeth as his cheeks formed big dimples. Approaching us on the airstrip alongside my mother, he took huge strides to reach us. "Glad to meet you kids," he said, giving us all bear hugs as if we were close relatives he hadn't seen in a while.

I instantly liked Mr. Howard's friendly, casual style. There was an easy, "what you see is what you get" air about him. But still, I was quiet during the forty-five minute drive to Doylestown. I looked out the station-wagon window while Mr. Howard and Mami discussed our living arrangements. Alberto was to continue renting the room from the Sandses' neighbors. María Elena would be sharing a bedroom with the Sandses' daughter. My mother, Roly, the twins, and I were staying with the Howards.

Each time Mr. Howard made small talk with us, I didn't say a word. Occasionally, I would catch him looking at me from the rear-view mirror with knitted eyebrows. I suspected he assumed I did not understand English very well.

When the car stopped in front of a looming red-brick Victorian house, my eyes scaled it with wonder, from the dainty wooden lattice work edging the peaked rooftop, down its ivy-covered brick walls, to the massive oak double doors on the front porch. The picturesque neighborhood was made up of Victorian terraced houses. The thick branches of colossal maple, oak, and elm trees arched over the sidewalks. Beneath their generous shade, the grassy yards spread out like an emerald blanket. As I poked my head out the window to look up at the towering trees, their soft rustling seemed to welcome me.

When we tumbled out of the car, the front doors of the house flung open. Four smiling children ran out to greet us, followed by a large caramel-colored dog. "Hi, welcome to our home!" they burst out sporadically, as if they were finally able to use the line they had been instructed to say.

"C'mere, kids," their father summoned them, lining the children up according to their ages. "This is Kimmy," he said, standing behind his oldest child and resting both hands on her shoulders. Then, glancing sideways toward the rest of his family, he continued: "And that's Dana, Judd, and Cory. Oh, and this is Hairy," he said, ruffling the dog's ears. Hairy sat by his owner's side, rapidly wagging his tail on the sidewalk, scattering the fallen leaves. With one ear upright and the other floppy, he surveyed us with his pink tongue hanging out of his mouth. I could not wait to pet this irresistible dog, the first I'd encountered since I had left my Lazy in Cuba.

Through the open front doors we spotted a giggling, barebottomed toddler dashing across the foyer on her tiptoes.

"Tracey-y-y...you come here *now*, you little rascal, you!" A woman trailing a diaper hurried after her. A few minutes later, Barbara Howard sprinted out onto the porch with an adorable red-cheeked little girl straddling her hip.

"*Hola!*" Her smile was almost as dazzling as her husband's. She was a willowy, strong-featured woman with a pleasant face and short brown hair. I felt sure by her mannerisms that Mrs. Howard had been a tomboy when she was young. As if synchronized, María Elena and I both dropped a curtsy when introduced to her. She chuckled, frowning at us. At the Sacred Heart Academy girls were taught the etiquette of always curtsying when meeting an adult. It was second nature to both of us. Noticing Barbara's quizzical expression, my mother told us we didn't have to curtsy anymore; girls in America didn't do that. But it took me a while to stop. I think deep inside I didn't want to let go of a gesture that connected me to my cherished school in Cuba.

For a few moments, both families stood facing each other on the sidewalk, the children awkwardly sizing each other up. But almost immediately, shy little smiles were exchanged, and we all headed into the house. Stepping onto the wooden porch, my mother admired a large planter filled with vibrant blooms.

"How pretty!" she commented, bending down to admire the delicate flowers.

"Impatiens," Mrs. Howard smiled. "They're my favorite." Walking behind the two women, I wondered if my mother was missing her flower garden, especially her stunning roses, which she had always tended with such care. Mrs. Howard put the toddler down and watched her scamper inside the house with Hairy. Casually draping her arm across Mami's shoulders, she said, "Welcome to our home, Ninina. Um… let's see, *mi casa es su casa.*"

"*Gracias*, Barbara," my mother replied, glancing at the flowers once more before going inside.

An impressive, wide staircase with thick wooden railings took up most of the foyer. Its broad, polished banister made me wonder if the Howard children often slid down on it. All along the staircase wall hung family portraits and pictures of the children and their pets over the years. We strolled from one ample, cheery room to another, each with high ceilings and deep windows. The aroma of cinnamon combined with the distinct wood scent of an old home washed over me like a soothing balm. A brick and stone fireplace gave the living room an inviting coziness. Warm-colored furniture with crocheted afghans and plump pillows, books, plants, antiques, toys, and tufts of dog hair here and there made the home look lived-in and comfortable.

Dominating the center of the dining room was a large, rectangular oak table Mr. Howard had made himself. A piano took over one corner of the room. On the opposite side, a mammoth stone fireplace, one I was sure I could stand inside, covered most of the wall. As we headed toward the kitchen, a soft mewing greeted us.

"Meet Helen, our sweet old kitty," Mrs. Howard announced, scooping up a black and white cat that was sitting on the kitchen counter. She gently squeezed the cat to her, gave her a kiss, and poured some kibbles in her empty food bowl next to the sink. I watched with delight as Helen dug into her food, sitting alongside pots, dishes, and a bowl of fresh fruit. *Consuelo would have a* patatú *if she saw this*, I thought. Just then, something warm and furry pressed against my leg. Hairy sat by me, looking up, swishing his tail. I dropped to my knees to pet his silky coat. He leaned in to my caress. I held his shaggy face in my hands. "*Hola*, Hairy." Feeling a fresh sense of loss, I thought of my Lazy in Cuba. Hairy did not leave my side for the rest of the home's tour.

Our new living quarters consisted of two large bedrooms and a bathroom on the third floor. Judd, Kim, and Dana had temporarily given up their rooms for us and moved into spare bedrooms on the second floor. Kim and Dana eagerly motioned us into their room, which my mother, Madeleine, and I would be sharing. I was expecting the two girls to act sullen at having to give up their bedroom. Instead, they behaved like cheerful guides, proudly showing us their things.

Hairy skirted past me and jumped on one of the beds. I set my suitcase down and scanned the bedroom while petting his head. Shelves loaded with books, dolls, teddy bears, coloring books and crayons, a pile of board games, and roller skates made me homesick for my room in Cuba. Who was sleeping in my bed now? Who was primping, sitting on the tufted stool of my old-fashioned dressing table with its pop-up mirror? Where did my favorite dolls, the ones Tita Lala had brought me from her travels to Europe, end up?

"Have you ever read Nancy Drew?" Kimmy chirped knowingly. She handed me a worn hardback. I shook my head slowly, my thoughts still lingering in Cuba. "That's one of my favorites." Kimmy had her father's huge smile, dimples and all.

"I love to read," I said, thumbing through the pages of *The Ghost of Blackwood Hall*. On the front pages of the book, Kimmy had scribbled *I love Nancy Drew* using colorful crayons.

"Me too, especially mysteries. You can help yourself to whatever you like." She walked over to the bookshelf and pointed to the top row of books. "These are all Nancy Drew. They're in numerical order, see?" Her eyes were a beautiful crystal blue. "Start with the first one so you really get to know Nancy."

Even at twelve years old, I was impressed with the sincere hospitality of this family. Their unselfishness in accommodating us, complete strangers, was remarkable. To me, their home was filled with a welcoming pleasure, an embodying friendliness generated by each one of them, Hairy and Helen included.

I was anxious to call my friend Kathy. I scurried down to the kitchen to use the phone. Perched on one of the wooden stools by the counter, I dialed her number.

"Hello, Kathy? It's me, Gloria. I know, can you believe it? I really am here." We chatted for a few minutes. "Yeah, I'll be starting seventh grade next week…uh-huh…I can't wait to see you either…okay…sure. I'll give you a call…okay, bye-e-e." I hung up the phone and jumped off the stool.

"So, you *do* speak English, huh, kiddo?" Mr. Howard was leaning against the kitchen doorway with his arms crossed on his chest, clearly amused by his discovery. He let out a warm, open laugh. It was the best sound I had heard in a long time.

"Yes, I do." I smiled, suddenly feeling happy, comfortable.

"You sounded just like a regular Yank." He let Hairy out the kitchen door. "Sure had me fooled." He shook his head, laughed again, and followed his dog to the backyard.

It was easy to adjust to life at the Howards' home, despite nine children running around the big house. I liked the rambunctious way they lived. Activity, fun, laughter, love, sharing, discipline, and tears all rolled up into one. They were what I construed to be a typical American family.

Their incredible Christian kindness and hospitality

aside, there was something else that set them apart in my mind. Then, one day, I knew. They had the puzzle piece that was missing in my own family. They had a father.

My experience living with the Howards gave me a glimpse of what my life could have been if Papi had been a well man. I believe that idealizing them was my way of paying tribute to them for their unknowing yet invaluable gift to me.

Returning to Our Lady of Mount Carmel School was just as easy. Seeing again the friends I had made in third grade made me feel like I'd never left. School was a short block away. On my first day back, Kathy and I headed for Hornberger's Bakery after school, just as we'd done in 1957. The familiar little bell jingled over our heads as we opened the door. Heavenly scents of fresh-baked bread and pastries wafted through the air. Tempting arrays of cookies, fruit pies, sweet rolls, and fancy cakes were displayed behind spotless glass counters. We splurged on some cupcakes with gooey chocolate icing and colorful sprinkles, two for fifteen cents. Remembering me, Mr. Hornberger gave us each a free bag of cookies to welcome me back to Doylestown.

On weekends, the Howards invited their friends over for cookouts so they could meet us. My mother introduced them to Cuban food. Mrs. Howard's favorite dish was *frijoles negros* with white rice. Mr. Howard's was *arroz con pollo*. Aware that we were searching for an affordable home to rent, a friend of the Howards' offered us her cottage, free, for as long as we needed it. Recently divorced, the woman lived on an expansive estate in the rural outskirts of town. She and her teenage children occupied a restored stone farmhouse surrounded by acres of cornfields and rolling hills. The caretaker's cottage had been vacant for several years. The Howards and the Sandses immediately mobilized their friends, neighbors, and church community to donate the basic necessities for us to set up housekeeping. In late October 1961, we moved into the little cottage on Cold Spring Creamery Road. Throughout the weekend, a barrage of items was continually dropped off: used furniture, beds, clothes, winter coats and boots, pots, pans, dishes, glassware, and silverware. Erma Sands had contacted our parish priest at Our Lady of Mount Carmel, and the church provided us with new linens, towels, pillows, and blankets. A young couple from our church donated a bright red pull-along wagon and two bicycles.

During the move, all of us younger children stayed out of the way by playing in the nearby barn where horses had once been stabled. I climbed up to the hayloft and sat, dangling my feet from the open double doors. Three feet below me, huge bales of hay were stacked against the barn, providing a perfect landing when we jumped off. Munching on an apple, I watched the parade of cars, trucks, and station wagons meander past the cornfields, down the long winding driveway to the cottage. Its passengers unloaded the many items that would turn the empty little house into a home for us.

Looking back on that crisp autumn weekend, I realize that the irony may have escaped me then, but it doesn't now. Only four years before we had donated our home's furnishings, appliances, and winter clothes to a destitute family in our very same church when we left Doylestown to return to Cuba.

By Sunday evening, the cottage was completely furnished, including curtains on every window. The tiny living room was aglow with the mellow light from a lamp's glass amber shade. The mismatched couch and chair were comfortable, despite their lumpy seat cushions. We even had a rocker. My mother made a makeshift coffee table using a sturdy cardboard box covered with a donated burgundy tablecloth. Someone had brought a bouquet of fragrant mums in a cream-colored ceramic pitcher. The narrow kitchen counters were laden with bags of groceries, several casseroles, homemade cakes, and plates of cookies people had made for us.

As the seven of us crunched around a small table for dinner that night, we passed our potpourri of plates for my mother to serve us. I noticed hers had a chip on its rim. Was she missing her wedding china, with its exquisite, hand-painted floral design? If she was, she didn't show it. Her face shone with sheer contentment, and she handled each dish as if it were Dresden porcelain. I recalled that evening in Miami when she resolved to make the move to Pennsylvania.

"You did it, Mami," I said, passing her the breadbasket. "We *are* living in Doylestown." My mother looked around the table at all of us, taking a few seconds to respond.

"I thought there was something special about this little town ever since the first time we lived here." She paused to open up her napkin. "The people were so warmhearted then, when we had everything. This time, we came back with nothing but each other, and thanks to their goodness and generosity...look at us now. We have everything we need."

Still, knowing that soon we would have to move again, I longed for a place we could truly call our own.

Our country life in the old caretaker's cottage was short lived. A rental home that Ed Howard had been eyeing became available for us. In late November 1961 we moved once again. The white Victorian duplex was on the corner of Maple Avenue, four houses away from the Howards. I was happy to live in town again. As much as I had enjoyed the Bucks County countryside, I was not going to miss our tight quarters and being so far away from everything. Even though we had only half of the house (the owner and his wife lived in the other half), *la casa de Maple*, as we christened it, had warmth and charm. The moment I walked through the front door I decided that this was a happy house. The large, sunny kitchen with an adjacent laundry room put a smile on my mother's face.

I had never been inside a turret. "A witch's hat," my father had called it the first time we saw one when driving through Doylestown in 1956. Our new home had a roomy one, with tall, wide windows and scalloped siding. Inside, the turret formed a cozy alcove off the spacious living room. Peering out its windows, I surveyed the small patch of lawn that hugged the front, side, and back of the house. Enormous maple and oak trees seemed to hover protectively overhead. The quiet side streets would be perfect for riding my bike.

Soon after we moved, my mother received a letter from my grandfather Bibi. Things were not going well in Costa Rica. Uncle Gus, an engineer, had been unable to find work. He, his wife, and their seven children lived with my grandparents in an apartment in San José, and this arrangement had almost drained Bibi of what little money he'd been able to take out of Cuba.

"We are desperate, *mi hija*," Bibi wrote. "Our hopes for a better life are in America with you and your children."

I felt an immense relief when my mother told us our grandparents would be coming to live with us. I had not seen them since I'd left Cuba nine months before. I had worried for their safety during their own exodus to Costa Rica and feared I would never see them again. Living with or near Mama and Bibi always filled me with a sense of security and emotional stability. Their love and support fueled my mother's strength.

Upon hearing the news, Ed Howard went into networking action again. He landed my uncle a job in a Philadelphia construction company and hired Bibi to work in his company's accounting department. Close friends of the Howards offered their homes to help accommodate my uncle and his family once they arrived in Doylestown. Meanwhile, neighbors and friends again rallied to help us round up the necessary things for our relatives to set up housekeeping.

On a cold and snowy evening in December 1961, another homeless Cuban caravan arrived in Philadelphia. My grandparents huddled together at the top of the tired-looking DC-6's stairway, looking anxious and cold. My aunt and uncle followed close behind, their seven children zigzagging between the adults, eager to reach the airstrip to enjoy their first experience with snow.

That night at the Howards' home, my grandmother kept smiling at Mr. and Mrs. Howard, exuberantly saying "*Zenk you, zenk you.*" Bibi spoke limited English, but

Mama did not speak the language at all.

My grandfather shook Mr. Howard's hand. His old eyes watered as he spoke the cautious English of an elderly foreigner. "I am proud to meet you, sir, and will be eternally grateful for all you and your family and friends have done for my family and for me." Mr. Howard flashed his broad smile and hugged Bibi sideways. "Welcome to America, Papa."

The following morning my uncle and his family moved into the cottage on Cold Spring Creamery Road where we had stayed. My mother must have truly loved her brother; after what he put her through in Cuba, stalling his move out of our home, La Coronela, she evidently held no grudges.

It was saddening to watch my grandparents settle in with us. The sorrowful expression on Bibi's face was unfamiliar to me. His half-smile was only a shadow of the bright one I knew so well. Though only in their mid-sixties, my grandparents suddenly looked old and fragile. They were lost in a way of life far different from the one they had known in Cuba. The language barrier was frustrating, the winter climate harsh on their arthritic bones so used to warm, balmy weather.

As soon as my grandmother walked into the bedroom she would share with Bibi, she cleared a small table by the window and set up the little altar for her Virgencita. Having the familiar statue, so lovingly venerated by our family, back in our lives again brought about a certain peace, a feeling that all would be right now.

Lying on my bed that night in the room next to theirs, I overheard Bibi telling Mama how grateful he was for their freedom in America but how he would never give up his dream of someday returning to Cuba. "That's the only way I can get through each day, Bebita," he said quietly. I imagined his disconsolate expression. "Will we ever be together again as a family like we were in Cuba?" Bibi lamented.

"*Ya*, Gustavo, *ya*," Mama soothed him. "You need to sleep now. *A ver, vamos.*" I could hear the sheets softly rustling.

"*¿Qué frío, verdad?*" he commented. I could picture him shivering.

"*Sí, horrible.*"

"But look, look at the falling snow, Beba. Have you ever seen anything so peaceful?" My grandfather's voice perked up, now full of wonder. "It's like nothing I've ever seen come down from the sky before."

I glanced out my bedroom window through the partially drawn curtains. The moon's silver beams cast a bluish light in the room. The snow was falling steady, swirling and dancing with an occasional gust of wind.

"*Sí, muy linda, pero no me gusta este frío horripilante*, Gustavo." My grandmother complained again about the cold.

"*Hasta mañana*," Bibi bid her goodnight.

"*Que duermas bien*," she purred back. But I suspected it would not be a peaceful sleep for my grandfather that snowy night, as his agonizing thoughts traveled back to the warmth of Cuba.

With Christmas fast approaching, my mother told us at breakfast one morning that we would not be able to celebrate the holidays as we had in Cuba. There was no money for presents or a Christmas tree. We didn't even have a *nacimiento*. I recalled my grandmother's beautiful nativity scenes in Cuba.

"But we will celebrate *Nochebuena*," Mama said gaily, as if reading my thoughts. "Barbara found a store that sells black beans. Isn't that wonderful?" She dunked her toast in her *café con leche*.

"And *tostones*?" Roly asked.

"*Sí*, they have plantain bananas and even guava paste for our *empanaditas*." My grandmother rapidly tapped her foot on the floor, which she did whenever she was excited.

"And we are all together," Bibi said, looking around the table at each one of us. "In this comfortable, pretty house. We have jobs, food, and caring friends." His eyes glistened, without a blink. "That is the best Christmas present we could ever hope for after all we have gone through." He paused and took a deep breath, releasing it slowly. "Celebrating *Nochebuena* with our Cuban dinner will be our Christmas gift to each other this year, *está bien*?" We nodded hesitantly, missing our gifts already.

Early that afternoon, our front doorbell rang several times. My mother welcomed the Howards in. "Hello-o-o everyone," they sang out.

"C'mon, Ninina, round up the kids. We're off to buy a Christmas tree," Mr. Howard announced, removing his red knit cap.

"I've got some goodies here for you, Mama." Mrs. Howard headed for the dining room with my grandmother close behind. While unpacking a grocery bag on the table, she held up two bags of black beans. "Yum-m-m," she smiled at Mama. "I hope this is what you need for *No-chay-bway-nah, sí*?" She nodded at Mama, who could not understand a word she was saying. That did not deter my grandmother from attempting to communicate.

"*Sí, sí, muchas gracias,* Barbara." Mama put her fingers to her lips as if throwing her a kiss. "*Muy bueno, sí.*" Then, taking both bags and pressing them to her chest, she rushed into the living room to show us.

An hour and a half later, we returned home with an eight-foot Douglas fir tied to the roof of the Howards' station wagon. The tree's fragrance immediately filled our living room. Bibi hung a wreath with pinecones and a red bow on our front door, while Mr. Howard set the tree up in the living room alcove.

That evening, the Howard family came to help us decorate our *arbolito*. They brought along several bags of Christmas ornaments, lights, and a big bowl of popcorn for stringing, a new Christmas tradition for us. We youngsters were so excited about trimming the tree with balls and tinsel that Mami, Mrs. Howard, and Mama ended up doing the stringing with the popcorn they salvaged from the boys, who kept eating it.

My mother brought in a tray of hot chocolate with Christmas cookies that a neighbor had dropped off. Kimmy and I played Christmas carols on her portable record player. The Howards and we children sang along while my grandmother caroled in Spanish. The stout *arbolito* almost filled the alcove in the turret. When Mr. Howard plugged in the colored lights, the tree seemed to reflect the joy that filled our living room that night.

"¡*Ay, que lindo!*" Mama's dark eyes sparkled above a child-like smile. Christmas had always transformed my chatty and bubbly grandmother into an even more enthusiastic, filled-with-the-spirit-of-the-season person. The fact that we were now in exile with barely enough to get by did not alter the meaning of *Navidad* for her.

Mama had made little ornaments with yarn remnants someone had donated, knowing my grandmother loved to crochet. She handed out the bright yellow stars, white snowflakes, red bells, and purple balls with wavy yellow stripes to everyone to hang on the tree. To me they were more beautiful than the brightly colored balls the Howards had given us. The half-eaten popcorn garlands were draped on the tree, and the *lágrimas de angeles*, angels' tears, as we called the tinsel, were carefully placed on the tips of branches.

"One more thing and I think we're done," Mrs. Howard called out, rummaging through a bag on the couch. "Here it is! Papa, why don't you do the honors." She handed my grandfather a bright gold star with shimmering glitter. He looked at it for the longest time. His lips quivered slightly as he stood on the small stepladder and reached for the top of the tree.

"*Cuidado*, Gustavo, *por favor*," Mama warned him, watching him.

"*Sí*, Beba, *sí*," my grandfather answered patiently. After anchoring the star, he turned to face us all. "¡*Feliz Navidad*!"

Christmas Eve morning I awoke to the tasty aroma of simmering *frijoles negros* and the sounds of my grandmother's prattling around in the kitchen. The night before I had helped her sort out the beans, separating the plump, pretty ones from *los feos*, the ugly ones. We then rinsed the beans in a large pot of cold water. I loved immersing my hands in the water to swish the shiny beans around. To soften the beans for cooking the next day, they soaked overnight with chunks of onions and green peppers.

All day long our home buzzed with activity in preparation for *Nochebuena*. My family had invited Ed and Barbara Howard and Don and Erma Sands to join us for our Christmas Eve Cuban dinner. We had to borrow a large folding table from the Sandses in order to accommodate all thirteen of us. My grandmother insisted it be adjoined to the dining table so we could all sit together like we had always done at Rancho Perea. Our table now extended out into the living room.

I was helping Mami set the table when Mama fluttered into the dining room, her cheeks flushed with excitement. She was holding something behind her back.

"*¿Qué tienes ahí*, Mama?" I asked her.

"*¿Sí, Mamá, qué jelenge te traes?*" my mother looked at her quizzically.

"*¿Pues ven?*" Mama unraveled the bundle she had been concealing. "Look what else I brought from Cuba." With both arms outstretched, she held out the tablecloth that we'd used for our Christmas dinners at Rancho Perea for many years. The white linen *mantel* with embroidered red poinsettias never looked more beautiful. In an instant both tables were covered with the cloth.

"*¡Perfecto!*" Mama declared, stepping back to admire the transformation. Of all the other things she could have squeezed into her one suitcase, my grandmother had chosen a simple Christmas tablecloth to remind our family of what we once had, what we had lost, and what we had regained.

After our *Cena de Nochebuena* of black bean *potaje*

served over steaming white rice, roast pork with all the trimmings, and *tostones*, we savored a special sweet treat of *turrones* from Spain that Lilí and Vicente, Alberto's parents, had sent us from Miami. I listened to the adults' conversation, heard their animated voices through the clinking of glasses and coffee cups.

"A February wedding!" gushed Mrs. Sands, clasping her hands. "It will probably snow." It was almost time to leave for midnight mass, and we were still talking about my sister's wedding; a very intimate celebration, with a small reception afterward at the Howards' home.

When we came home from mass, my grandmother announced that she had a special surprise for our family. Bibi gave his wife a knowing little smile. Half-asleep, I watched my grandmother open the hall closet, and teetering on her tiptoes, she reached for the top shelf. She brought out a large shoebox, which she had covered inside out with brown corduroy material, and placed it on a TV table next to the Christmas tree. In our rush to leave for church, no one had noticed her draping a white cloth over the little table.

Taking a small bundle out of the box, she then set the box on its side, the opening facing us. My grandmother had saved some greens from the tree's bottom branches. She deftly arranged them on top of and alongside the box. Mama had glued together twigs to create makeshift stalls inside the box. As if drawn by a magnet, we gathered around her. Slowly, Mama's arthritic fingers unfolded the little bundle. Unveiling the figurines, my grandmother identified each one: "*La Virgen María, San José, y el niñito Jesús.*"

She then reached into her sweater pocket and took out a plastic bag containing a wad of hay from the barn at

Creamery Road. Pinching small bunches, Mama covered the entire bottom of the box with it, all the while smiling and tilting her head as she marveled at her creation. Admiring the familiar little statues in the rustic *nacimiento*, I was amazed at what my grandmother had created. Bibi put his arm around Mama without saying a word.

"Mama, your Nativity scenes are still the prettiest," I said, looking at her work. I remembered my grandmother's elaborate *nacimientos* that occupied a quarter of her formal living room in Havana. This *Navidad* there were no neighbors dropping by to see Mama's Nativity scene, no maids serving refreshments and Christmas treats.

Folding her hands in prayer, my grandmother began to sing: *"Noche de paz, noche de amor."* Singing "Silent Night" with my family late that Christmas Eve, I thought of the Sacred Heart nuns and how often they had spoken to us about a spiritually moving experience: something that touched our hearts, that connected us to God and our loved ones at the same time. *This must be what they meant!* I realized, as our voices reached the highest note—"sleep in heavenly peace"—and the infant Jesus smiled back at me.

At bedtime, the cold winds howled outside my bedroom windows. I snuggled contentedly, thinking of the old shoebox downstairs next to our *arbolito*. I reveled in the pride I felt in my grandmother for having brought the three Nativity figures from Cuba that now looked resplendent in the Bucks County hay. As I drifted off to sleep, my thoughts shifted to the next day. My grandfather's poignant words and my grandmother's shining example of the true meaning of *Navidad* could not erase my disappointment as I thought of Christmas morning without gifts.

Early the next day my brothers' voices hurled up the stairs, waking me up. They were calling to my mother to come see something. On their way to shovel the walkway, they had discovered a large cardboard box with a huge red bow sitting on our snow-covered porch. A small card tied to the bow simply read: "Merry Christmas from Santa."

By the time I came downstairs for breakfast, my mother had taken out gifts for each and every one of us from that box. Our *arbolito* glistened with lights and presents. We never found out who Santa was, but he left me my first two Nancy Drew books: *The Hidden Staircase* and *Mystery at Lilac Inn*, along with a bag of caramels, my favorite, and a beautiful red sweater.

"I'll never forget this Christmas as long as I live," I heard my mother say while watching us children open our presents. That Christmas in 1961 we had so little, yet we had everything. We were far away from Rancho Perea, the family bastion that had brought us together every weekend and especially during the holidays. And yet while experiencing our first *Navidad* in America, I felt a different family tie binding us closer, much closer than we had ever been before.

After breakfast, I sat with my grandfather in the living room alcove. I dove into one of my books. Bibi filled his pipe with cherry tobacco, his gift from Santa along with a cream-colored wool scarf. Drawing a first puff, he let out a long, satisfied sigh. I peeked at him over my book. A trail of faint smoke circled his head as he gazed out the window at the falling snow.

"*Doylestown de mis amores,*" he murmured. "*Como me acordaré de tí.*"

I shared in my grandfather's sentiment. *Beloved Doylestown. How I will remember you!*
I have never forgotten.

Chapter Nineteen

LIKE A PALM TREE IN THE SNOW

I always knew where to find my grandfather. Our living room's turret became Bibi's special nook. The sunny daylight streamed in through its tall windows, creating a warm coziness. He loved his *butacón*, an overstuffed armchair, its seat cushion flat and faded. The back of the chair had a dent where previous owners had leaned for many years. Bibi propped himself comfortably with two brightly colored pillows that Mama had made. An afghan from a church parishioner was always nearby to throw over his legs. A feathery Areca palm thrived in its sunshiny corner. Next to the chair, an old radio sat on top of a small wooden table, its badly scratched surface concealed by an ivory-colored doily my grandmother had crocheted.

My grandfather spent much of his time in that alcove, reading, listening to classical music, smoking his pipe, and remembering Cuba. I learned how to play chess, his favorite game, in that cozy niche. Each time I won, the twinkle in his eye revealed that he had given me the game.

Our first major snowstorm of the season kept us home from school one day in early January 1962. I could see streams of white between a gap in my bedroom's sheer curtains as I lay in bed reading, killing time until *American Bandstand* came on. Now a teenager at thirteen, I loved American music. Every day after school I watched Dick Clark's popular program, my eyes glued to the round screen of our donated black and white TV, as I rated new songs and rooted for my favorite dance couples.

The rich scent of cherry tobacco floated faintly into my room; a serenade of sweet-sounding violins followed. When I trotted downstairs, my grandfather seemed lost in the melancholic music. He looked sad and distant, peering pensively out the window at the fast-falling snowflakes. The evergreen trees in our yard were draped in snow, and every limb of the black walnut tree had a thick coating of white.

"What are you listening to, Bibi?"

His body perked up as I interrupted his thoughts. "'Ello, m'dear." He loved imitating a British accent. His eyes brightened, and I basked in his warm smile.

"It's so pretty," I said, perching on the arm of his chair. I casually wrapped my arm across his shoulders and leaned my head against his.

"You are listening to Vivaldi." Bibi pronounced the Italian name with pride. "'Autumn' from The Four Seasons, Opus #8." It was Chinese to me, but the violins' music, escalating to a frenzied joy, almost made me cry. Then, a single violin played a remarkably sad solo.

"*¿Estás triste?*" I asked, noticing my grandfather's downhearted expression. He puffed on his pipe, the cherry tobacco sweet and woody.

"I was remembering Cuba, the beautiful palm trees swaying in the tropical breezes." Bibi's voice was filled with emotion as he spoke of his homeland. "When I think of those palm trees on a bitter cold day like today, it warms my tired old bones." He sighed. "I try to imagine *palmas* here, but we both know that they cannot make it in the snow." The violin solo reached an exquisite high note. "Sometimes that is how I feel: *como una palma en la nieve*—like a palm tree in the snow." We both looked out the window. There was something soothing about the silence of the snowfall. I felt sorry for my grandfather, for his sadness that would not let go.

Every day without fail, Bibi sat in the alcove and waited for my mother to arrive home from work. Mami had left her job at the hosiery factory and now cleaned rooms at the Doylestown Hospital, a much closer walking distance and better pay.

"¡*Ay, por tu vida*!" My grandmother bustled in with Bibi's afternoon espresso. "The snow is getting worse, Gustavo," she exclaimed, opening the curtains wider for a better view of the sidewalk across the street, where my mother would soon become visible. "¿*Donde está* Ninina?" Mama wrapped her bulky sweater snug around her.

"Thank God she doesn't have far to walk," Bibi said. The snow was almost blinding. Then, through the white blur, a dot of turquoise appeared. Snowy gusts flapped my mother's uniform skirt under her jacket.

"There she comes!" I cried out. "I'm going out to meet her." A wave of relief washed over my grandparents' faces. The deep snow crept into my boots as I trundled across the front yard; snow missiles landed roughly across my face. While waiting to cross the street, I turned back to wave at them. Bibi raised his hand slowly, and a far-off smile shadowed his face. I knew his thoughts had returned to Cuba, where the sun was shining hot and bright and where the lofty palm trees were basking in that tropical sun, missing one palm tree, a palm tree in the snow.

* * *

My mother did not keep her job at the hospital for long. Her drive to do better was relentless. Detail-oriented and with an aptitude for numbers, Mami convinced the manager of Green's, a five-and-dime store in town, to hire her to do office work when she heard they were looking for help. She took an accounting course and a month later she was promoted to office manager. Her first raise came just in time for the wedding.

Erma Sands had been right. The weather forecast called for snow, lots of it, on February 10, 1962, the day of my sister's wedding. The night before, my mother helped Mr. and Mrs. Howard clean their house and decorate it with white streamers, paper wedding bells, and fresh flowers for the reception. At home, my grandmother was in her glory, baking the wedding cake and preparing a fruit punch for the luncheon. Friends and neighbors offered to bring appetizers, casseroles, salads, and little sandwiches to help with the meal.

The day of the wedding was one of the coldest that winter, yet the sun shone intermittently with frenzied flurries of snow. In our bedroom, I, the maid of honor, helped María Elena dress. She had borrowed her gown from Alberto's sister, who had recently married in Miami. My royal blue velvet dress was borrowed from a neighbor's daughter. Slipping into my first pair of stubby black heels,

I felt quite grown up, despite a bit of wobbling. A small headpiece of dainty mauve flowers with a demi-veil and white gloves completed my outfit. My sister had done my hair up in a French twist, and I wore my first dusting of blush and a dab of her new rose-colored lipstick.

I was in awe of seeing my first bride. María Elena glanced at herself in the mirror one last time. "Okay, I'm ready," she said. Then, turning to me, she added, "*Bueno*, let's do it."

The front pews of the chapel-like church of Our Lady of Mount Carmel were sprinkled with the small group of family and guests. In the chilly vestibule, Bibi stood tall wearing a black hand-me-down suit with a white rose on his lapel. Papi was not able to come to his daughter's wedding. None of the Fernández family came. My grandfather gave María Elena away in marriage.

* * *

As soon as he stepped out of the car, the loving smile I yearned for bathed Papi's face when he saw me sitting on the steps of our front porch. He and my grandmother had come to spend a few days with us in May 1962. The spring weather and the fact that my father was calmer had encouraged Tita Lala to travel with him.

Papi had gained a little weight since I'd last seen him in Miami, eight months before. He sported new tortoiseshell rimmed glasses, and his bronzed skin radiated a healthy glow. Relieved, I banished the apprehension that always plagued me each time I was to see my father. I never knew what to expect. Would he be responsive and loving, or nervous and strange? I dreaded finding out.

"Yoyi, look at you!" Papi dropped a small duffel bag on the sidewalk and opened his arms to welcome my hug. "*Una señorita ya.*" He engulfed me in an eager embrace. "*Sí*, I'm almost fourteen," I boasted. "How was your trip?" I looked up at him, leaving my arm around his waist and feeling the comfort of his arm across my shoulders. "*Pues, muy bueno.*" He looked around and smiled. "It's good to be back in Doylestown." My father loved Pennsylvania, *el norte*, as he referred to it.

Papi and Tita Lala stayed in town at the Doylestown Inn but spent all their time with us. My grandmother visited mostly with Mama and Bibi and behaved civilly toward my mother, but the tension between them was obvious. Tita Lala acted like an observer, obligated to be there because my father needed to see his family.

My father remained relaxed and talkative throughout their visit. He tossed the football with my brothers and was cordial yet cautious with my mother. They smiled politely at one another, and if standing together for a picture, both would instinctively put their hands behind their backs. There was a boundary drawn between them now, and each kept to their side.

Papi and I sat out on the porch one sunny afternoon and talked about school, music, and movies. I even shared my secret crush on a boy from school. A warm breeze picked up, carrying with it the sweet scent of blooming hyacinths lining the porch. Red tulips and golden daffodils flourished in the spring sunshine. I gazed at my father's handsome face as he leafed through a book I was reading for English. For a brilliant jewel of a moment I felt like I had a normal father.

Unlike during most visits, Papi was cooperative when it was time for them to leave. He blew us a kiss as we children stood on the porch and waved goodbye. That weekend with my father in the spring of 1962 was a gift, one that would have to tide me over for many years before I was to see him again.

I was right about our home on Maple Avenue. It was a happy place, despite our hardships. We drew strength from being together as a family. We learned to appreciate what little we had, rarely stopping to mourn what we had lost. We held on tight to our hopes for a brighter future.

But all too soon the *desparramo de familia*, the scattering of our family, took place again when my sister and her husband decided to move back to Miami. With the loss of their income, my mother could no longer afford *la casa de Maple*. My grandfather was still working at Mr. Howard's company in Philadelphia but had to cut back his hours drastically because of his worsening circulatory problems. We moved to a smaller duplex in a similarly quiet residential area of town.

Determined to help their daughter and four grandchildren in any way they could, my grandparents continued living with us. Their spiritual and emotional support was the glue that held us together, even though to them, exile was a sentence of insurmountable sadness—a constant longing to see the rest of their family, a painful, unbearable yearning to return to their homeland.

 By the fall of 1964, the harsh winters, language barrier, and separation from their two other children began to take their toll. My grandparents moved to Colombia to live with their daughter Milly and her family.

My mother took on a part-time job in order to make ends meet. In addition to her full-time job at the store, on Saturdays she worked at the S & H Green Stamps store in town. I helped our family by babysitting and working in a department store.

The Howards and the Sandses remained a consistent and supportive influence in our lives. The Sandses' shoe store provided us children with two new pairs of shoes each at the beginning of every school year. They also invited us every year to share Thanksgiving dinner with them. Knowing how much we enjoyed our rice, Mrs. Sands always made a special side dish of wild rice just for us.

By the time I turned sixteen, I had fully embraced life as an American teenager. My closet door was plastered with posters of the Beatles and Dr. Kildare. It was a tight race for my affections between Paul McCartney and Richard Chamberlain. I listened to records, mostly of the Beatles, day and night on my portable phonograph, although I did have one 45 of Richard Chamberlain's called "Dream." I enjoyed looking at Dr. Kildare better than listening to him sing.

The latest issues of *Photoplay* took the place of comic books, and a diary became my new confidante. The phone was almost always for me. I was a sophomore in a whirlwind of high school activities: football games, drama club, color guard, yearbook staff, library assistant. I kept up with my studies; French and history were my favorite subjects…and so was Bill.

He asked me out to the movies. My first date. My mother said absolutely not, not without a chaperone. It was the end of my world. I reasoned, argued, pleaded, and cried. Mami clenched her teeth. I knew what was coming next. It was what she always said to us, dramatically, when she was at the end of her rope arguing with us. *"¡Yo no nací para esta batalla, qué vá!"—I was not born for this battling, no way!* Defeated, I ran upstairs to my bedroom, slammed the door, and played "She Loves You" full-blast. I flung myself on the bed. "YEAH, YEAH, YEAH!" I sang along with the Beatles, stressing the word louder than usual. *This can't be happening to me. I'll be the laughingstock at school. I'm the only girl in America who can't go out on a date without a chaperone.* Despite the loud music, I heard the faint ringing of the telephone out in the hallway.

"¿Qué tal, Yoyi?" My grandfather's voice instantly alleviated my fury.

"Bibi! How are you? How's Colombia?" We chatted about life there and the family, then he asked me about school and things in general. My grandfather knew me too well.

"¿Qué te pasa?" he asked me. I told him. *"No te preocupes."* His voice was reassuring. "Don't you worry. I'll have a talk with your mother about this."

"Oh please, Bibi, will you?" My spirits soared.

"Is he a nice boy, this Bill?"

"I know you would really like him, Bibi," I gibbered away. "He takes Spanish in school and practices with me all the time. *¿No es perfecto?"* He chuckled.

"Sí, ya veo. You cheer up now and be patient. This is hard for your mother, you know, but I think she'll come around." My grandfather's open-mindedness on this diehard custom surprised me.

"Gracias, Bibi. I wish you were here." I twirled the phone cord around my finger. "Give Mama a kiss from me."

313

"I will."

"Bibi, I love you so much."

"*Yo también,*" he said, his voice catching. After giving my mother the phone, I prayed and I waited. I turned the music down. My mother's expression was grave as she came into my room. I was sure Bibi's efforts had been in vain.

"You have your grandfather to thank for this," she said curtly. "I still don't think this is proper." Mami surveyed my posters, then looked at me. "You can walk to the movie matinee with Bill on Sunday." She furrowed her eyebrows. "And you come straight home afterward."

I gasped. "*Sí,* Mami, I promise. Thank you," I said, in my best kiss-up voice. *Be quiet, don't push your luck.* As soon as the door closed behind her, I played another Beatles record. *Love, love me do…you know I love you…*I sang along, rummaging through my closet for my favorite pale pink blouse with Peter Pan collar to wear on Sunday. *And pleeee-ee-ease…love me do…oh yeah, love me do.* I held the blouse up against my mauve sweater. "God bless America," I said aloud. "And God bless Bibi."

That Christmas of 1964 I was invited to my first formal school dance. Realizing she had three more teenagers on my heels to contend with, my mother gave in to the American system of dating. Sitting in Bill's rented Bonneville, I lifted my beautiful wristlet corsage of white and red sweetheart roses to my nose, inhaled deeply, and bid good riddance to all those chaperones I would never have to endure.

In January 1965 my mother started a new job as a teller at the Doylestown National Bank. "¡*Al fin!*" she rejoiced with us the day she was hired. "At last I have found a really good job." Later on, when an irate bank customer complained that he could not understand my mother, she enrolled in evening community classes to improve her English. Less than a year later, she became assistant head teller. Shortly after, she was promoted to head teller. I was proud of my mother's accomplishments, but most importantly, of her amazing determination to better herself.

Where was Papi? I wrote to him faithfully, but his sporadic letters stopped coming altogether in the summer of 1965. He now lived alone in a one-room efficiency unit in Miami. My heart ached because he was living a lonely life isolated from us. Even though my grandmother provided financially for him, was he emotionally strong enough to live by himself? Did he know when to take his medication, and worse yet, did he? What did he do with his time? Through María Elena, we learned that he had been hospitalized several times. My sister was our only source of information about Papi.

For the next couple of years, a scattering of birthday and Christmas cards and an occasional scribbled note were my only contact with my father. I knew that the long silence meant he was not doing well. It was as if he did not exist. I never stopped missing him. Nothing could soothe the yearning in my heart, nothing except seeing him again.

In early 1968, Papi wrote Mami telling her he had moved to an apartment in Hialeah, Florida, near the hardwood company where he worked. Papi was working. A good sign, I felt sure. Soon after, a torrent of letters to me confirmed that. My father was back in my life full-force, like never before.

Mi linda Yoyita, he addressed his letters; they were beautifully written, informative, affectionate, and lighthearted. Reading Papi's strong, flowing penmanship, I clung to the lines where he wrote how much he missed and loved me. His words filled the empty spaces in my heart with the love I had been longing for. Through our missives, at long last, I felt connected to my father.

Papi was extremely proud of his job. The company imported lumber in log forms and serrated wood from Colombia and Brazil. It was headquartered on the Amazon River, the area from which most of the lumber was imported. Papi worked in the accounting department, "where I get to use all that I learned about that subject at the University of Havana," he wrote. He especially liked doing statistical work with tally sheets and reports of the imported wood. It reminded him of his job at his father's lumber business in Havana.

Papi was focused, holding his own. Letter after letter, I began to know him like I never had before. What he thought, how he felt, what he enjoyed doing, and, most importantly, how he felt about me. As I did so often as a child, when my father seemed normal to me, I found myself hoping once again: this is it. Maybe this time Papi would stay normal for the rest of his life, a life that destiny kept refusing to let me share with him.

* * *

Bill had long since been replaced by several high school crushes. Then, one night in the spring of my senior year, in 1967, my final crush burst into my life when the phone rang and someone yelled, "Gloria, it's for you!"

The outgoing voice on the other end belonged to Lee, a freshman at Delaware Valley College of Science and Agriculture, in Doylestown. He was majoring in ornamental horticulture, played a Martin guitar, and sang in a folk group. I felt instantly comfortable talking to him and, at the same time, somewhat uneasy not knowing what he looked like. Lee, on the other hand, had spotted me in church one Sunday, and having met a couple of my girlfriends at college mixers, he had learned the identity of the girl with the long, dark brown hair wearing a Spanish *mantilla*.

I told him that I had a boyfriend. He knew that. Unbeknownst to me, Lee also learned from my girlfriends that I was heading toward the end of a two-year relationship. The phone calls became more frequent, and I found myself looking forward to them—and not feeling guilty that my boyfriend didn't know about them. *It's only a telephone friendship*, I told myself. The friendship kept building for a month. By then, I had broken up with my boyfriend.

"I think it's time we met this mysterious admirer of yours," my mother said under her breath, handing me the phone when Lee called. "Why don't you ask him to come for a visit?" Even though my broken heart wasn't in it, I reluctantly followed Mami's advice.

"Great! I'll be there in five minutes. I know where you live." I gaped at the receiver after Lee hung up. *He's on his way!* I thought, suddenly panic-stricken. I knew I liked who he was, but what did he look like?

Mama and Bibi were visiting us at the time. "¡Ay, qué bueno!" my grandmother exclaimed when I told everyone Lee was coming. "We want to see who is *este muchacho*." Bibi smiled at me as he puffed on his pipe. Giving in to my uneasiness, I asked my sister Madeleine to scout Lee out when he came to the door. If he was cute, I would brave it; if he was strange or nerdy-looking, I was not feeling well.

Mama was assigned to open the front door, something she always loved doing. Behind her, Madeleine would be at her lookout post on the stairway landing. A few steps above her, I would be waiting for her report. The doorbell rang, and my stomach lurched.

"Ah-loh!" Mama greeted Lee cheerfully.

"*Buenas tardees. ¿Coma aystah yusted?*" I heard him sing out to her. My grandmother's happy voice filled the living room with fast, chattering Spanish. "No, sorry, that's all I know. I don't speak Spanish," Lee tried to interrupt her. My sister bounded upstairs.

"Okay, he's cute."

"Are you sure?" I shot her a suspicious stare. Maybe she was getting back at me for not letting her borrow my new kilt.

"Yeah, honest," she said convincingly. Meanwhile, my grandmother was enthusiastically ushering the cute guy with sexy sideburns into our living room and into my life.

María Elena and Alberto returned to Doylestown in the summer of 1968, after living in Miami for nearly six years. They missed living in Pennsylvania.

They and my mother bought our first home in America. The impressive old Victorian with a wraparound porch occupied the entire corner of Union and Shewell near the center of town. I loved that house. More than a hundred years old, it had colorful stained-glass windows in the foyer above the main staircase. A stone and tile fireplace was the focal point of a room that was once the parlor, next to the formal living room. It was disappointing knowing I would live in it for only a year, since I was engaged to be married in June 1969. But what a grand place it would be to have my wedding reception.

My joy was unbounded when Papi wrote that he and Tita Lala would be coming to my wedding. After six years of not seeing him, all I could think about was walking down the long aisle of Our Lady of Mount Carmel's new church on my father's arm.

In May 1969, my grandparents came back to Doylestown to live with their son and his family. In the years since they'd left our home in 1964, they had lived with their daughters in Colombia, then in Miami. Mama and Bibi wanted only to be with their children and grandchildren. Like two outcast gypsies, they quietly adjusted to each new lifestyle and never complained.

Mama's buoyant personality had remained unaltered. As soon as she arrived, she set up a little altar for her Virgencita in the nicest corner of their bedroom. The votive candle shone brightly, and whenever possible, a bouquet of fresh-cut flowers was at the statue's feet.

My grandfather had changed drastically. His tall, erect figure now drooped at the shoulders. There was a fragility about him, and the impish gleam in his wise old eyes was gone. All I saw there now was sadness.

Two weeks before the wedding, my father called. He and Tita Lala were not coming. Papi told me he could not leave work, but I knew that was just a front. We later found out that my grandmother didn't feel up to traveling, and my father's doctor stressed that he not make the trip alone.

As when my sister was married, no one from the Fernández family was coming to my wedding.

The next day during my lunch hour I went to see my grandparents. I did that as often as I could. Mama and Bibi spent most of their days in their bedroom at the very back of the house. "Our gilded cage," Bibi called it. It had all the comforts they needed, including their own private bath, TV, and telephone, but they felt isolated from family life. My grandparents' faces lit up each time I stopped by for a visit.

The fragrance from the bouquet of lilacs I had brought for the Virgencita perfumed their bedroom. My grandmother bustled about blissfully arranging them in a vase as I sat visiting with my grandfather.

"Bibi, Papi won't be coming to the wedding. Will you walk me down the aisle?" My voice sounded unrecognizably distant to me. He stopped cleaning his favorite pipe and looked at me, his hazel eyes swimming with affection.

"*Sí, mi'jita, como no.* I'm sorry your father won't be here," he told me. "I know how much you were looking forward to that." I nodded, looking over at my grandmother putzing with the lilacs, trying to ward off my tears. "I will do my best to take his place that day, m'dear." Bibi pushed up his glasses; that old twinkle danced in his eyes again. I gazed at this wise, kind man who had been a part of my life for as long as I could remember. The irony of his words moved me deeply. Throughout my life, he had taken the place of my father so many times. I had never loved my grandfather more for doing so than at that very moment.

I perched myself on the arm of his *butacón* like I had done since I was a child. I rested my right arm across his frail shoulders and kissed his forehead. "*Gracias*, Bibi." The familiar scent of his Old Spice cologne comforted me. With his right hand, he squeezed mine, the one resting on his shoulder.

"*De nada,* Yoyi, *de nada.*"

I also had a favor to ask of my grandmother that day. I wanted to place the Virgencita on the Blessed Mother's side altar at church during the wedding ceremony. It was to her, the statue of Our Lady of Mercy, the one my great-grandfather had salvaged from a burnt chapel in Artemisa, Cuba, and the one that had watched over our family since then, that I wished to offer flowers while the soloist sang "Ave María" during the mass.

My grandmother held my face in her soft, gnarled hands. A tear trickled from the corner of her eye.

"*Sí, sí, sí, mi amor, como no,*" Mama said, radiant, and kissed my cheek. "*Que Dios te bendiga.*"

They say when a door closes in your life, God always opens a window. A door had been slammed shut in my face when I went to visit my grandparents that summer afternoon. By the time I left an hour later, the wooden shutters of a big Spanish colonial window had been flung wide open.

Chapter Twenty

MI GUAJIRITA LINDA NEVER FORGET WHERE YOU CAME FROM

"How's married life with your *Americanito*?" Papi asked in a letter awaiting me when I returned from my honeymoon. He regretted not having been able to come to my wedding. *I have your framed bridal portrait on my desk at work, that way I see you every day,* he wrote me. In every letter, Papi promised to make a trip to Doylestown with Tita Lala as soon as he could.

I wrote to my father as if I were talking to him: gushing over my new life, describing my secretarial job, boasting about Lee's accomplishments in his last year of college, and sharing our future plans. Papi wanted to know what we did on weekends, what hobbies I enjoyed, how much snow we got in the winter, what music I listened to, what records I had and wanted, what car I drove, and what movies I had seen recently. *Tell me what TV programs you watch so I can watch them too,* he wrote.

Above all, my father was very interested in my Cuban cooking. *Give Lee a dish of black beans, white rice, and picadillo and see what happens—let me know. Keep our tradition going.* When I wrote back that my first attempt at *picadillo* with white rice was a grand success and how much Lee liked our food, Papi sent me a *ranchito*, a care package with all kinds of Cuban groceries that I couldn't find in Pennsylvania. A note inside the parcel read: *Para mi guajirita linda. From now on I will call you 'mi guajirita' because even though you have lived en el norte for so many years, you still love all things Cuban. I know your heart is Cuban. Never forget where you came from.*

I looked forward to my father's letters. They were my constant assurance that he was still doing well, was productive at work and content with his life. *I'm so happy to be alive and healthy, enjoying everything that life has to offer me plus the true love of my dear children.* When I read such words, it seemed too good to be true that this healthy period in Papi's life had lasted a year.

Feeling nostalgic, as I often did when writing him, I once confessed to Papi my fear that since we hadn't been able to live together as a family, and I hadn't seen him for eight years, that he had forgotten what I was like. My father's reply was immediate: *You ask me if I remember you. You can be assured, my beloved Gloria María, that you are always in a little piece of my heart, no matter how many years have passed. Even though destiny has not permitted us to live as a family, my immense love for you is engraved in me until death and after that, forever in eternity.*

There was that horrid word again. Destiny, my archenemy. Maybe this time I would triumph over destiny and rightfully reclaim my father.

It was during this lucid and endearing period in my father's life that I made an indelible connection with him. In our copious letters, we shared our passion for Cuba, our *patria*, and our mutual love for all things French, history, art, traveling, and especially literature and writing.

During the early part of 1970, Papi developed a deep desire to write about Cuba. He immersed himself in Miami's Cuban environment; *I caught the exile's fever,* he wrote. He became up to date on all political anti-Castro activities and wrote passionate, patriotic articles, sending them to local newspapers and magazines, where a few were published.

"Pepe Millán," his beautifully written, moving account of his brother Oscar's brother-in-law who died valiantly during the Bay of Pigs invasion, was published in Miami's *Diario de las Americas* newspaper on February 10, 1970. He entered the piece in a contest in honor of Cuban patriot José Martí and the anniversary of Cuba's independence. He received an honorable mention award that was presented to him during a ceremony in Miami on May 20, 1970, the actual anniversary of Cuba's independence. Then, in the early summer of 1970, Papi received an offer to write his own column in a local newspaper called *El Crisol de la Libertad.* He named his column *Desde Mi Trinchera*—From My Trench.

An all-consuming ardor was ignited in my father. In a letter dated April 15, 1970, he wrote: *I believe that the beautiful rainbow of peace and prosperity will shine again over the meadows and mountains of Cuba. My writing feels like a vocational calling from God. I feel it. The words pour forth onto the paper so easily, a flow of ideas about our enslaved homeland Cuba. I have a deep conviction that this vocation will be with me until the end of my days.*

Meanwhile, in Doylestown, my grandparents were preparing to leave for Miami. After spending a year with their son and his family, they decided to live on their own, hoping to find the peace of mind that kept eluding them.

"A room with a bathroom is all we need," Bibi told his family when we all gathered for dinner the night before they left. "We don't want to be a burden anymore. This is the way we want it to be until the day we can return to Cuba or until the day we die."

Despite their family's concerns and our opposition to them living alone, Mama and Bibi settled in a modest boardinghouse near their daughter Pucha. My grandparents made do with Bibi's Social Security income and financial help from their four children.

I'm living at the Ritz! my father wrote in his letter of November 21, 1970. *How swanky is that?* He was now living in a hotel room on Flagler Street, in the heart of Miami. Papi wrote that he was busy at work and with his column and involved with the freeing of Cuba.

My father strongly believed that the liberation of Cuba could be achieved only by the work of Cubans on the island. The United States could not help because of their pact with Russia. He felt confident that once Cuba was freed, the U.S. would then give economic aid to help rebuild the island and establish a strong democracy.

He wrote as if its liberation would take place any day now, and when that happened, he would be among the first to return to his *Cuba libre*. His letter read as if he were saying goodbye: *No matter what happens, always remember my love for you is rooted very deep in my heart. I will be your father until I die.*

What was happening to Papi? This letter was different. Toward its end, it seemed to unravel wildly. On the last page, his neat penmanship grew larger and larger, switching frantically from English to Spanish and scribbling unevenly all over the page. Instead of the familiar Papi with the oversized dot on the *i*, this time he signed "Big Fat Daddy."

The following Sunday, when I visited my mother for dinner, I shared my concern over my father's recent letter.

"Papi makes it sound like there's another Cuba invasion brewing in Miami and he's ready to go with it." I stopped tossing the salad and looked at my mother. She heaved a sigh.

"*Ay, m'ija*, so much of what your father says is fabricated in his mind."

"He's not doing well, is he?" I put the salad aside.

"All we know is what we hear from him through his letters or phone calls," she said. "Nobody from the Fernández family ever calls to tell me anything about your father."

"Do you know if he's seeing a psychiatrist, or if he's taking the meds he's supposed to be taking?" I pressed on.

"I don't know, I don't know anything," my mother said abruptly. She slammed the rice fork hard on the counter. An argument was itching under my skin.

"Well, who's taking care of him? Does anyone check on him to make sure he's all right?" No reply. "Mami, what are we going to do about it?" I demanded, aware of the mounting impatience marking my voice. "He's been doing so well for the past two years. I don't want him to get sick again." Destiny was breathing down my neck. "Am I the only one in this family who cares?" Tears of frustration stung my eyes.

"*Cálmate*, Gloria," my mother said sharply. "There's nothing we can do. Your father *is* sick, and he's in your grandmother's care now." Her words grated me to the core. I did not want to be reminded that Papi was a sick man.

"I will talk to him next month when I go to Miami for Mama and Bibi's wedding anniversary." My mother's "in charge" demeanor momentarily reassured me. "I will also talk to Tita Lala and try to find out what is going on with your father." Mami turned around and faced the window over the kitchen sink. Her hands grabbed the edge of the basin.

"Someone has to help him before he gets worse." My tone was final. My mother nodded slowly. Then, staring out the window, she said, "There's just so much I can do." The conversation was closed, like a box with a sprung lid.

Miami ended up being the best place for my grandparents. With many of their relatives and friends from Cuba living nearby, the tropical weather, and the extensive Spanish-speaking community, Mama and Bibi were content with their newfound independence.

On January 1, 1971, my grandparents celebrated their fiftieth golden wedding anniversary with a mass and dinner party, surrounded by their four children and many of their grandchildren, relatives, and friends.

"It was the happiest I've seen them since they left Cuba," my mother told me when she returned from her long weekend in Miami. "But it was heartbreaking when we had to say goodbye."

My father had written me only twice since his upsetting letter in November. I knew what the silence meant.

"How is Papi doing? Did you see him? What did he say?" I fired away at my mother. She had come to our apartment for dinner and sat at the dinette table while I cooked.

"I called your grandmother first to find out how he was doing. She had to hospitalize him for a few days a couple of weeks ago." Mami paused and sipped her wine. "He had to quit his job at the lumber company. That's why he moved to Miami, so he can be near Tita Lala and the family. Your grandmother set him up in a hotel room downtown."

"Yeah, the Ritz," I said sarcastically and stopped stirring the *ropa vieja*. I turned around to face my mother. "So, now he's not working anymore?"

"*No, m'ija.* He can't. He's very unstable again."

"His newspaper column." My words struggled to come out. "Is he still writing?"

"Yes, he's really immersed in his writing about Cuba. He finished a booklet titled *Cuba en Llamas* and is hoping to have it published."

"Thank God! I'm so glad at least he still has that. But you didn't get to see him, huh," I guessed, disappointed.

"No, your grandmother suggested I didn't." Mami shook her wineglass slightly, watching the ice clink against its sides. "But at least I was able to talk to him." An air of sadness flitted across her face.

I resented my mother's complacency with Tita Lala. I would never have tolerated my grandmother not allowing me to see my father after almost nine years. At least, not without an argument, I reasoned.

I was prepared to wage a battle with destiny. I was resolved to fight the good fight to keep my father in my life, and to somehow see him again soon.

"My father the writer," I said aloud to myself, while holding his business card in one hand and his first published work in the other. *Cuba en Llamas* was published on February 5, 1971. It was a compilation of poems and articles, including his previously published piece "Pepe Millán."

Reading my father's work, I discovered a side of him that was foreign to me. I visited his very soul and there was surrounded by a pure emotion for something for which he cared deeply: his *patria*, Cuba. His poetic, eloquent words were intelligently written in a formal Spanish unfamiliar to me. In parts Castilian, it evoked a profound patriotism.

My father's accompanying letter was what I had hoped for. Once again, he was optimistic and affectionate. My Papi was back.

You and Lee have to come to Miami so we can celebrate, he wrote. But money was tight. Lee was finishing his last semester of college, and my secretarial job was our only income. Knowing we could not go, I proposed another idea.

"Why don't you and Tita Lala come visit us this summer?" I asked my father when I called to congratulate him.

"Well, if you and Mr. Lee can't come, then I'll be heading for *el norte* soon." I imagined Papi's smile as I heard him chuckle comfortably, imagined that slow-motion unfurling of his lips that created a friendly expression. He had not yet met my husband and jokingly referred to him as Mr. Lee.

I proposed the visit to my grandmother.

"We'll see, Yoyi." Tita Lala brushed it off when I first called her. But I was relentless. My bombardment of calls and letters to my grandmother finally paid off. After nine long years, I was finally going to see my father again, in August 1971.

"Oh look! There's Papi!" I cried out as we drove up to my mother's house. "That's my father, Lee, there he is!"

He was by himself, leaning against the front-porch siding, smoking a cigar. Since he didn't recognize our car, Papi's eyes followed it curiously as we pulled into the short driveway. As soon as he spotted me bounding out of the '62 Chevy Impala SS, my father's hand went up in his trademark stationary wave. He quickly put out his cigar and held his arms wide open.

"Gloria María!"

"¡Papi, *al fin!*" He took me in his arms and held me against him. "Papi!" I whispered into his crisp cotton shirt as my cheek pressed against it. I took a deep breath, taking in as much of the scent of his Guerlain cologne as possible, so as to never forget it, to always have it with me. My father did not say a word. I felt his chest heave a soft sigh. Papi kissed the side of my head twice. Looking at his relaxed face, I noticed he didn't look much older, except for a silvering in his mustache, dramatic against his bronzed skin. I squeezed his midriff, hugging him again. His right arm pulled away from me.

"You must be Mr. Lee." Papi's voice sounded scratchy. He cleared his throat. I turned around, still nestled in my father's one-armed embrace.

"Pleased to meet you at last, sir," Lee said cheerfully, shaking Papi's hand a bit too fast.

"That's quite a car you have there." Papi gave my shoulder a squeeze. "She's a beauty."

"Yeah, it's a great car," Lee said proudly, turning to gaze at the turquoise-colored Chevy gleaming in the summer sun.

"*Sí*, that beauty is my rival," I quipped. Behind us the screen door opened.

"Yoyi, *mi niña*," my grandmother greeted me. She

reached for me and held me softly tight. I took in the scent of her old perfume from Cuba as I kissed her cheek. Her jet-black hair was now silver around her scalp, but the skin on her face was still smooth, unwrinkled.

"¿Abuelita, *qué tal?*" I hated calling her granny, but she loved it and insisted her grandchildren now call her that instead of Tita Lala. I quickly liberated myself from my grandmother's embrace. I felt uncomfortable. At almost twenty-three years old, I was fully aware of what had transpired in our family since we had left Cuba. I sensed the friction between my grandmother and my mother, and I was hurt that I now felt shunned by my father's family… and gnawed by the frustration that there was nothing I could do about it.

As it always seems after anticipating a special event for so long, Papi and Tita Lala's four-day visit seemed to evaporate. Throughout the weekend, Papi had been at ease and talkative. But by Sunday, during a family picnic at our apartment, his mood had changed to an eerie remoteness. He seemed restless and constantly hounded my mother about living with her again in Doylestown.

As we said our goodbyes, it took all of us children to reassure my father that we would see him again soon. We encouraged him to continue with his writing and stressed how important his commitments in Miami were. A calm washed over Papi, and he was able to leave us amicably. It felt wrong, making empty promises and banishing my father back to his lonely life in a hotel room.

Papi remained dedicated to his writing. Soon after his August visit, he penned a short story that was published in a Spanish magazine. His next goal was to write a novel.

But by late fall 1971, his letters became erratic again. In his now sloppy, uneven penmanship, he wrote that somehow he would find a way to move to Doylestown as soon as possible. During this time, Papi wrote to Mami incessantly, often calling her collect. He was adamant about living with her again. He claimed that they had been apart for too many years, that he missed and loved her and his children and wanted to make up for lost time.

When my mother separated from my father, she had told her parents that as soon as her children were on their own, she planned to live with her husband again and devote her life to helping him. Divorce was out of the question for her. To Mami, this painful yet necessary separation was only temporary. She explained to Papi that she still had the responsibility of raising three teenagers but that someday they could talk about living together again. Papi would not hear of it.

You cannot deny me my children, he wrote her. *I'm still your husband and their father.* Fearing Papi's increasing determination to come to Doylestown, my mother worried what he would do next.

By mid-February 1972, my father stopped writing to me altogether. He wrote only to my mother, the same implacable letters about coming to Doylestown. I continued writing him, telling him about our new dog, a sweet, smart, Shepherd-collie mix we named Bessy, and of our move to a roomier apartment in nearby Solebury. Still, no letters came. His silence augmented my awareness of his mental anguish and my desperation that I was once again losing my father.

In late February, Mami showed me a letter she had received from Papi. *They are after me because of what I've written about Cuba. They're going to kill me, Ninina. Please help me. Let me come and stay with you.* At the end he wrote, *If you won't let me live with you, maybe I can stay with Gloria and Lee until I find a place of my own. Give my love to my children. Tell them I will see them soon.*

"What's going on, Mami? When is Papi coming?" As I held the letter in my hands, my father's agony seared through me.

"He cannot come," my mother said with a harsh finality. "If he calls you and asks to stay with you, you have to say no." I looked at the wild, uneven handwriting.

"Doesn't Tita Lala realize how bad he is?" I asked, incredulous. "Is Papi under psychiatric treatment?"

My mother lit a cigarette and inhaled deeply. She was smoking more than usual these days. "I've called your grandmother twice about this. Each time I talk to her, she tells me the same thing. She says that your father is doing fine, good days and bad, and for me to stop exaggerating."

I could not believe that no one in my father's family acknowledged his paranoid behavior and his frightening, deteriorating emotional state. Worse yet, that no one was doing anything to help him.

I heard from Papi on a cold, gray Sunday in early March 1972. "*¿Yoyi, como andas?*" He sounded nervous.

My stomach churned hard. "Papi, where've you been, *pillo*? I haven't heard from you in ages." Did he notice the shakiness in my voice as I tried to sound upbeat? We talked about his novel, his newspaper column, the weather in Miami, and how Lee and I were doing. I knew I was stalling for time.

"Yoyi, I want to go to Doylestown and be near my family again." My father's voice grew serious. My heart raced, throbbing in my neck as I waited for what I knew was coming next. "Can I live with you and Lee for a while until I settle on my own?" Sitting on a kitchen chair, I leaned forward and put my face in my free hand and closed my eyes, struggling against the words that were ready to burst out of my mouth.

"I'm sorry, Papi, we have no room," I said flatly, the guilt of my lie weighing me down as I thought of our empty guest room. I was torn between doing what my mother had asked and helping my father in any way I could.

"Oh…" he started, broke off. "You were my last hope."

I winced. "I'm sorry, Papi." I got up and walked as far as the phone cord would stretch, then leaned against the hallway wall. "Maybe now is not the time for you to come to Doylestown. You can…"

"No, no, no. I have to go now. I have to leave Miami immediately." The panic in my father's voice frightened me.

"But Papi, listen,"

"Don't worry. I'll find a way and I will see you soon. I have to go. It's not safe for me to be on the phone too long. I love you, *mucho, mucho*."

"*Espera*, Papi, wait!" The line went dead.

I hung up in slow motion. The kitchen walls seemed to close in on me. Air. I needed air. I couldn't breathe. Bessy sprung up from her nap on the kitchen rug and sat by me, her thick brindle fur pressed against my jeans.

Wagging her tail rapidly, she sprinted to the front door and pranced around.

"You need to go out, Bess?" I asked her, mechanically grabbing my jacket, knit cap, and gloves. The dry, wintry air smacked my face. Odd, I didn't seem to mind the cold like I usually did. I was glad I didn't have to use a leash on Bessy. Even though our apartment was on a thick wooded lot, she listened well and always stayed close by. Bess romped through the tall, thin trees, exploring, poking her nose under snow-covered fallen branches, and occasionally looking back to check on me.

We reached a clearing where Lee had dug a small pit for campfires. The stones he had found in the woods formed a sturdy low wall around it. I sat on the hollow log that was our makeshift bench while Bessy investigated a nearby tree stump. The setting sun's last rays cast an amber glow around me. My mind kept replaying my father's plea to stay with us. My response stung my conscience.

The outline of a luminous crimson sun glimmered through the towering elms, oaks, and walnut trees surrounding me. "God, why can't I have my father? How much more suffering do you need from him?" *Never ask God why,* the Sacred Heart nuns' voices reverberated in my head. *There are no answers here on earth. We must learn to accept without asking why.*

"Why?" I heard myself question God once more.

I waited for Him to answer, to give me a sign, something, anything to help ease my misery. A few snowflakes floated softly through the air. Their rhythmic descent reminded me of the first time I saw snow in Lumberville with my father. We had sat and looked out at the imposing Delaware

River from our living room window. Papi's eyes were filled with the same wonderment that I felt as we watched the snowfall together. I felt a sudden peace, recalling painfully normal moments shared with Papi. Times when I believed I did have a father.

As the sun dipped into the horizon, in the stillness of the Bucks County woods that my father loved so well, my tears mixed with the snowflakes that landed on my face.

By early April 1972, María Elena had ballooned gracefully into her seventh month of pregnancy. As the baby's future godmother, I embarked on preparations for a surprise baby shower at my home on April 30.

My father had relented on his letters and phone calls to Mami about coming to Pennsylvania. None of us had heard from him in the last month. One Saturday morning, while my mother sat at her kitchen table knitting a baby blanket, I was sitting across from her, addressing shower invitations. The sudden shrill of her ringing phone pierced the quiet comfort in the room. My mother was surprised to receive a call from her brother-in-law in Miami. She listened intently, placing the blanket on the table, the knitting needles clanking loudly. Mami's face went pale, her lips parted slightly. Uncle Wilfredo told my mother that Papi had gone to see him at work the day before. He said my father looked unkempt and acted extremely nervous. What greatly disturbed my uncle was that Papi had asked him for help in buying a gun for protection. My uncle told him to forget about such a dangerous idea. He warned my mother that Papi had been in bad shape when he stormed out of his office, yelling out the door that he would find a gun on his own.

Mami immediately phoned Papi's sister Emma in Miami. There was an urgency in her voice as she told her about Uncle Wilfredo's call. My aunt insisted that Papi was doing fine. How could Aunt Emma not be concerned? I was terrified, imagining my father, in his unstable frame of mind, wandering the streets of downtown Miami in search of a weapon. What if he had one already? While I worried that my father would hurt himself, Mami feared that and worse. Was he angry enough to hurt her because she denied his pleas to live with her? My mother sought legal counsel.

"He cannot come to Doylestown. He is a grave danger to you and your children in the state of mind he's in," the lawyer stressed to my mother. He advised her to divorce Papi. She refused. After all she and my father had gone through, Mami would not do that to him now, not while he was in such pain, even though she feared for his life and hers.

The lawyer urged my mother to get a restraining order against my father. Again, she refused to do anything that would implicate my father with the law. And so we continued waiting for news from Miami that my father had calmed down, praying that someone in his family was watching over him.

Unbeknownst to us, Papi spiraled deeper into paranoia. On April 24, 1972, alone and afraid in his hotel room, he shot himself in the shoulder and leg with a .22 caliber gun. According to the police report, at 3 p.m. a maid down the hallway heard his cries for help. She called the hotel manager, who found my father conscious, lying on the floor of his room by the door. Papi admitted to the manager that he had shot himself.

He was rushed by ambulance to the hospital. No one in the Fernández family called my mother to tell her what had happened to her husband. Two days later, a blood clot developed in Papi's brain as a result of his wounds. The doctors informed my relatives that an immediate risky operation was the only option to save his life. If Papi survived the procedure, he would probably be left partially paralyzed. My father was operated on that day.

As I wrapped my sister's baby presents and fussed over the last-minute details for the surprise shower, my father lay paralyzed in a coma in critical condition. Still, no one called my mother.

Another two days passed. On Friday, a Fernández relative, without the family knowing, finally called my mother.

I clung steadfastly to the hope that Papi would survive. I wanted to run to his bedside, hold his strong hand, breathe my life into him.

My mother insisted we carry on with the shower plans. I went through the motions robotically; my whole being was in Miami with Papi. Tears blurred my eyes as I wrapped bunches of almonds in white netting and tied them with pink and blue satin ribbons, all the while praying that my father would live to see his grandchild. But he never regained consciousness. That Sunday morning on April 30, six days after shooting himself, my father died of a cerebral hemorrhage. He was fifty-one years old.

My mother had received the call from Aunt Blanca while getting ready to leave for the shower. Mami waited until the party was over to give us children the heartbreaking news. She did not tell my aunt that we would be in Miami for my father's funeral.

Our flight was packed. The coach cabin's stale, warm air was near nauseating. To my left, my mother sat quietly in the aisle seat. To my right, my nineteen-year-old sister Madeleine looked out the window as the luggage carts sped away from the plane. My brothers, nineteen-year-old Jorge and Roly, twenty, sat in the row in front of us. Because of her advanced pregnancy, María Elena's doctor advised that she not make the trip to Florida.

The engines started humming, roaring louder as the aircraft lumbered onto the runway to gain acceleration for take off. Within seconds, the jet was climbing toward the clouds. Leaning my head back, I closed my eyes. A pristine vision of my father engulfed me, saturating my thoughts with memories of him.

I'm coming, Papi.

The powerful thrust of the jet engines made me glance at my watch. *We'll be landing soon*, I thought. The roar of the plane propelled the feelings welling and raging within me.

Pity and sorrow were the first to claim me. My mind was tortured by visions of my father's last moments before pulling the trigger of a weapon no one knew he had. I forced myself to sense his desperation, his lifetime longing to be with his wife and children cruelly denied by his mental illness. I related to his yearning, similar to the one I had always had for my father.

I was sickened by the immense feeling of rejection he must have felt, thinking that all whom he thought loved him actually did not care for him. That included me. In his dismal hotel room, before shooting himself, did Papi cry out one last time at the life that had given him so much suffering?

Anger. It barreled through my other emotions, surfacing in the tears that stung my eyes. Destiny drove a hard bargain with my father. The attention that Papi pitifully craved cost him his life. I reeled with the agony of defeat, seething at destiny's victory in its relentless battle.

The sudden opening of the airplane's flaps thumped beneath us. The aircraft angled toward descent, slowing down, pulling back. A smooth landing.

I'm here, Papi.

During our short taxi ride to the funeral home in Miami, my mother seemed in perfect control of her emotions, exuding an air of composure. Tensing her jaw, she looked straight ahead at nothing, her eyes brilliant. I worried about the feelings I was sure were churning deep within her unnerving silence.

Our unexpected entrance at the funeral home was like an apparition to the gathered guests. The sight of my mother caused a sudden silence in the crowded room, as they paused their conversations to take in her presence. My siblings and I flanked our mother. The five of us, abreast, walked confidently toward the open casket. Sporadic gasps, whispers, and quiet comments broke out as we filed by.

"It's the widow and her children!"

"Oh my God, it's Ninina!"

My mother didn't pause. I supported her elbow with my hand; she leaned hard into it. Her fixed expression announced *get out of my way* to everyone in the room. Mami's eyes remained focused on the coffin. We looked straight ahead, like advancing soldiers, not stopping to greet anyone. Straight ahead to Papi.

Stopping several feet from the casket, I let go of Mami's arm. She took a rattling deep breath. Then, slowly, she walked up to my father by herself. My mother's dreadful, keening wail pierced the now deafening stillness of the room. My heart broke for her despair.

"¡*Ay*, Rolando, *mi amor!*" She clasped her hands, holding them to her chin as she gazed upon his lifeless body. "*Solo tú y yo sabemos lo que hemos sufrido*—only you and I know the suffering we have endured." Then, spreading her arms open, my mother leaned forward and collapsed on my father's torso. She laid her head on his chest and sobbed bitterly.

I was not prepared to see Papi reposing so peacefully. I choked a gasp. No tears. I stared at him, willing his brown eyes to open, his lips to part, forming the smile that had always warmed my heart. But my handsome father's face remained unchanged, reflecting only his deep eternal slumber.

The tension between my mother and my father's family was intensely evident throughout the viewing. Tita Lala, especially, appeared incensed that Mami had come, yet she was extremely affectionate with me.

"Abuelita, I'm so sorry," I said softly, greeting her. She folded me in her arms and wept, shuddering. A great tenderness sprang up in me, melting away my irreconcilable feelings. I understood with certainty that my grandmother did love her son. Terrified of his illness, she had been unable to come to terms with it, yet Papi had unfailingly loved her deeply.

I also realized that the friction and resentment between

my grandmother and my mother had nothing to do with me. She was my *abuelita*, my father's mother, and I loved her. In her eyes, I saw clearly the pain of her loss.

"*Pobrecito* Rolando, *tu Papi*," she said, caressing my face. "At last he is at peace."

The following morning, at the funeral home, Mami and we children waited for family and guests to pay their last respects before the casket was closed in preparation for burial. There was soft weeping all around me. Where were my tears, my intense feelings of loss? When the room was almost empty, my inconsolable mother walked up to my father, looked at him for several moments, then gently embraced him one last time. I stayed behind while my sister and brothers accompanied Mami out to the lobby to await the limousine that would drive us to the cemetery. I was alone in the room with Papi. The silence was heavy, consoling.

The folded paper quivered slightly in my hands as I inched closer to the casket. I knelt down on the padded kneeler and prayed for my father's soul. The flower arrangement that we children had sent him was placed at the head of the casket. Without thinking, I reached out and plucked from it a white carnation, Papi's favorite flower. Standing up, I leaned over and inserted it in the eyehole of his suit lapel. Then I slipped my folded letter into the left pocket, right by his heart. Holding my hand over it momentarily, I was astounded at the hardness of his chest. *Papi is dead.* My heart was seized with an all-consuming pity for my father's wasted life. I was ambushed by love for my Papi—by regret for the family life we were never able to have.

The darkness of unhappy memories tormented me as my childhood welled up in my mind.

Destiny robbed me of my father. I defied the thief and forced myself to produce loving remembrances of my Papi. A few precious vignettes intertwined with the first years of my life fluttered elusively in the corners of my mind. I recalled going for ice cream at El Recodo and then for long walks on El Malecón. I could feel my father's firm grasp as he held me while I stood on the promenade's low stone seawall, both of us looking out at La Punta fortress and El Morro castle looming across the harbor. Spending lazy summer days at the Biltmore Country Club—Papi pushing me in my boat swing on the beach playground, swimming with him in the warm ocean, celebrating birthday parties that lasted all day long. These memories seemed like faded photographs of someone who loved me once, so long ago I scarcely remembered. Yet my heart compelled me to keep these treasured mementos that destiny left behind.

My eyes focused on Papi's face. His countenance radiated a tranquil expression, as if finally free from the emotional turmoil that had devoured his life. His face, bronzed by the sun, just like that day in Kawama when we walked the beach hand in hand. I looked down at my wrist, at the gold bracelet with dainty seashells that he had given me for my twelfth birthday. His voice sprang out from the ashes of my childhood: *So you always remember Kawama*...it was then, in the cold viewing room, redolent with the intoxicating scent of the flowers that surrounded his corpse, that I mourned my father with a despair I had never known.

I lingered for quite a while until the funeral director entered the parlor and headed for an adjacent room. Soft sounds coming through the open door told me it was time to leave.

I said goodbye to my father, quoting the closing words in my letter; they were his words, written to me not so long ago. *Even though destiny has not permitted us to live together as a family, my immense love for you is engraved in me until death and after that, forever in eternity.*

I kissed my fingers and tenderly touched his cheek. Then I left the room in search of my mother.

After the funeral, Mami, my siblings, and I spent the rest of the day with Mama and Bibi before our flight home the following morning. My grandfather's health had deteriorated greatly since October 1971, when he suffered prostate gland problems and underwent an operation. The stress of the surgery proved too much for his heart, causing a massive attack immediately after. Though Bibi's health remained fragile, he and Mama insisted on continuing to live by themselves in Miami.

Their home was an old-fashioned boardinghouse with a small veranda. Palm trees, colorful crotons and hibiscus, and areca palms bordered the property. We headed down a long, dark hallway toward their room, greeting friendly seniors along the way. The faint smell of medicines, antiseptic, and stale coffee wafted from the rooms as we walked by. *This can't be where my grandparents are living*, I thought, unprepared for the sight that awaited me.

As we passed an open doorway, the sounds of a TV blasted, while a white-haired woman swayed gently in her rocker. Hearing our echoing footsteps in the tiled hallway, she turned her head abruptly as we walked by. An anticipating smile lit up her face. It broke my heart to see how quickly it faded as she realized we were strangers on our way to make someone else happy with our visit.

At the very end of the hall, framed by the light of a window, the silhouettes of my grandparents were unmistakable. *Mama y Bibi.* The tall, lean physique of an old gentleman standing ever close to the stout, diminutive form of his long-standing lady. They stood waiting for us by their doorway, my grandmother waving gaily. It had been two years since I'd seen Mama and Bibi. His almost seventy-six years hung heavy on my grandfather's delicate frame. It was startling how prominent the veins were on his tanned, transparent skin.

Mama's arthritis had accentuated the hunch on her back, and the pain in her legs caused her to move slower, but her spirit was undaunted as she cheerfully welcomed us into their unit.

Inside their nutshell of a room, a dismal contrast to Rancho Perea, I was surrounded by the sad summation of my grandparents' lives. Immaculately neat and clean, the cramped room had two single beds, a dresser, a chair, and a tiny bathroom. An old air conditioner hummed steadily on their windowsill. In the corner of the room, next to the bathroom, Mama had created a little kitchen; a small wooden table held a box refrigerator, a hot plate, toaster, and blender. Next to that, a narrow bookshelf held groceries. They ate their meals on TV tables, and my grandmother washed their dishes in the bathroom sink.

A scant nighttable between the two beds was transformed into an altar for their ever-present companion. There, as beautiful as I always remembered her, was their beloved Virgencita. The votive candle burned brightly, and a bouquet of jasmine scented the room.

We sat on their beds and visited while my mother put away the two bags of groceries and staples she had brought her parents. Mama opened the box of chocolate-covered cherries, her favorite, that we'd brought, then served us *batido de mamey* and my favorite Cuban cookies, *galleticas de María*. I marvelled at my grandmother's dexterity in her constricting quarters, how she maneuvered things so easily in her makeshift kitchen area, as gracefully as she had done in her huge, bright kitchen in Havana.

While Mami and Mama talked about the funeral, Bibi comforted me on my father's passing. Time stole silently away. I wanted to stay longer, much longer, and console my grandfather, this proud and loving man who had been the one true father I had ever known and whose spirit was so painfully broken.

Looking past the sadness in his face as he spoke to me, in his lively hazel eyes, the eyes of a man who possessed such wit and intelligence, I recognized the protective and much-adored patriarch of our family, strolling around his beloved *finca*, wearing his favorite *pantalones mecánicos*, plaid shirt, and comfortable leather boots. In my mind I clearly heard the joyful shrieks and peals of laughter coming from the gaggle of his grandchildren in Rancho Perea's swimming pool. I wanted to reach out to that past that would never be ours again, lost forever in the blink of an eye.

As we walked outside to our waiting taxi, Bibi's arm in the crook of mine, a fragrant wind blew softly into my face. Vibrant red, coral, and white hibiscus bloomed along the sidewalks. In the honeyed light of late-afternoon sun,

I missed Cuba with an overwhelming desire.

Remembering that snowy day in Doylestown when my grandfather had yearned for his palm trees, I said to him, "Look at all these *palmitas*, Bibi. It's almost like being in Cuba."

With the same wistful glint in his eyes I had seen then, he smiled at me. "*Sí*, but they are not la Palma Real de Cuba. Do you remember? So tall and regal, with smooth, white trunks. Someday, when we go home again to Cuba, you will see why they are so special to me."

It would not abate, that heartbreaking longing that had possessed my grandfather since the day he left his island home. After eleven years, my grandparents still clung to the hope that any day the communist nightmare in Cuba would be over and they could return to their life in Havana, to the golden days before Castro's revolution.

The struggle to constantly be with their children was over. My grandparents were now resigned to wait in Miami: for their children and grandchildren to visit them whenever possible, for the liberation of Cuba, for the day God would take them home.

I knew in my heart that this was the last time I would see my grandfather. I felt the warmth of his love as I hugged his frail body and kissed him goodbye.

Unabashed tears streaked my face as I threw kisses to my grandparents out the taxi window. They stood close together, their arms around each other, smiling and waving goodbye. I watched their forms grow smaller and smaller until they disappeared in the distance.

As Mama later told us, at bedtime one night in November 1972, Bibi seemed unusually melancholic. While she turned down the sheets and brought him his glass of water to set on the nightstand, my grandfather sat at the edge of his bed gazing at the Virgencita.

"Bebita," he said to his wife. "Let's say our prayers together tonight."

"*¿Estás bien*, Gustavo?" Mama stopped folding back the bedspread and frowned at him. Bibi patted a spot on the bed next to him and nodded slowly.

"*Sí, sí*, I'm just a bit tired tonight. *Ven*, come sit with me."

"*¿Qué te pasa*, Gustavo?" Mama cooed, sitting close to him.

"I'll never see *mi Cuba* again." He looked around at his spartan surroundings. "*Más nunca*."

"*Ay, viejo*, don't talk like that." She tapped his knee gently.

"I wish that I could die *en mi patria*—in my native land." Bibi laid his hand over Mama's.

"*Lo que Dios disponga, mi vida. Bueno*, let's say our prayers. *En el nombre del Padre, del Hijo y del Espíritu Santo…*" As my grandmother crossed herself to pray, Bibi leaned against her. She turned and caught him as he slumped forward. "Gustavo! Gustavo!" she cried out, cradling him in her arms. She looked over at the statue of the Blessed Mother. "¡*Ayúdame, Virgen mía*!" she pleaded. "¡*Ay, no*, Gustavo, *no*. Don't leave me!"

Darkness.

The bright glow that was my grandfather's love was extinguished in my soul the day Bibi died of a heart attack.

The very heart of my Cuban being stopped beating with the passing of our family's patriarch. The anchor of my life had been set free, leaving me adrift in an ocean of emotional uncertainty. I felt an unspeakable emptiness. Yet, in my sorrow there was consoling joy, for I knew my grandfather's spirit was home at last, basking in the tropical sunshine with his beloved Palmas Real de Cuba.

Epilogue

Every family has a historian, the torch carrier of each generation.

After their deaths in 1972, it was as if my father's and grandfather's longing to see Cuba again was passed on to me. I grasped the torch and began gathering information about our family's past, listening to my older Cuban relatives recall their life stories. When I gave birth to my first child, in 1976, it was then that the thought of writing this book came to me—the sweet ache of nostalgia became an insistent desire to pen down the story of my Cuban youth and exodus to America. Our lost culture, richly woven with ancestral roots, ethnic traditions, and indefatigable Cuban spirit, needed to be preserved for the generations that follow. I wanted my daughter to know about the Latin blood streaming red through her infant veins. It was her heritage, a precious gift to pass on to her.

It seems a lifetime ago, when that twelve-year-old girl stood on the tarmac in Miami, next to the airplane that flew her to freedom.

In 1961, I became a statistic when I fled Cuba as part of Operation Pedro Pan, one of the largest political exoduses of children in history. Between 1960 and 1962, approximately

14,000 children were sent out of Cuba by panic-stricken parents to protect them from a future under communism. Around 7,000 of these children, myself included, arrived in Miami, unaccompanied. Some were not as fortunate as I; they didn't have relatives to live with until they could be reunited with their parents. These children were taken to temporary camps in Miami until provisional homes across the country were found for them.

After mourning my losses, I tucked away the memories of those traumatic experiences in a far corner of my mind. I suppose it was a survival mechanism, allowing my youth's resilience to kick in and help me accept and embrace my new life in America.

But I'm still an exile in Neverland: perennially waiting, holding on to the dream of someday seeing Cuba again. My heart skips a beat each time Fidel Castro's name is mentioned on the news. I stop what I'm doing and turn up the volume on the TV, paying total attention. Is it over? Is Cuba finally free of communism?

I plummet into disappointment again. Does the world really want to know that Castro tripped and fell while giving a speech in Havana?

As my mind sifted through the memories, at times it seemed as if they happened to someone else, not to the Americanized version of the woman I am today. But that someone else *is* the other version of me—what makes me a Cuban-American.

I became a citizen of the United States of America in Philadelphia in March 1973, a privilege I had to earn and today treasure with my life. I experienced that momentous event with my husband, Lee, and with Ed Howard, who, to me, will forever embody the good and giving heart of the American people.

Standing next to the famed Liberty Bell, I ran my fingers over its crack. Liberty. The word evokes unforgettable memories of my family's, especially my mother's, struggle to attain it. On that day I promised myself I would never take for granted the precious gift of that freedom—the freedom for which my family, without looking back, left their possessions, their lives, and their beloved homeland.

As I was sworn in before a judge along with a large group of immigrants, my feelings were conflicting. *I am an exile, not an immigrant,* I remember thinking. I was driven from my native land. I did not come into a foreign country on my own free will searching for a new life and a permanent place to live. It was supposed to be for a little while only, wasn't it? Only until the *barbudo* Castro was kicked out of Cuba.

And yet, I felt immensely grateful to this benevolent country for allowing me to live freely after fleeing the communist oppression that continues to tyrannize my homeland. Before I was pronounced an American, a wistful sadness washed over me. I felt I was betraying the land of my birth. That day I pledged my allegiance to the United States of America, my eyes welling with thankful tears as I proudly recited the words *with liberty and justice for all.* But in my heart I also pledged my fidelity to Cuba. I have, to this day, a divided loyalty to both countries. At that solemn, patriotic moment, which belonged to America only, I made a firm resolve: I will never forget that my roots are Cuban. *Yo soy Cubana.*

My father was right about me; my heart will always be Cuban.

As time passes, I am acutely aware that I am not as American as I thought I was. I have often felt oddly different in the ways I think, act, and even practice my religion in this country. I am keenly aware that something about me is incompatible with my American identity—something, despite the many years of adapting to a new culture, that I have never wanted to change. *Yo soy Cubana.* At times I have felt out of place, as if temporarily waiting to be back where I belong. I now realize that that place exists only in my memories.

My childhood memories belong to Cuba.

Although as a result of my father's illness, my youth was not always stable, my school years at the Sacred Heart Academy helped maintain one aspect of my childhood on sure ground. My longing for that part of my past was somewhat satisfied many years later in a small chapel in Rome.

Throughout my cherished years at the Sacred Heart, I had a deep devotion to Mater, the Blessed Mother and patroness of our school. The last time I saw the beautiful life-size statue of Mater was in February 1961, shortly before I fled communist Cuba. I feared I would never see her again. Years later, I was planning my first trip to Europe in 1999. It was a fast-paced group tour providing only one free day in Rome. I was determined to see the original fresco of Mater in a church in that city.

On that glorious fall morning in *bella* Roma, the first thing I did was ask our hotel concierge to call the Sacro Cuore Convent for me to see if I could visit Mater. She dialed the number and after a brief conversation in Italian,

Epilogue

the young woman covered the mouthpiece with her hand and gave me a blank look.

"I'm sorry, *signora,* there are no visiting tours today," she informed me in a snippy tone.

"Oh no, please." My voice was desperate as I plunked down both my hands on the countertop in front of her. She glanced down at my hands, then looked at me, raising an eyebrow.

"Please tell her I've come all the way from America and only have today to visit Rome," I pleaded on. "And tell her I was a student at the Sacred Heart in Havana, Cuba." She rolled her eyes. I wanted to pull out the pins of her fancy up-do and cut off her long French manicured nails. The animated Italian conversation continued. By the concierge's dour expression, I could see a final no coming. But before she could speak a word in her broken English I implored one last time.

"Please tell her I am a child of the Sacred Heart of Jesus." Feeling like I had just used a secret password, I watched her lips intently as she rattled off my plea in Italian. I waited for the final response.

"Gratzie, multo gratzie." The young woman placed the receiver back on its cradle. *Sí, ben*e. I was in. I had been granted special permission to see Mater.

My husband and I immediately took a taxi to the top of the Spanish Steps and got off in front of Trinita dei Monti Church, adjacent to the Sacred Heart convent. I pulled much too hard on the rope of a little brass bell next to a window by the entrance. A young *hermanita* opened the sliding glass pane and greeted me with a cheery *buon giorno,* motioning me to come in.

355

A few steps inside the cloistered convent and I was instantly back in time, overcome with the familiar tranquility. The sunny courtyard was an identical replica of the one in my school in Cuba. I stood stunned for a moment, surrounded by long-ago memories. An elderly *Madre* greeted us, then led the way to a formal foyer. Pointing to the stairway that led to the chapel, she smiled at me knowingly and said, "Mater." The *Madre* nodded gently and quietly left us.

On my way up the worn marble steps, I stopped on the landing to admire a protrait of Saint Madeleine Sophie. Suddenly, I was a little girl again. My eyes filled up as I allowed the reverence of the place to envelop me. *Is this really happening? Am I truly here?* Slowly, I walked up the remaining steps.

"I found you, Mater," I whispered wondrously.

Then I saw her, the original 1844 fresco of Mater that the nuns had told me about. I knelt down on an all too familiar wooden kneeler before the beautiful painting—the miracle—surrounded by fragrant white lilies. I looked up at the Virgin, at the exquisite face I had not seen for thirty-eight years. Joyful emotion welled up in me like a long-forgotten spring, making me aware of an intense connection to my past. Mater's sweet gaze welcomed me to a fond childhood memory, if only for a short time.

As we left and I closed the convent's door behind me, a moped whizzed by on the narrow street, plumes of black exhaust trailing behind it. Souvenir vendors lined the *calle* while tourists clambered up the famed Spanish Steps before us, pausing to take pictures as they wove through the crowded staircase. Rome awaited at my feet.

Before descending into the sea of people, I turned to

glance at the Sacro Cuore Convent one last time. I thought of Mater in her quiet nook by the chapel inside. *You brought me all the way to Rome to see you. Ciao, bella Mater.*

When I think of *mi patria*, the glistening, forbidden island in the Caribbean where I was born, a tidal wave of longing hits me. Those few formative years I lived in Cuba have remained the firm core of my being. The influence of my native Spanish culture and traditions has never left me; I won't let it.

I would think that anyone who was abruptly uprooted from their youth's secure, loving setting would inevitably, as the years pass, look back on those early years as idyllic. If the uprooting resulted in exile in a foreign country, the longing for that past is intensified in later life.

I long to return to *mi tierra*. I have treasured my mother's stories; they are my legacy. I have proudly held the torch high, kept the neverending vigil over Cuba, waiting. I have willed the hope of someday seeing my island home again to remain alive in my heart. Someday when Cuba is free from the rusty chains of communism that have enslaved her for more than half a century, someday when it is a democratic republic like my father dreamed it would be. But how much longer must I wait? Now I understand how my grandparents felt, their deep sadness of leaving home. The merciless years roll on; time is running out.

I'm often asked by people, including many relatives who don't wish to return, "Why would you want to go back to Cuba? It's nothing like it was when you last saw it. Don't you want to remember it that way?" My mother sadly tells me, "I can never return. It would break my heart."

She lays her hand on her chest. "*Yo llevo mis recuerdos de Cuba, aquí.*"

My mother's sister and my godmother, Milly, could best answer the incredulous questions from those expatriates who want nothing to do with Cuba: "The only things that Fidel could not destroy in Cuba were her palm trees, or the sky, or the sands that shift in her turquoise sea. He only destroyed our nation and the lives of all of us who lived there. For me, my roots, for me, my country, for me, Cuba is the most beautiful. The sky of Cuba, the climate and colors of Cuba, you cannot find that in any other country in the world, *niña,*" she told me passionately. "*No, eso no se encuentra.*"

I know that the Cuba I once knew died with Fidel Castro's revolution, and yet, so much of the island, especially Havana, has remained the same, despite the decaying homes and buildings in great need of repair. The few cars of today, vintage relics of the 1950s roaming the island's crumbling streets, are like the ones I rode in as a child. Our only relative who stayed behind still lives where she was born and raised, in her parents' Spanish colonial mansion in Reparto Kohly in Havana. Recent pictures show the home and its contents eerily the same as I remember them the last time I was there, in 1960.

Even though life went on for the people who stayed behind and made new lives for themselves, viewing these unchanged images makes it seem as if time stood still when Cuba lost its thousands of fleeing citizens. It's as if the island was left behind by history, untouched, its ancient beauty awaiting the return of her exiled Cubans.

Reflecting on what I've learned in writing this book, I

recognize that racism and a lack of social welfare programs were key problems in pre-Castro Cuba. But brutal revolution and communism were not the way to fix such a rigidly race-based, classist society. I'm glad when I think of all the African Cubans who could finally enjoy an education, health care, and their own home. But it's a devastating shame that that end was achieved through the means of the government robbing other Cubans of their wealth, properties, and, in some cases, their lives.

I need to return to my lost pearl of the Antilles; to wade in its crystalline turquoise waters, my senses enveloped by the constant, consoling sound of the sea; to feel the warmth of the tropical sun on my body. To sink my toes in Varadero's sugary-white beaches and wander the sands with the ghosts of those I knew and loved.

I yearn to feel the island's sultry, sensuous energy, share the joy of life and irreverent sense of humor of *mi gente*, my Cuban people, whose indefatigable spirit is inextinguishable even in difficult times.

I long to feel the balmy tropical breezes welcome me home as I breathe in the sweet air, fragrant with gardenias, jasmine, and citrus. With my head held high, I will gaze at Bibi's beloved lofty palm trees, rustling softly and eternally in the trade winds, and my soul will be soothed. Then I will proudly acknowledge my Cuban roots shining bright within me—*Yo soy Cubana*—and recall a time in my life when I had no doubts about where I belonged.

I am part of the last generation of Cuban exiles in my family. After us, those who journey to Cuba will be our children and grandchildren, born elsewhere in the world, carrying our torches, honoring our memories, and curious to experience a semblance of the sun-drenched Caribbean island that was once our home.

As I age, the stubborn clarity of nostalgia makes my life in Cuba seem more recent in my memory. It illuminates the good, dimming the bad. It's been fifty years since I left the island, yet I haven't forgotten how to get to Rancho Perea:

Guatao Road, past Batista's *finca*, Kuquine, on the right. Left at the corner where the split palm tree grows out over the road. The little winding road past the *capilla* and the Our Lady of Lourdes grotto. Through the dense areca palms ahead, on the right, a chain-link fence, the emerald-green lawn clipped smooth like a golf course, the rambling front porch, set back a ways from the gravel road…Mama and Bibi's *finca*.

I want to walk in the meadows and fields where my grandfather's *finca* once stood before the *milicianos* ripped it away from him. I will stroll down Rancho Perea's long driveway and reclaim the memories of my interrupted childhood.

So I keep waiting for the day I can return.

If I am unable to see *mi Cuba* again, I hope that together, my two daughters will make that return journey in my name. This book will serve as their guide. It will help them to mentally sift through the ruins of my youth, embrace their heritage, and appreciate my romantic leftovers from Cuba.

ACKNOWLEDGEMENTS

When I first decided to write this book, I went to my mother, Ninina.

She was sitting in her rocker by her bedroom window, knitting. I asked her to share with me her memories of when she first met my father, Rolando—her memories of Cuba. The knitting needles ceased their busy work and rested on her lap. That was the start of our many hours of reminiscing. *Gracias*, Mami. Your invaluable stories were the foundation of my book.

In memory of my dear "Mr. Howard," who passed away in January 2011; with a grateful heart I will always remember that spring day in the early 1990s when I visited him for an interview for this book. Barbara Howard had recently passed, and Ed was selling their home on Maple Avenue in Doylestown. We sat in the sunny side porch, a favorite of Mrs. Howard's, where she spent her last days battling cancer. I strongly felt her presence as Ed recounted their selfless involvement in our family's resettling in Doylestown.

I would like to thank Margery Guest, for her insightful editing of my book's first draft. I am also grateful for her invitation to join her writers group, an ensemble of engaging, creative women including Jean Bahle, Laura

Bennett-Kimble, Catherine Frerichs, Diane Herbruck, and Marty Ayres White. My deep appreciation to all of them for believing in the concept of my story, and for their ever-constant encouragement. Their comments and helpful suggestions were instrumental to my work and to my growth as a writer.

To Peter Honsberger, Principal, Cold River Studio, my sincerest thanks for guiding me through the pitfalls of publishing with patience and sound advice. His loyalty to his authors can be matched only by his passion for their work and his efforts to make their books the best they can possibly be. One such example was the design of my book's cover, his creation, which had a stunning effect on me. Working with him has been a rewarding experience.

Above all, my loving gratitude to my daughter, Amy Strassburger Van Stee, who was my first reader and my editor. I need to acknowledge her remarkable perception and unbiased critique throughout the many hours that she labored over my revisions. Amy's unfailing support and encouragement but most importantly, her belief in *Palm Trees in the Snow*, were the wind beneath my wings. A sweet irony of life—as my first child, Amy's birth ignited in me the desire to pen down my family's story. Later in life as a professional editor, she was able to join me in the last leg of my long journey in writing this book as my most excellent editor.

When we completed the last revisions of my book, Amy clipped a note to me on the hard copy of her final edits. They were kind, editorial words of support and praise for my work. But in the last paragraph, she switched to daughter mode: "I feel like I know my grandfather and

Acknowledgements

great-grandparents because of this book. What a tremendous gift. Thank you for writing it! I love you, Amy."

It all came down to that note. The guiding force that drove me for so many years to write this book made itself known to me through my daughter's words. The validation that I yearned for came from the very person who inspired me to accomplish what I did. I knew then, that my work was done.

It warms my Cuban heart to know that with this book, I am passing on to both my beloved daughters Amy and Ana María, my legacy, to be shared with our family's future generations to come.

Gloria María Strassburger
November 2011

Gloria María with her niñas lindas, Amy (l) and Ana María (r) making Nochebuena dinner on Christmas eve
—Michigan, 2007

About the Author

Gloria María Strassburger was born in Havana, Cuba, and educated at the Sacred Heart Academy. Once in exile, she grew up in Doylestown, Pennsylvania; married and had two daughters; and now lives in Michigan with her husband and her two Havanese dogs.

Visit the author's website:
www.gloriamstrassburger.com

Author Photo: Amy Strassburger VanStee

CPSIA information can be obtained at www.ICGtesting.com
Printed in the USA
BVOW08s0908070716

454620BV00002B/75/P